A LIFE IS TOO SHORT

A LIFE IS TOO SHORT

AUTOBIOGRAPHY: VOLUME ONE

NICHOLAS FAIRBAIRN

QUARTET BOOKS

London   New York

First published by Quartet Books Limited 1987
A member of the Namara Group
27/29 Goodge Street, London W1P 1FD.

British Library Cataloguing in Publication Data

Fairbairn, Nicholas
A life is too short: autobiography.
Vol. 1
1. Fairbairn, Nicholas   2. politicians ——
Scotland —— Biography   3. Lawyers ——
Scotland —— Biography
I. Title
344.11′0092′4   DA822.F3

ISBN 0-7043-2643-3

Phototypeset by AKM Associates (UK) Ltd
Ajmal House, Hayes Road, Southall, London
Printed and bound in Great Britain by
The Camelot Press PLC
Southampton

To my three little women,
Charlotte,
Anna-Karina
and
Francesca

A LIFE IS TOO SHORT

CHAPTER 1

Authors who want to be fashionable claim prodigious recollection of their earliest experiences. Anxious as I am to vie with them in that ambition, it would be taking a holiday from probity if I were to claim that I recall my conception. It was, I sense, unenjoyed and unintended by the half-consenting adults who were the unsuspecting parties to it, and little can they have appreciated the pain which such a risk would cause for all concerned – especially me. But Priapus won the day, – or rather the night. The skill which my male gamete demonstrated in slipping through the customs to improlificate my female component on that occasion created (in the mature zygote) an ineradicable urge to frustrate sterile authority at all times, and the pain which my conception caused to the keeper of the unsuspecting egg has ever since filled me with two resolves – to ingratiate myself in propitiation to the female species and to do all I could to frustrate unintended conceptions of my own.

Women may be anxious to be liberated from men: 'Can man be free if woman is a slave?' But ever since I was liberated from my mother I have always wanted to be re-united with her and with womankind again. 'Woman,' says the Koran, 'is your field: get into her as you will.' It is the duty of man to love woman; they are most lovely when they are most loved. I endorse the exhortation of Oscar Wilde: 'The only way to behave to a woman is to make love to her if she is beautiful and to somebody else if she is plain.' We come into this world alone: we leave it single: we should be close in between and generous with love. We cannot avoid birth and we cannot avoid death – let us mightily enjoy the interval between.

My memories *in utero* are few. As the months passed life became increasingly restricted, bumpy and suffocating. A palace became a cupboard – such is the overtaking predicament of the human race. I liked being there but I disliked the dark and I still do. The process of gestation is however inevitable:

1

Ay, there's many a beam from the fountain of day
That to reach us unclouded must pass on its way
Through the soul of woman.

I was upset by the distortion which I caused to my mother's delicate figure, never intended to carry such weight. I distinctly remember not enjoying the parturition, though now tocologists say that it was not at that time that my distortions arose. Birth is inevitably traumatic: from comfort and luxury, from being centrally heated, air conditioned, drip fed, protected, warm and asleep, and united with a woman, we are suddenly squeezed with great pain into a cold world, severed, slapped and washed. Helpless, we are forced to do everything for ourselves. No wonder children resent their parents. The pain and resentment of that first rejection and its consequent loneliness and the equal and conflicting fear of bondage and incarnation which precede it form the basic structure of the torments and passions of life and love. The violence of crime, the din of arms, the rage of politics, the orgasm of music and painting, the passions of love, the fervour of religious faith – all these are the echoes of the thunder of the concussions of the human soul in its search for the resolution of these early traumata. Sex, art, war and God are the complete channels of catharsis open to men. Sex brings sleep; art, tranquillity; war, peace; and God, the hopeful balm of everlasting life. Heaven – in all its forms.

I had given notice of my intended exit a few days before I decided finally to undertake it, and this feint, as the first vital act on my part, caused – as so many have since – great inconvenience to others. My mother's obstetrician, John Sturrock, had arranged not only to deliver this prospective whitling to a waiting world, but also to introduce his prospective fiancée to his Aberdonian parents. With a sense of duty which only so dedicated a physician and so devout a Christian gentleman would have contemplated, he sent his trepid fiancée to Aberdeen alone and stayed behind to deliver this intrepid infant to his doting – or doubting – family. Greater love hath no man than this – that he deserted his fiancée for his patients.

The significance of my birth was universally acclaimed throughout civilized Europe. My first memory in the fresh air on that sunlit Sunday morning was the church bells of St Mary's Cathedral in Edinburgh ringing out to acknowledge my arrival. Glout detractors have since tried to claim that since I was born at 10.50 on a Sunday, Christmas Eve, the bells were ringing out to will God's people into his womb – and not me out of mine. Whatever the reason, I had a decent Christian start: I

2

was an Easter present from my father to my mother and a Christmas present in return.

I was born in my mother's bed at the hands of a midwife, a regrettably infrequent occurrence nowadays. That habit gave every monster or weakling a merciful chance of being put face down on the pillow before the mother's sentimental feelings for the poor creature were stimulated by fondling so deformed a wretch.

So 1933 saw the arrival not only of Hitler but of myself. The distinction is that I'm the better painter of the two, though he thought he was. I regret now that I didn't describe at the time my real feelings and fontal experiences inside my mother. This might have exposed the thrilling secrets of the birth of time and illustrated the imaginings of Freud, but it would not have tempered my urge to return to the site of my entrance to this world.

I was born with an unfortunate flaw. I was tongue-tied at birth. For the first twelve whole days and nights of my life I regret to record I was prevented from either making a speech or taking a drink. This terrible defect was eventually cured by the flick of a knife and my liking for drinks and speeches, and my loathing of knives have never left me.

Now the nurse who pulled me silent and reluctant into this world and who looked after me in those first hectic days, when input and output were unregulated, was promoted to the rank of godmother for her kindness to me and to my mother. Shortly thereafter she married a famous surgeon, Sir Harold Stiles, whose considerable contribution to medicine is perpetuated solely in Cunningham's *Anatomy* by a drawing in cross-section of the male member 'after Stiles'.

I was proud of my titled godmother, though not for that reason, but I confess to having enjoyed the romance of titles ever since. If we don't have titles, we have to invent them: Miss World, The Coal Princess, the Chief Environmental Health Officer, the Braw Lad and so on.

The promotion of my nurse to my godmother and the resignation which such status required left me in the tender hands of my beloved nanny for the next seven years, when to my intense grief she left, following a terrible parental row of which I was bitterly conscious. In those formative years, she was the closest and only friend I had; my squabbling, if affectionate, parents were distant figures. She contrasts in my memory with a succession of tyrants yet to be endured. She was small with a round face and grey silken hair and spoke with a gentle Scottish voice. Her laugh was a constant chuckle. Her open face was ever lit with a smile. She feared mice, heights, ghosts, darkness and lightning. Goodness and kindness were her stirring qualities, sustained

3

by the shy fears and genuine awe of a simple Christian faith. She was a true innocent. Never a cross word or an unkind thought crossed her lips. Endlessly humble and truly good, she inspired in me a tolerance and forgiveness I was only able to retrieve from the resentment of the traumas to come some twenty years later, by which time she had retired with her gentle sister to a cottage in the village of her birth. No one can tell the ultimate effect of early allegiances, but whenever I feel angry or ungenerous, I calm myself by thinking of the loving soul of Nanny Wilkie now buried in the graveyard at Kirknewton.

So far as I know my mother's tiny breasts were not the source of my initial sustenance. Sister Laura had to do instead. I was thus deprived of the inestimable advantages of a mother's milk – later described to me in the class of medicine by Dr Mary Pickford, a distinguished lecturer in the heartless science of physiology, as being 'always available, of the right consistency, at the right temperature and coming in such attractive containers'. Basically I agree, although the goatskin bag of Biblical description is unwelcomely common. Sucking, however, through a cigarette or from a glass, remains a central compulsion to the human soul.

I was born in what seemed to me a huge house – 18 Landsdowne Crescent, Edinburgh. It had four floors, the basement being the empire of the servants and the attic being the habitat of nanny and of us. 'Us' was my sister who was six years older, always old enough to appear maternal, and my brother who was half-way between and young enough to be my companion and keeper. We had a day nursery which was light and a night nursery which was dark. We had a back garden which was tiny and private into which we rarely went (because one had to go through the kitchen and laundry to get there and that was not allowed) and a front garden which was public and in which the habit of the exhibition of children was regularly indulged.

Landsdowne and its twin crescent, Grosvenor, are dominated by the Episcopal Cathedral of St Mary which was built by the munificence of the Misses Walker and designed by Giles Gilbert Scott. It was to this sunless sarcophagus, full of gloom and wailing prebendaries, that I was taken to protest my rejection of the devil and all his works by two devoted and beloved godparents who like all of their kind kept, to the letter, none of the promises which they took.

The names I was given were Nicholas Hardwick, the first an allusion to the time of my birth. The name Nicholas imposes mighty obligations on an infant: being translated it literally means first to be champion or victor of the people. Such an achievement would entitle one to

4

canonization and thus imposes upon the infant Nicholas the patronages of the saint of that name – virgins, scholars, sailors, thieves. I haven't done much for sailors but I've given of my most indulgent to the rest. My second name, Hardwick, was bestowed in tribute to my only English ancestors of note – the family of Bess of Hardwick who befriended Mary Queen of Scots. Both names were given different connotations at school and since. I cannot think why my mother agreed to a name from my father's family except perhaps that being unintended I was his child and he could call me what he liked. The fact that I was my father's child and not hers was confirmed in my mother's eyes by my red hair at birth. I thus enshrined the vibrant reflection of their mutual resentment of each other.

And so I was conditioned to worship my father and despise my mother; to see everything from his cosy point of view; to reject all her trusts and favours; to be partial and one-sided. As the years went by her loneliness increased our betweenity. It did me great harm and great hurt but every advantage has its tax and every pain has its reward. In the aftermath I learned that there are two sides to every story; that the underdog feels under and needs allies and that everyone would be much nicer than they are if they could help it. They frequently can although they frequently don't. By a twist of irony, it is my mother's tastes, attitudes and horizons, more than my father's, which I have developed. 'Violent antipathies,' mused Hazlitt anticipating the science of psychiatry, 'are always suspicious and belie a secret affinity.' The reverse is also true as many marriages discover. I hope that the reader and the objects of my observations in the pages to come will retain Hazlitt's wisdom in mind. In retrospect I find it easier to comprehend and forgive my mother's torment – born of a terrible loneliness – than the narrowness of the base upon which my father constructed his long, wise, scholarly views. For some reason, parents seem surprised that their children have strong emotional reactions to every aspect of their behaviour. Early impressions of kindness and resentment are not easily erased and mine made me short-tempered and long-suffering, and blunt and sharp at the same time.

The memory of my first three years is scattered and almost entirely all bad. I remember throwing a biscuit with green sugar icing out of my cot; being injected by a loathsome doctor whose death I prayed for when I heard he was coming to do it again; having croup, and being steamed up by the fish-kettle. Croup is now out and so are fish-kettles, and if we don't watch it fish will be out too. I remember the rompers I wore in the back garden were prickly. I remember rows downstairs. I remember adults coming, and having to go to the drawing-room and be embarrassed by their condescension and boring talk. I remember the pleasures of sitting on a pot and roaming around on it on the linoleum floor of the nursery. I remember how I loathed being watched performing. I hated fish, a hatred that was created by steaming rolled herrings and finnan haddock. I remember the luxury of going out in my pram. Why can't we adults be wheeled around the garden in bed? I'm all for prams. I remember having to do what I was told – in theory anyway. One of the greatest resentments of being a child is that you have to do what you are told. Adults can do what they like. You have to wear what you are told to wear. Adults can dress how they want. You have to go to bed at a set time. Adults can get up and go to sleep as they please and when you are in bed they go out and enjoy themselves. It's all wrong! All our lives we remain children – sugar-coated or armour-plated, but children, however much we haughtily try to disguise it.

Nursery food was never as good as the downstairs food. How delicious the dining-room food seemed when you couldn't have it. Occasionally we were allowed to go down to the dining-room to say goodnight. The dining-room was filled with very beautiful furniture collected by my grandfather when Georgian and Sheraton furniture were unfashionable. The walls were covered with paintings which my grandfather bought for a few shillings and my father, alas, sold for a few pounds. One item which remains is a long Scotch Sheraton sideboard, inlaid with Prince of Wales feathers, which my grandfather bought for nineteen shillings, painted green in a laundry.

My two worst dreads were dancing-class and parties. Both caused me acute embarrassment. Dancing was cissy and I had to wear my kilt, which was then considered cissy too, though I have worn it with pleasure ever since. Unsuitably for a little Scot, I had to wear some slimy green pants under my kilt – my brother, on the other hand, had tartan pants which matched; it wasn't fair. One morning I got up early and went through to the day nursery. I hunted out Nanny's scissors and cut my slimy green pants to ribbons and then slipped back, innocently to bed. I had committed the perfect crime, and I had the complete defence – an alibi – I was in bed in another room when the crime was committed. But I made one basic mistake, for the last time . . . I overlooked the other person's view. 'O, wad some Pow'r the giftie gie us, to see oursels as others see us!' I was the only slimy-green-pants-hater in the house. No one else had a motive to commit pants-slashing. The accusation quickly produced a confession of guilt. But who said crime doesn't pay? I do not remember the punishment but I know that I never had to wear slimy

6

green pants again, and I got a beautiful tartan pair like my brother.

But there was one diversion at dancing: our dancing mistress, Miss Gardyne. A cheerful woman with a scarlet bust. We were fascinated when she demonstrated a right cross beat, or the Highland Fling, as her bosoms bounced up and down, sometimes in tandem and sometimes in turn.

Parties were my second real dread. Once again it required the wearing of my hated slimy green pants under my kilt – but even more than dancing it meant being among a crowd of strangers – often rough strangers. I've always been anxious among a lot of people whom I do not know, except in Edinburgh where I have often been more uncomfortable among a lot of people whom I do know. We had to play all those classic children's games like Musical Bumps and Pass the Parcel, but what was worse one had to pretend to enjoy oneself and to say thank you and how much one had enjoyed oneself – when one hadn't. I was quite happy to be generous with my gratitude; it was the hypocrisy which stuck in my throat.

What I enjoyed most were visits to Nanny's friends. My early world was peopled with humble Scots folk like her mother, and Agnes Knox, and Lizzie Milne, and Katie and Effie, who were on the staff in the house. People with good hearts, good manners and goodwill. They were all natural. Their language, like their habits, was entirely Scotch which was the mark of their perfect naturalness. They dressed and spoke as they chose. Their views were forthright and unstuffy. Their manners were a pleasure to see and a delight to recall. There was nothing scruffy or third-rate in anything they did. They were the salt of the nation. I get on best with unstuffy, unpretentious, and unassuming people – and goodness shone through all of Nanny's friends.

I was never very keen on cakes and fancy food which adults in those days imagined that children dreamed of as one of the necessary characteristics of Elysium. I always preferred the good plain tea and home-made baking which was provided in those humble, kindly homes. I also had an aversion to crusts. One day at tea at Lizzie Milne's, I hid my crusts in a circle under the rim of my plate, imagining my crime in leaving them was thus hidden, but of course I was discovered and that taught me the second rule of successful crime: Think ahead! The charge of refusing to eat what you don't like has always been a particularly heinous offence in the code of the adult to the child, motivated partly by a puritan sadism dating from Victorian times when children's food was chosen partly for its unpalatability, and partly from an arrogant condescension that 'Adults don't leave their food so why should you?'

7

Well, this early conviction for crust-hiding at Lizzie Milne's was forever to stand me in good stead. I learnt the art of slipping unwanted food of all kinds, unseen by watching eyes, into a handkerchief on my lap and those same goodies I committed later to the sea through the loo – as they would have been anyway; they just didn't pass through me on the way. I used the art at my prep school to dispose of such essential wartime delicacies as artificial fried sausage rounds, regularly provided every Wednesday and Saturday for tea; cooked dehydrated banana, a luxury reserved for a Sunday lunch; frog-spawn pudding – Monday's treat which first entered and emptied our systems in 1944 to celebrate the liberation of France – and government laxative jam, or 'free squish' as it was called. At prep school the method of food disposal was crude and messy if devilishly effective and the motive was selfish. By the time I had reached digs and university my technique and my motive both improved. In my digs I kept an empty glucose tin on the table into which rejects were cast. Especially the gallimaufry which was the weekly diet at Wednesday lunch, not just because I didn't want to eat them but because it hurt dear Mrs Miller, the landlady, and her faithful dwarf maid, Ruth, if one rejected the good food they had taken such trouble to cook for us.

Very early in my life, two educational glories were wisely introduced to me – music and French. Children should be introduced to languages and music at an early age, when the power to imitate sounds is at its best. We have an ability to imitate any noise we hear when we are young, an art most of us lose after the first five to ten years of life, so we should all learn to speak languages when we have the ability to imitate sounds. We don't learn English from a grammar book, and we shouldn't learn other languages from rules of grammar either. We should learn them by imitation. My introduction to French was in the nursery. Once a week Mademoiselle Duranton and later Mademoiselle Picabier came to tea and spoke French, and you got no jam until you said 'Pweesh avwahr la confeetoor seel voo play'. This excellent system was repeated at my prep school by Colin Mason (the brother of James Mason) who successfully taught us to speak French. Many a little boy who couldn't say 'Pweesh traversay la coor' wet his pants instead – he soon learnt. Music, or the piano, was then, however, too much for me to learn. My mother played confidently and well on her beautiful Bechstein piano. It fell to the 'unfortunate Miss Kinross to attempt to overcome my entrenched prejudices and incapacities. I loved chassefont which seems to have disappeared, but the piano I loathed and after making, I was told, a particularly amusing remark about Ginger Rogers which is, alas, lost to posterity, I closed the lid with some firmness on the sensitive fingers of the good Miss Kinross thus silencing for me her melodies for good. Other lyrical hags later took up the struggle at my prep school. My report underlines my lack of interest and their lack of success: 'Fairbairn does not practise – and he does not seem to concentrate during lessons.' Eventually I summoned up the courage to ask my father if I could give it up and he agreed with alacrity. That term was the only time I went back to school feeling happy. My love of music survived these early storms and has grown ever since. But my indulgence alas is confined to listening. I would love to have been a conductor.

Every summer we went to Straton House, my grandmother's house in Montrose – a beautiful, old red-brick house down a close. It had been a smuggling-house and commanded fine views of the sea and the lighthouse Skirdyness, and had a most exciting cellar on the roof of which we used to burn our initials with candles. I remember those summers as the happiest times and the house as the most romantic and important influence in my early life. I was deeply attached to it. It had the greatest number of smells of any place I have ever known; every room, every passage, every staircase, every drawer had its special smell. I loved them all and I can still smell them all. The household we joined consisted of two cousins, Harry and Robin More Gordon, and sometimes their father; Bella the cook and Barbara their nanny. All was presided over by my grandmother. She was always a very old woman in my memory. When I first remember her she had been a widow for some years. Time had been dealing with her and she walked with a stoop, but she was venerable and doughty. She had great dignity, great wit and great charm, very high standards and very fixed views. She was very Scottish, independent and proud, and deeply cultured, like my mother, in music and books. Her eyes were piercing and twinkling and she spoke with a very clear enunciation, over-emphasizing her 'r's and making each syllable count. She was a living example of the philosophy and generosity of country life; she valued straightforward people and beautiful things – flowers, taste, dignity, manners, kindness and class. Class was not something to be ashamed of, nor to boast about. It represented a level of responsibility and a level of behaviour in the search for excellence. It involved a dignified culture, a sophisticated taste, a rare duty and a better life. My grandmother was superior – not in any arrogant or unjustified sense, but because she had wider horizons, better taste, higher aspirations and a justified confidence – necessary

9

characteristics of any society which hopes to advance or even to survive and to produce, or to patronize, great music, great architects, great art or great civilization in any form. The biggest myth is that all men are equal, or can be equal. Some are very much better at some things – and some in all ways – than others and in the aim to do the best or to be the best the training and tradition of generations help. Those who spend their time in betting shops know this philosophy. They bet on those horses which have the best-bred parents, who have the best training (i.e. education), and the best chance. Egalitarians accept Eton and Christ Church for horses, but not for man. If you had to sell punters the idea or theory that every horse should be given an equal chance to be backed and that Arkle was no better than any other, that they should be forced to put an equal part of their money on each horse regardless of its upbringing, there would be an outcry amongst them. Bettors prefer better horses and resent better men. The absurdity of such a suggestion illustrates the absurdity of socialist life. Forcing people to treat the unequal as equal is bound to failure. There is no shame in a governing class where entry is open to all classes. There is no better system of government or society than a transferable aristocracy. What we are creating now is an immutable kakistocracy – a society with no deep values, no standards, no parts, no heights, no depths: only myths and jealousies. The values of the country community are abiding. Though unequal in station, to each is accorded the respect due to every human being that his capability commands, and the love which his personality evokes. Mass-activity, mass-production, mass-licence blend with one another to produce grey, stereotyped man. We have destroyed worth.

My grandmother had a cook called Bella Cobb. B-B-Bella spoke with a quiet st-s-stutter. She was the most benign woman I have ever met. She spoke broad Angus. She had cheerful eyes, a sad face and bad feet. She had cook's arms and hands and normally wore a scarf round her grey hair when she was cooking. She was full of chuckling humour. Humility was her strength and cooking was her genius. She got enormous pleasure from our enjoyment of her cooking – she had no recipes. She lived in a little room next to the morning-room which was Attic in its starkness. The baubles of life were superfluous to her fulfilment, the sole objects of luxury she deigned to own being the squared fawn coat and pot hat she wore when she went out. Her empire was the kitchen with its large, clean, scrubbed dressers and Wilton ashets and the iron-range on which she concocted her excellencies. She loved my grandmother. Both women were the same age. One had to cook for her living, the other ate what she cooked. Each had her own life but shared the other's life. It would have been 'fairer' if both had had to work for their living, and neither had had a cook. But would it have been better? Both women would have been much less happy. As it was each was totally fulfilled and satisfied. Bella made the best gingerbread on earth – round like a cake but it fell to a quarter-inch in the middle and was soggy and scrumptious. I asked her for the recipe after she retired, on my grandmother's death, to her little house, kept spotless and neat up an outside stair, but she could only remember she used to make it with cold tea. All her cooking was done by art – she had no need of a higher degree in jam-making, or social science or any other bogus highfollution. As a result, her food was exceptionally good. I can taste it still – her broth and her lemon puddings. None of the standard listed dishes of a restaurant, under the impostor's title of 'International Cuisine', came from her job. Bella, however humble with her quiet stutter, however untrained, was the élite. I watched her fade into the Lord's mansions. I hope she's cooking for Him. If she is He will sup well.

Our summer days consisted of mornings at the freezing beach and afternoons on picnics, or going for walks round the harbour where we saw the seal who lived in a little tank on the pier. Poor seal: I hope he knew how much pleasure his confinement gave us. I had a fear and horror of the sea and, looking back, I've no doubt that my dread was partly created by the temperature of the North Sea, because I have been a committed thalassophile ever since I sampled the pleasures of the welcome warmth of the Mediterranean. One fateful day we set out in a boat for the Elephant Rock. I lay screaming in the bottom of the boat all the way, thinking of the appalling distance from the surface to the bottom. It is a long way after all, and I had no desire to measure it. But there was another strand to my anxiety for I recently had become acquainted of the fact that Britain was an island and surrounded by the sea. We were trapped. I never liked geography after that, though I've always thought that the British Empire should have consisted only of all the islands in the world – it would still be there – invincible. On our picnics, all of us usually had an ice and one of us was usually sick. The great-aunts made pipes out of rushes for us to pretend to smoke and we picked heather and rowans and bilberries and learned the names of all the wild flowers which the aunts took home to press and dry in their little villa in White's Place where they had resided under the watchful eye of Mrs Hadden ever since they had been evicted from Charlton, the family estate near Montrose.

The house at White's Place was filled with the paintings of these two ancient and excellent women and characteristic furniture rescued from a large Victorian mansion. Aunt Jane, Aunt Georgina, my grandmother and Mrs Hadden – each was an example of an indomitable breed of independent Scotch ladies: strong-headed, high-spirited and warm-hearted, full of wisdom, laughter, and spice – spice above all. They were pious in their devotion in religion but the freedom and forthrightness of their views on all subjects, sacred or profane, and on the human state would excite the horror of those who give such prissy tone to matters of religion nowadays. Their Christianity was blunt and generous. Each was merry even in solitude; each was resolute; each was utterly individual, standing out like rocks from the sea. Each believed her high values and her right to be herself which was accorded with equal justice to others.

They were all racy – each in a different way. Each had her place, which was kept – and granted – with dignity and pride. Miss Georgina and Miss Jane were always 'Miss Georgina and Miss Jane' to their servant and mistress Mrs Hadden, and Mrs More Gordon, their sister-in-law, was always 'Mrs More Gordon' to them. For each of them life was to be lived to the full. People were to be explored. They were part of the wonder and order of the world, part of the splendour of life, for both of which – weekly in church and nightly on their bony knees – they mightily and meekly thanked God. One by one these ancient cosmo-polites, the Misses More Gordon, died and they were buried in the Howf near Charlton, a burial hill where the family collects under the beech trees on their death. Each week, unknown to Mrs Hadden, they put the rent which she paid them towards an annuity to provide for her in her old age. And when they died safely in their home, they left her the house where she lived happily till failing sight compelled her to move to Dorwood House where she lived in the kindly atmosphere of a good old folks' home until her death at the age of 103. When she reached her hundredth birthday in 1975 I took Mrs Margaret Thatcher to her birthday party. All the residents and her family assembled in the hall where she was surrounded by flowers and presents and cards. When a photographer asked her to hold an empty glass, she indignantly retorted: 'Aw, naw thankyee: Ah'm strawng enough wi'oot ony o' yon.' Margaret Thatcher enchanted her, and so did she Margaret Thatcher: 'Well, ah'm tellin yi: I've tocht Nickee tae gie it tae them stricht from the hairt – wi naw nownsense.' I hope I was a good pupil. She still retained her zest, her zip, her sparkle, her ardent spirit, her strident voice, her standing no nonsense. Her forthrightness was inspired by the humblest and kindest heart in the world. Loving life as she did, she was utterly unafraid of death: 'Ah think they've furgutten ahn awld buddie

12

lark me up yawnda,' she crackled. I'm glad they did.

At Straton House the grandchildren had certain restrictions – they were not allowed to use the beautiful front stair, with its wrought-iron balustrade, or to go into the drawing-room unless by command. We lived in the morning-room where we played with our rocking-horse and Hornby trains and had our meals surrounded by rows of books bound in leather and more of the aunts' paintings of Montrose and Italy. There was a giant clock which struck the Westminster chimes or a variety of other cosmopolitan tintinnabulations. We only had lunch in the dining-room on very special occasions. The dining-room had at one end a beautiful, tall semi-circular sherry cupboard built into the wall – a feature of many Scotch houses. At the other end it had a glass case containing the last and best remnants of a collection of beautiful stones and minerals which my grandfather's eldest brother, Uncle John, had amassed in exchange for almost the whole of what modestly passed for the family fortune. This was responsible, eventually, for the sale of the family estates of Charlton and Kinnaber. These remnants were presented to Montrose Museum on my grandmother's death by my uncle. I wished they had been presented to me. Museums are all very well and the urge to turn over your family possessions to them is no doubt founded in a desire to immortalize one's mortal self. But they are essentially filing-cabinets in which the contents are ordered but isolated from the vitality of people and cease to serve the sensitive purpose for which they were created so lovingly or collected in the first place. These stones gathered on a shelf in Montrose Museum epitomize that death.

My Uncle Harry was an officer in the Gordon Highlanders. He was very gifted as a child and very good-looking as a man. As a boy he had a perfect voice and sang solos in St George's Chapel, Windsor, for which talent he received the Coronation Medal. His son Harry, my cousin (the eldest is always called Harry) inherited this bird's ability to sing and often had to sing 'O for the Wings of a Dove' in the drawing-room and O, if he had had those wings far away would he have flown! The drawing-room smelt of pot pourri and was dominated by Corinthian pillars on either side of the fireplace, flanking which were two beautiful crayon portraits of my mother's grandmother and grandfather, both of whom had striking, kindly and handsome faces. At the window was a tit-box where my grandmother fed succeeding families of those delightful fluffy friends. It was a very noble and a very graceful room.

One of the great treats of our holidays was the fruit garden where we were allowed to pick gooseberries into a rhubarb leaf. I was allowed to pick strawberries because I was thought too young for such unshaven and hairy fruit. In late summer the vast pear tree on the west wall produced its massive load of delicious pears and we glutted ourselves on them in preparation for the dismal return to town life.

On Sundays we all went to the Episcopal church of which my grandmother was a staunch pillar and a regular communicant. Our boredom during Matins was distracted by various characters in the congregation who were always there demonstrating an unassuming eccentricity. Those I recall were Mr Piggins – who kept budgerigars and who sang louder than the whole of the rest of the congregation – and various purple straw-hatted friends of my grandmother, such as the Misses Lyall and Dolly Woodward. Canon Millar was the ancient and apparently immortal rector. He was an old man with small eyes and white hair, very deaf, and a very dear friend of my grandmother. We always walked home from church down the closes which are so much a feature of Scotch towns, of which Montrose is a supreme example.

And so eventually, each summer, as the nights lengthened, we got ready to go home. Nanny stitched up the pram in sacking with a vast bodkin needle. We were all allowed to buy a tin of 'Officer's Buckies' and some 'Seaside Donkeys' – both now extinct alas – to take back to the boredom of life in town. And then we would set off to the station for the exciting train journey home. What an excellent thing is a train! A travelling house – vast, comfortable, affording endless views. Who wants to be sucked like a bullet through the stratosphere, or crammed in a self-propelled tin trunk on a road competing with every articulated brontosaurus and dawdling dwarf on earth? Who prefers to be crouched in a bus where you can't read or eat? The train is indeed the transport of luxury. The humanity, dignity and leisure of trains is expressed by the personality of all railwaymen – they are a league of friendly and kindly gentlemen. No wonder I wanted to be an engine-driver as a child.

Back in Edinburgh two public events stand out in my pre-war recollection – the Jubilee Visit of King George V and Queen Mary in 1935 and the Coronation of George VI and Queen Elizabeth in 1937. I remember the thrill of putting out the decorations on the house – the red, white and blue banners and the crown and the flags of the Union. We watched the coruscating and clinquant parades pass along Princes Street under the knaggy rock of the castle – which Dr Johnson observed would make a good prison in England – from the balcony of one of the independent Scotch shops which my mother patronized: Ferguson's, Birrell's, Jamieson's fruit shop, Wilkie's Furs and a hundred others, each of which had character and belonged to a family who knew their customers, now alas displaced by English conglomerates. Progress they call it. These grand state occasions made a great impression on my tiny mind and the visit of King Olaf brought them vividly to mind again. Edinburgh is a splendid city for pageantry with its grand volcanic silhouettes, and its historic royalty and pageantry is a splendid entertainment for everyone.

In winter we had tea once a week with my father's mother, my other grandmother, who lived opposite us at 18 Grosvenor Crescent. She stood very erect, dressed in black and was always garlanded with Victorian necklaces down to her waist where a pair of lorgnettes hung. Even in great age she walked with great elegance, and possessed the remains of considerable beauty in her face, and great and just pride in her only son. She had very high standards of rectitude and bestowed love upon all around her to the end of her days. She was very kind to us and would put a sixpence under each of our plates. Our favourite treat was sugar mice made by Miss Aitchison, our grandmother's cheerful and friendly housekeeper. Although equally old, equally kind to us, and equally self-demanding as my mother's mother, these two aged women, living daily in the service of God, could not have differed more basically. Granny Fairbairn, although she was brought up on a farm at Hovingham in Yorkshire, had married my grandfather – a surveyor – and had lived in Edinburgh ever since, where she had adopted all the demanding and narrow views of the professional worlds of Victorian and Edwardian times. Nature and culture – which were so much of the fabric of Granny More Gordon and the foundation of the breadth of her soul – were unimportant to Granny Fairbairn. She was concerned rather with the fussy niceties of her own daily life and the routine gentilities of her social station. These restrictive horizons she enclosed around my father. He and my mother, therefore, approached everything from different worlds. He was a zoo animal; she was born free. Perhaps that is why whenever we were asked what we wanted to do on Sunday afternoons we always chose the zoo. It may be the dominant gene.

I never knew either of my grandfathers, but both have been described to me as gentlemen of great gentleness and wit. My father's father, Thomas Fairbairn, bought the Red House at Morningside – then in the country – when he married my grandmother, Cecilia Leefe of Hovingham. And there, after much trial and more error, they conceived their only child – my father, who was brought up in the stifling care of an adoring Victorian mother. They moved during the First World War to 31 Drummond Place, latterly the home of Sir Compton Mackenzie, whom I visited very often there. My mother's father, Harry More

Gordon of Charlton and Kinnaber, succeeded to the estate on the death of his spendthrift elder brother, John. He had spent his life thus far attempting to grow tea in Ceylon with a commanding lack of success – and he spent his life thereafter attempting to run the family estates with commensurate failure. He was, however, a superb fisherman and spent his days on the river. He married my grandmother – his first cousin – late in life, and they had one son, my Uncle Harry, beloved because he was male; and one daughter, my mother, rejected because she was female. However these two siblings were devoted to each other until an incident occurred when I was three or four which struck them apart forever. My uncle asked my mother to buy a leopard-skin coat for his lover. With the devotion of Juliet, my mother repaired to Messrs. Wilkie, then the supreme furriers in Great Britain, to oblige. 'But why leopard skin?' the assistant enquired with the uncharacteristic shop-keeper's urge of trying to save the customer some money. 'Ocelot is much cheaper and no one can tell the difference.' So the fatal seed was sown. No sooner had the furry token of my uncle's love fallen into the greedy hands of his rapacious mistress than she sped to the nearest furrier to price the measure of his devotion. 'Ocelot indeed! So I'm not good enough for leopard! Your love, like this skin, is a pretence' – a pretence incidentally that was kept up for the next twenty years! And so the whipped fury passed along the line until, like the seventh wave, it burst upon my unsuspecting mother and deeply wounded her spirit and her mind. The loss of her brother's devotion and his affection to a mistress confirmed the loneliness of her early life. Ever thereafter, and always in my memory, she was a tormented and unhappy woman.

Christmas as a child was the greatest fun. I've always been very receptive to presents, though I prefer giving them, and since my birthday fell on Christmas Eve, I got a double dose. Two events always preceded Christmas – the stirring of the plum pudding and Aunt Nannie's sale. It is not recorded what I wished for in my first two years, but in my third I wished for a cow. My father had some Freudian interpretation of this vaccine longing and I had to wait until I was thirty-three when we bought Vantage Farm for that to come true. On my fourth Christmas I wished for a jelly, no doubt hoping to emulate Thomas Cromwell who bribed Pope Julius II with a jelly to build the harbour at Boston. The darkening clouds of war interrupted this developing lottery, but they never interrupted Aunt Nannie's annual sales. Aunt Nannie was a widow all my life; indeed every female in the family I ever met was either a widow or a virgin except my mother who was, to all intents and purposes, both. God knows what they did to their men. My mother's mother had a sister, Aunt Beatrice, and a brother, Harry. Aunt B – Miss Beatrice Macbean – was witty and seductive though somewhat plain. A prospective seducer, whose eyes fell upon her at a ball and whose hands were hoping to afterwards, asked her if she would care to dance. Hopefully he held out his programme: 'Number 5' she said wickedly. Not knowing her name but pretending to, he asked her how to spell it. 'With a small b,' she replied. Not being a gentleman perhaps he didn't see the joke.

Aunt Nannie was the widow of Harry Macbean. She remained identical during the thirty-four years that I knew her. She was small, dressed in black, and had twinkling eyes, white hair and little red veins on her cheeks, a chirpy voice, and slept for four hours a night and was a vegetarian living on one 'ague' (as she called it) a day. Fortified by these simple and frugal victuals, she generated a tireless energy. Like the old Edinburgh cable trams she only had two speeds – full on and full off. She was a pillar of the fabric of St Giles and the Grassmarket Mission and many a lonely soul had the solace of her cheerful company in their homes in the Grassmarket or the Canongate till the very last days of her happy life. Her annual sale at Bank House in Morningside Road became an essential event for the faithful of St Giles. Neither warfare nor changing fashions altered the range of available purchases, all of which were hand-made, such as emery bags for cleaning rusty needles and parchment book-marks inscribed with such hopeful brocades for those with prostates and constipation as 'The music of the stream is caused by obstruction.'

Our Christmas present was always a red sixpenny savings stamp. As I grew up I began to question the sufficiency of this investment so I wrote at the age of seven a rather formal acknowledgement: 'Dear Mrs Macbean, I have received my savings stamp with thanks. Yours faithfully, N. Fairbairn'. This missive was fortunately interrupted by parental censors for it would have wounded a most generous heart. One day, when she was very old, in 1968, she fell over in bed and died as she lived – cheerful, brisk, Christian and Scottish, a bright, kind little buddy to the end.

Aunt Nannie was responsible for one more Christmas delight – she lent my mother her Christmas-tree decorations and fairy lights. Decorating the tree with its trumpets and bells and birds and animals was an annual excitement, which still gives me a thrill with my own children. I love all the ceremonies of Christmas, but I'm glad it only happens once a year.

Christmas Day had a standard routine – church, boring old church. In the morning the inaudible, chanted mysticalia in the gloom of St Mary's Cathedral, then the monotonous intonement and unending sermon by the Provost, Canon Gooderham. He had a face like an eagle and on his ample nose there perched a pair of rimless pebble glasses, so thick that his eyes were like pins, and his voice was nasal to the point of incomprehensibility. His wandering thoughts were as abstruse as his diction was pompous. His instructions did nothing to incline children to the worship of God. He seemed to preach for an aeon of time, especially when Christmas lunch and presents were waiting. Eventually he committed us to God's gracious mercy and protection and to Christmas lunch in the dining-room consisting always of more goodies than anybody, child or adult, could comfortably contain. Then we listened to the King's halting speech, while trying to contain our lunch, standing self-consciously to attention in the drawing-room during the National Anthem. At last, all ceremony dutifully done, came the great moment of presents from the tree. It is the unwrapping that makes the parcel such an excitement – that is why I have always been against the current custom of *déshabillé*. Women should wear the least that makes the most of what one would be pleased to see and the most that makes the least of what one wouldn't.

The rest of the day was spent fighting indigestion and depression at the thought that 364 days must past before the next round of gold, frankincense and myrrh. Then there was tea in the drawing-room with a selection of the virgins and widows of which my relations were almost exclusively composed. Apart from Aunt Nannie, two irresistible regulars were Aunt Elsie (Mrs Hunter) and Uncle Hamilton, the sister and brother of my father's late father. They lived together at 37 Granby Road in a stone villa decorated with aspidistras and antimacassars as one would expect. Uncle Hamilton was almost stone deaf and was the spit and image of Freud. His walk was a sort of whiffle. Aunt Elsie was very dominant, rather prim and had an almost superstitious fear of it being suggested she had ever sinned. As Dr Johnson judged the Prioress in France – she lived life not so much for the love of virtue as for the fear of vice. She was as Presbyterian as can be. Her sister Margaret smashed the entire family collection of Georgian glasses to prevent alchohol being drunk out of them. Such was the strength and weakness of the faith of those worthy Scotch ancients.

One person who was always welcome at Christmas was my godfather, Angus MacNiven, who was the Medical Superintendent of the Gartnavel Hospital in Glasgow. He was a West Coast Highlander with Dundrearie whiskers and spidery spectacles. He always produced very generous presents. Much later in life I saw a lot of him in the witness-box in Glasgow High Court where he gave his credible evidence in his incredulous voice, telling which of my clients were really soft and which were really hard. A natural and beloved eccentric he was a true Scottish gentleman and lives where he was born and as he was born – unmarried in Mull.

Scottish gentlemen will frequently appear throughout this story so it is as well to define the term now – it was invented by Graeme Murray, of whom more will be told later. A 'Scottish gentleman' speaks unselfconsciously in the Scotch voice of his locality. A Scottish gentleman is deeply cultured, steeped in the history and love of his country. He is well read. He is eccentric, unselfconscious and original; drinks a good deal, regarding drinking as a virtue rather than a habit or merely a pleasure. He is deep, wise and cheerful and neither gives damns or cares figs. They are men upon whom flies settle at their peril. It will be apparent from this definition that intellectuals, snobs and sociologists do not qualify. They are a strong breed utterly devoid of the taint of fanaticism.

When I was young we saw very little of our parents at home. My mother read a good deal – three or four books every day – and incessantly listened to music and regularly to evensong on the wireless. My father spent his days, from dawn to dusk, listening to endless wallop which his cod patients resurrected from the torment of their mothers' wombs. At night he wrote these stories up and his theories down. As a result, my mother saw little of him either and she deeply resented his being locked up in his consulting-room with a succession of weirdies and beauties on his couch, like an artist with eight different models a day. Inevitably, psychoanalysis, to which my father made a formidable and original contribution as a pioneer, was my mother's unfavourite subject. It was probably for this reason that when I was four, having reconsidered my application to join the NUR, I decided to be a doctor like my father; besides, I wanted to become more like my father than my brother was going to be and he wanted to be a schoolmaster, which he became to the great satisfaction of himself and the gratitude of all who have benefited from his gentle instruction. So far as I remember, very few people visited the house at all, except for patients, some of whom were still coming back for more thirty-five years later. I remember the odd psychoanalyst coming to stay – indeed, I remember some very odd psychoanalysts staying – but only three or four friends came to the house and they all became friends of mine when I grew up.

When I was four my father engaged a resident secretary – and she very nearly engaged him. He only ever hired one other secretary. The war intervened between their reigns. The second succeeded where the first failed and became my stepmother when he married her in his old age to her inestimable benefit in April 1959, he having resisted for fifteen years.

No child could live with a father whose insights into the workings of the human mind were so profound or so wise and so beneficial to humanity, without being greatly affected. In my own case, the effect was undoubtedly much greater and more stimulating than in the case of my older brother and sister for several reasons.

During their formative childhood years, guarded in the nursery by Nanny, the atmosphere in the house was normal, very social and very happy. My father and mother were still in love. Neither had yet become inimical to the other. When that sad sea change occurs in marriage the effect upon children of formative age is profound. It is schismatic and the resultant effects of turmoil may either develop the child or wound it critically. Alas, certainly by the time I was born and probably even by the time I was conceived, that terrible sea change had occurred between my father and my mother, as if the poles of their magnets had been reversed and those virtues which formally attracted one another now came to repel. My father increasingly withdrew from this pain into the fascination which his work provided and his theories of human motivation, as revealed by his analysis of his squinted patients. The more he probed the more he found, the more he found the more he withdrew from the society of my mother and his family and all their friends into his private investigative world, even to the point of taking his consulting rooms out of our home to the other side of the street in Grosvenor Crescent to emphasize the more bitterly his new priorities. My mother, as I have described already, broken by her climacteric row with her adored brother over the ocelot coat, retreated forlorn and resentful into illness, loneliness and dipsomania. My father had removed from her the mainsprings of her life, the fun of his love and his company, the good talk with many friends, dinner parties and the excitement of travel, the thrill of music and art and the discussion amongst sophisticated people of all the intellectual matters of the day. She was left alone to read, to drink, to listen to her beloved music and evensong on the wireless and to develop her lonely resentments. But worse, she was reminded of the neglect which her adored father had visited upon her and from which she had been saved by the devotion of the brother from whom she was now estranged. My father was rigidly insensitive to my mother's emotional suffering, in stark and resented contrast to his concern for the emotional suffering of the women on his psychiatric couch, locked up with whom he spent his day. It is not difficult to see how each partner justified their retreat, blaming the other, which is the story of love gone wrong.

Into this dismal turmoil of failure, frustration and hostility, I arrived, by that time if not unintended certainly unwanted. At birth, I looked like my father and was immediately identified by my mother as 'his child', not hers. My rejection by her sounded a profound echo in my father who, as an only child, had suffered his own mother's scolding rejection of his imperfections which she saw as an attempt to perfect him by criticism. That experience produced a man of intense sensitivity and kindness within a shell of stiffness, formality and aristocratic reserve. My father both consciously and sub-consciously recognized the traumatic wounds of emotional rejection or neglect of a male child by his mother, whether well or ill-intended. He therefore adopted me as *his* child in accordance with my mother's taunts. He saw in me the lonely child of his own childhood, the child of whom special success was expected, and he comprehended only too well the morbid wounds which parental neglect could effect and the violent forces for good or ill which such could unleash – as evinced by Churchill on the one hand and Hitler on the other. Accordingly, he adopted an almost maternal role towards me. He was, in psychoanalytical terms, trying to save himself from his experience by saving me. From the earliest times of my memory, he treated me as if I were an equal adult. He took me out to watch the bombing, at the age of six, long after midnight. He sent me out to look for the leftovers of war, such as anti-aircraft shells which had fallen to earth. He discussed with me the wisdom or folly of Hitler's dilemma of conquering the oilfields of the Crimea, rather than taking Stalingrad and the Russian armies. He took me to Carstairs Hospital where, week after week, he examined those who either were made mad or claimed to have been made mad by war and were in any event terrified by it. Whenever he could spare a moment, I was by his side and treated as if I was his equal and his confidant. Throughout that time, my mother was ill and unmentioned and no friends or visitors that I can recall, except for his psychological chronies, ever entered our household at all.

This relationship had profound effects upon me. Firstly, it enabled me to withstand the trauma and rejection which I felt and which I experienced but, more importantly, it enabled me to feel secure for the rest of my life against any misfortune or rejection which might come my way. It also made me profoundly in awe of father figures and left me with a consistent feeling, which I have to this day, that I am still a child. Apart from teachers at school and nannies, he was the only adult in my life and for the next twenty years or so until his degeneration into old age, we remained locked like twins in discussion about the motivation of the human mind, about the urges of art and music and their sources and the manifestations and causes of sexuality and homosexuality, crime and psychopathy, literature, politics, religion and power. Despite the lack of maternal affection, my father's affectionate role, both intellectual and emotional, prevented the suffering which I would have otherwise had and improved my incisive understanding, not only of others but of myself. So I learnt at the knee of a great intellect to enquire into the raging cauldron of human emotion about the forces which produce uncontrolled rage and sadism and the same forces which produce art and music, courage and daring. My father's personality was formed by the remarkable combination of distant smothering affection and harsh and scolding abjuration to which he had been consistently and confusingly subjected by his proud and ascetic parents. And it was his desperate need to escape from and yet to be worthy of those parental expectations which caused him to explore and fundamentally to explain the object relations of the personality. Thus by chance is mankind gloriously rewarded.

In September 1938 I went to my first school – Queen Margaret's PNEU School – in Darnaway Street. My only recollections of this school are three: first, doing blobs with Miss Strachan, the headmistress – fat, motherly, indevirginate and prim, one of that generation of wise and principled dominies now alas extinct except in the country; second, I remember a colleague who had the capacity like a rhinoceros of retromingency and took particular pleasure in piddling through the holes in the seats of our wooden chairs during Scripture; and third, I remember a dramatic thunderstorm in which it became pitch dark at 10.30 in the morning and lightning struck the dustbin on the pavement outside.

The subject I remember liking most was chassefont, apparently now extinct, a device used to teach children the rudiments of music. It was a box of metal minims and sharps and crochets and rests which we had to place on bars and trees and other shapes. It was such fun . . . I suppose it has gone forever. Anyway, it would be plastic if it came back.

One particular delight of our childhood in Edinburgh which lasted into my university days was our visits to the little shop in Morrison Street baldly entitled 'Confectionery'. Alas, it is no more. It had a brown front and very little on view in the window but inside it contained an assortment of unique and unequalled treats. First among these were the confectioners themselves, Miss McCraw and Miss Paterson, very much in that order, who produced, in partnership and independence, the most delicious sweets a tongue could ever taste. It was rare to see both these characters at once, or indeed at all, for in my experience, Miss Paterson rarely emerged from the kitchen at the back where I imagined she was chained to her chocolate hob. Each wore a black satin overall and their hair was disciplined into a tight bun at the back. They rarely smiled but when they did it was the reflection of a loving soul under the restraint of timidity. Miss McCraw was at the sharp end. She had the daunting task of confronting customers face to face. She had a harder and more hirsute face than Miss Paterson, whose countenance was round and seraphic. Her every act was undertaken with caution and care. Her every syl-la-ble was most de-lib-er-ate. They referred to each other as if they had never met, in terms of deference befitting two strangers, though they had spent the whole of their proud and rewarding life together in this tiny shop. None of the first-name sycophancy of contemporary guilt affected them. They had status. Each sweet had status too, being personally baked by Miss Pat-er-son who passed them with an armless hand through the woollen curtain which divided their empires. It took a long time to obtain half a pound of Miss Pa-ter-son's pep-per-mint choc-o-lates, as Miss McCraw called them, because not only were they in-div-id-u-ally se-lec-ted and per-son-ally wrapped but the wrap-ping pa-per was cut up with huge scis-sors in-to in-di-vi-du-al strips and the card-board box-es had to be man-u-fac-tured in each case to contain them. Fur-ther-more if Miss McCraw sensed the slightest whiff of inclement wea-ther she insisted on imprisoning the parcel in war-rterproof pa-per and string as if the chocolates were too good, which they were, ever to be eaten. But time was never better spent. The vulgarity of Sellotape would have been an unthinkable come-down in the standards they set themselves. The judgement of the world is puff! – it is the standards we set ourselves which matter. They were perfectionists, for them nothing but the best would do. What did they achieve? The pride that comes alone from a fulfilling life, the joy that comes of providing nothing but the best and selling it not for their reward, which was subsidiary, but for yours; and the satisfaction of their certain excellence and exclusive independence. What did they give? Their hearts and their arts. What did they keep?

Their pride and their dignity and a modest sufficiency to fund both, which the avaricious wage-earners of today, whipped on by their union task-masters and by the devaluation of money which their gluttony causes, would deride and reject as a pittance. No pair were ever richer.

CHAPTER 2

In the summer of 1939 we went as usual to Montrose but this time for two reasons I was left behind. My mother was ill and Hitler had gone mad. My mother was quickly cured, but Hitler was not, so I went to school in Montrose with Mrs Forbes and I was very happy there indeed. The outbreak of war occurred on my way back from church, and I ran all the way along Montrose High Street in the sun to the frightening and hellish scream of the sirens. I was terrified as were, no doubt, those sounding the sirens and those causing them to be sounded but children do not credit adults with the fear they feel themselves, nor adults recall sufficiently their childish fears.

By this time Nanny had left and I was looked after by a succession of young women, who, apart from my grandmother and Bella the cook, were the only other occupants of Straton House. They all had names which I forget and they came and went in rapid succession as a result of their preference for older men. The first, Margaret, failed to return at all after her night out and I awoke in terror alone in my room at the very top of the house with the air-raid sirens wailing. My absent guardian was dismissed by my grandmother with rancour on her eventual return at midday – I hope her (k)night was worth it. While her trespasses were nocturnal, those of her successor were diurnal. She and I went for our usual morning walk to the beach where she had either arranged to meet, or spotted, a soldier who took her fancy. In order to distract me she asked me to look out to sea at a non-existent boat. I gazed long and in vain at the ocean and on turning round to report no sighting I was astounded to see that she had vanished like the ghost of Hamlet's father. I waited and hunted in vain and eventually set off on my lonely journey across the dunes. Unfortunately a hungry alsatian spied me, alone, far from cover in the dunes and decided to have me for its lunch before I could get home for mine. As he tucked into his hors d'oeuvre of my leg there appeared, as if by magic, two of the ancient women in purple straw-hats with fluffy skin who peopled the congregation of the

Episcopal church. They rescued me in my plight with the skill of gladiators. Armed only with their furled umbrellas for tridents and without nets these two intrepid grimalkins fought off the demented wolf and took the remains of his tattered morsel home. My errant guardian did not return for several hours – she had in fact fallen into the arms of a passing Hamlet in soldier's uniform who took her for a quick bite of love behind the beach pavilion. Her quick bite must have turned into a full-scale meal. She was full of remorse – what about I wasn't very sure. All I know is that I never saw her again and probably neither did her soldier.

The apparent inability of Montrose to provide suitable young women to look after me, and my obvious loneliness resulted in my return to Edinburgh in October or November 1939 to a house utterly transformed: all the windows were either painted black or papered over and there were very few bulbs in the lamps and those that were, were mostly blue. The house was full of fire-shields and tin buckets filled with sand or water; the cupola that lit the vast staircase had been painted black so night occurred all through the day – the steps were painted white so that you didn't fall up them. My mother was very ill in a nursing-home, and all the maids had vanished except for Mary the cook. My father's secretary had been absorbed into the Air Force; and in the nursery was installed Edinburgh's answer to the lovers of Montrose, Miss Ellsden, a horrific spinster who quickly earned the title of 'Loopy Lion'. She was eventually ejected from my life for forcing me, by threat of drowning in my bath each night, to hand over to her, one by one, such of my toys as she fancied for her repulsive niece. A vast crate of the toys which she had accumulated were found under her bed when she was despatched. I was deeply attached to my toys, as children are – they are an extension of their personalities. Nor are possessions less important to an adult. Borrowing is not enough; they must be exclusively 'my own', hence the importance of property. The urge to own and not to borrow or share explains in part the motive of marriage and the fact that the interest often dwindles when exclusive property has been established explains in part the frequency of divorce.

Since there were, apparently, no British females left out of the war who could be trusted, and since the PNEU school had been evacuated, and my mother was in a nursing-home, my father decided I should board at Dolphinton House in Peeblesshire, where the school had gone. I was just six. I remember crying for many nights after my arrival. What for, I do not know, but I can imagine: home, safety and security, love, my toys, the familiarity of my nursery – all the chords of loneliness and insecurity struck at once. With a brief interval in 1941 I was to be confined in institutions for the next twelve years. I detested from that first moment institutional life and all it represented – the lack of freedom and the mindless routine. I have the greatest sympathy with those who have to go to prison, though I recognize that some only feel at ease in a cage. After all, I did twelve years, the equivalent with remission to eighteen. Prison must not overwhelm the redeemable with despair, nor must it provoke the irredeemable to a more cruel and audacious defiance.

To the gentle staff who had taught me in Darnaway Street had been added a camp commandant in form of a matron, Miss Thompson – 'Sharp Tin' we called her. She was a cruel woman, unsympathetic to the nature of children to such a degree that she could only torture them into whimpering obedience or pickthank submission. My brother and I spent not only the terms at this hated place but also the holidays. One day, out for a picnic, we had to cross a river by walking along a tree; Miss Thompson came last. As she reached the middle I wobbled the tree. To the delight of all but her, she fell in and we watched with glee, in defiance of her protest, the removal of her soaking clothes from her hideous form. The shame was complete. Justice had been done. She left soon after, but we had suffered terribly under her hagship. I prayed frequently in the wrath and torture of her tyranny that Adam had died with all his ribs intact, though having grown up I have come to the opinion that no better creature than woman was ever made out of a chop.

Amongst those who were left in the holidays was the entire family of Douglas Dickson: Malcolm, Betty, Hester, and Joan. They were a very musical family and played instruments endlessly, and with great talent, but it is not their music that I remember most at Dolphinton. Malcolm was much older than us and compelled my brother and myself to conform to his every whim. The slightest deviation attracted punishment which ranged from being shut in a drawer until we acknowledged his superiority, or held out of the top-floor window by a foot until fear turned pride into submission. Little boys are horrid to one another but most grow out of it, as Malcolm did. His father, Doctor Douglas Dickson, was the kindest and gentlest of men but my first memories of him are different. On the climacteric day of the Battle of Britain I took a stroll along the lengthy drive to the school gates. I was caught short and took my modest relief behind a tree. Upon my satisfaction I spotted some lurid puff-ball toadstools. Hating and fearing these strange shapes I began to kick them over one by one. Suddenly, from behind a tree, the

27

furious figure of Douglas Dickson appeared, uncharacteristically, in a rage. He was a great connoisseur of what are doubtfully called 'edible fungi'. He accused me of destroying the nation's food supply in the hour of its greatest need. I can never forget the extent of his wrath. How odd the impressions of childhood are, for he was the gentlest and kindest of men! Once I grew up I had many happy and lyrical times with all the members of this most sensitive and musical family.

At the end of 1940 when invasion no longer seemed inevitable we returned to Edinburgh. Once a week my father visited Carstairs Hospital, which is now a criminal lunatic asylum, but was then an asylum for soldiers in blue suits who tried to convince him that they were too frightened to fight. He sometimes took me to see these poor tortured beings. A colleague, Dr Gorson, had a donkey which he thought we would like to ride. My brother went first. We were put in the charge of one of those blue-suited gents called Sennet. Now Sennet, it should be appreciated, had a strong motive – like all his fellow inmates – to prove to the doctors that he was daft. Here was his chance. He whipped and tormented the donkey until the enraged beast rampaged into a wood where – like Absalom – my brother was plucked up by a tree, but – unlike Absalom – he survived it. Sennet never had to go to war again. On such great evidence the psychiatrist depends. Carstairs was a horrid place and bitterly cold – I feel for those whom I have advised or defended who have ended up there, because those who enter rarely leave – alive.

My memories of the early war years are scattered. I remember watching the raid on the Forth Bridge and seeing the barrage balloons going up and asking if I could go to see the body of the first German pilot to be shot down and killed which lay in state under the Nazi flag at Portobello. My request was refused.

I was very upset when they took away all the railings that no one ever made into bullets, and put air-raid shelters and water tanks in the gardens of Edinburgh. When the siren wailed we went down to the shelter in the basement. The window there had been bricked up and the ceiling had been strengthened with metal beams and sandbags which were expected to sustain all the weight of the masonry above if it were bombed. It was a maid's room before the war and therefore had bars on the windows already, and the universal smell that maids' rooms have – of maids. Only the smell survived the war.

One night I was woken by the whistle of a falling bomb which landed on a nearby whisky bond at Gorgie. There was no siren because single planes were not accorded the honour of a welcome and this was a stray unloading its bombs on its way back from Glasgow. My father took me out to see the wasteful blaze – whisky running in the gutters, sometimes burning, and old men scooping it up with tin mugs. I dare say there were some pretty ill men next day. Thereafter I slept on a camp-bed in the shelter, sharing it with the stores which my father had laid in, in anticipation that some commodities might run short. He bought enough lavatory paper to last the whole household for the duration of the war. In the morning, I went out and collected the noses of anti-aircraft shells that had come down to earth. Assuming one did not realize the possibility of death, it was fun to be alive in war-time.

The overwhelming memory of those days was listening to the growing challenge of Winston Churchill's speeches in 1940. My father, knowing the Germans from his years studying at Kiel, Cologne, Berlin and Strasbourg Universities, and understanding human motivation in general and psychopathic behaviour in particular, had been an ardent anti-Munich person. He had analyzed Hitler as 'the repository and embodiment of many forms of soul-destroying hatreds' and abhorred the lunacy of pacifist policies almost to the extent that Churchill did. He taught me Cicero's great query, quoted by Pitt in the House of Commons on 3 February 1800: '*Cur igitur pacem nolo? Quia infida est, quia periculosa, quia non potest*' ('Why therefore do I refuse peace? Because it is treacherous: because it is dangerous, because it cannot be.') He admired Churchill therefore and I remember him coming into my bedroom to tell me that at last a great man was Prime Minister. He let me listen to all his broadcast speeches. How I loved them. But, in my estimation, the greatest speech he ever made during the war was his speech at St James's Palace on 12 June 1941 to the conference of Dominion High Commissioners and Allied Countries' Ministers, though one prediction he made was, perhaps happily, inaccurate: 'it will not be by German hands that the structure of Europe will be rebuilt, or the union of the European family achieved'. I'm not so sure.

Neither Churchill nor Hitler could have been accused of pacifism for both separately declared their horror of war while, in quite different ways, they each relished its art. But one of the observations my father made was that his pacifist patients were inspired to be people of peaceful intent by the inner conflicts of their minds which were so intense that those feelings must be overtly lidded and denied. Hatred is the parent of pacifism as it is of the urge of those who claim a passionate detestation of animal suffering. And certainly all the evidence of the actings of those who claim to champion either of these causes confirms my father's

29

diagnosis – that so resentful and hateful is the child that, in the one case, he feels compelled to deny his aggression in the search for the peace of his inner mind and in the other that he transfers his sense of suffering and outrage to an animal object with whom he feels compelled to identify.

Thus it was that I was inspired to enquire of my father that as every decency and virtue seemed to be only explicable as a denial of its opposite or certainly the product of the pains of emotional torture whether a placid, responsible and safe upbringing, unaffected by trauma and schism, angst or deprivation, could ever produce a man or woman, be it Churchill, Beethoven, Cezanne or whomever of greatness or consequence, or whether quiescence would inevitably produce only the bland and the dull. I also asked him whether we had to risk the tyrants and tormentors of the world to obtain the great men of creation and of courage, whose mainspring came from the same dynamic boiling source. However often I asked him, he could never bring himself to agree with my implied diagnosis because he was too kind a man, and his belief in the eternal Christian good prevented him from pronouncing such a stark and wicked diagnosis. Yet he was too true a philosopher and a thinker to admit that my diagnosis was in any way wrong or to advance an alternative thesis to it.

He found the same strength of hatred in his patients to be the root cause of male homosexuality, which has a totally different form and strength of cause from lesbianism, female homosexuality. The male child is conceived in the womb of its prospective love object. Throughout his sojourn there, he is drip-fed, centrally heated, cosseted and protected, but as he grows it appears to him that his adored landlady is pulling on the walls of his palace until one day he is confined in a cupboard and she ejects him painfully and without notice, only for him to have to beg as a supplicant at the breast of his most loved and hated rejector for food. If thereafter by smothering attention, or tendentious neglect, she thwarts his significance she will build up hatred of such intensity that it will cause him to deny her as the worthy love object and turn into himself as the wrongly unloved and rejected Adonis. That is the rage of male homosexuality. Since the female child is also born of her mother, her rival is not the object of her ambition, which is the father object. The trauma of birth rejection does not therefore have the same ragious implications, although the homosexual recourse of narcissism is also a denial of unbearable feelings of resentment and rejection. To suggest, as many do, that homosexuality and heterosexuality are a mere sexual preference, like the high road and the low road, is to misunderstand and overlook the morbid psychopathological hatreds which give rise to these deviances.

Similarly, in art and music my father identified the positive as opposed to the negative resolutions of the forces of hate, extremism, resentment and power. He explained to me the aggression and sadism for instance of Rembrandt and Beethoven, the controlled pacifism of Botticelli and Bach and the schizoid detachment which produced the works of Dali and Picasso.

Thus I acquired not only an insight into human nature and an understanding of the manifestations of human behaviour and personality but also, most useful of all, an endless interest in the motivation of human kind and the urges that made the horrors and the glories of human creation. Nothing could have been a better preparation for a life in the high court of Glasgow amongst the most helpless wicked, or the high court of Parliament amongst those who imagine they are the most helpful exalted.

I now went to a split new school – Buckingham House School which Miss Kathleen Martin had opened. I was the first pupil and arrived in my kilt. No child who went through Miss Martin's hands emerged other than confident, well educated and improved.

The British market having failed to provide an honourable nanny, my father turned his search to the resources of our enemies instead. There was a ready source of German Jewesses who had fled from persecution. We had two in turn – one dreadful, one darling. The first was Fräulein Irsch. Her pale, haunted face betrayed the hostility which had been visited on her and which in turn she visited on us. She walked awkwardly and spoke guttural English with bad breath. No language is more incompatible with feminity than German – except perhaps Swiss German – its sounds grate against all beauty. From the very beginning all of us disliked her and were firmly convinced that she was a spy and we were all delighted when she left us. No doubt she reported the sea-borne defences of Angus to the Führer. She was supplanted by Cilli Marx, whose very first act was one of kindness. She put a bar of chocolate under our pillows. It taught me to remember that children love treats and surprises. She was cheerful and kind and remembered us every Christmas. She came to my wedding and now lives the evening of her life in Manchester. She taught me an invaluable and early political lesson: it is political systems that are bad. Never judge ill those that have to live under them. She and the pilot at Portobello, whom I wasn't allowed to see, broke my hitherto unshakeable belief that all Germans were bad Germans.

31

It was suggested by our doctor that it would be good for me, recovering from whooping cough, and for my mother – who was by now convalescing from many illnesses – if we spent the summer in the country. My father leased a house called Bolton Muir, one mile from Gifford. It was modelled like a ship, appallingly badly designed, though it looked more like a bijou residence in Broker Belt than anything in Scotland, but we loved it and spent a very happy summer *en famille*.

It was in the next holidays that it was announced that sweets were to be rationed, and we went to the village to stock up with Maltesers and soor plooms from Mrs Nicol's Shop. All these delicacies thereafter instantly disappeared.

In September 1941, I went to my preparatory school, the Nippers at Loretto. My brother was already there as were my two cousins, Harry and Robin More Gordon. I was accustomed to boarding away from home and was not too apprehensive or unhappy. I was thrilled by the red blankets on the beds. At seven years old I weighed three stone five pounds, standing four foot one and a quarter inches. I was very small and as a result became something of a mascot. During the early days of my first term I was constantly called to the matron's room or the headmaster's house to be exhibited to some worthy member of the Loretto family. I was put in Form IV under the gentle instruction of dear Miss MacDonald, a plump little woman with a round face like an apple out of which, occasioned by her natural timidity, her deep, sunk brown eyes blinked like an owl. Her skin was like a ripened peach tinged on the cheeks with little red veins. She always wore a brown cardigan whatever the weather, being a creature of controlled order and routine. The dimples on her cheeks were barometers of her displeasure. Her instruction like her handwriting was meticulous. She cared for the things that matter – reading, spelling, arithmetic, good English clean manners, and God. Kindness was her pleasure.

Latin was taught by S.T. Hutchinson who was, to us little boys, the perfect man. Hutchie was the son of an English divine from Lincoln. His hair was immaculately brushed and parted in the middle. He had an aquiline nose and a powerful resonant voice. He was a tease and a taskmaster and being beaten by him either with a puddox stick or for serious crimes with his thin wicked cane ('Long John') was neither welcome nor easily forgotten, but he was a supremely gifted teacher, a lithe and swift athlete, and he instilled in us immediately the pleasures and disciplines of Latin. And so I rushed through the early pages of Hillard and Botting and Kennedy's 'Shortbread Eating' Primer. In

French, the first lessons egotistically teach one to say 'I am' and possessively 'I have', but in Latin the very first lesson is appropriately 'I love', even if for a bit the object of affection is only Cotta or a table. I often wondered who those barbarians were that dear Cotta kept attacking. I know now, I've met many of them since. It was not long before we learnt to decline years, boys, masters and wars, judges, kings and soldiers, flowers, virgins, couches and fathers and mastered the arts of conjugation. We learnt the prepositions which take the accusative by such devices as this:

> Ante, apud, ad, adversus
> We'll get in if you reverse us.

I soon formed at school a lasting and ineradicable aversion to rugger and PT, Sunday walks and the smell of the Esk, a river whose bed was a cesspit of black, stinking slime. On Thursday and Friday afternoons we had singing practice for which we had to walk through the territory traditionally occupied by the boys of St Peter's School, a well-disciplined guerrilla force of clustifists, or keelies as we say in Scots. Having passed through the Thermopylae of St Peter's, the next terror was the Persian hordes of Upper School. I apparently resembled a cartoon figure called Henry, who appeared in some pre-war journal and kept getting into trouble, so I had to cross the ash court to cries of 'Hiya Henry' from the giant boys of Upper School. I was terrified. I was so small some of them used to pick me up by the neck. These periods of singing were in preparation for Sunday chapel which we attended in our kilts, black jackets and Eton collars, and in summer with a flower in our button-holes. All the boys had to sing in the choir, so I learnt by heart all the hymns and psalms and the canticles and anthems of the English Church, which were contained haphazardly in books of different colours and were hard to find. I have never ceased to love the music of the English Church, especially when sung in the resonant acoustics of the great English cathedrals by a boys' choir. The treble solos in chapel were sung by Harry More Gordon who had, to my ear, a better voice than Ernest Lough. Paradoxically, it was my brother – who like me was a musical mute – who won a singing scholarship to the Nippers, and not my cousin. The chaplain was the Revd Basil Snell who preached at aeviternal length. I remember the last three words of his last sermon at Loretto and no others: 'learn to pray'. I have often had to.

Our only other regular visit to the Upper School was to the torture-house of the gym where our torture was orchestrated by Sergeant Major

Edwards, commonly known to us as Baller George. For a man of the age of sixty he had a breathtaking agility which he retained until his death and an equal capacity to tell stories that even the most youthful and credulous did not believe. Despite his sadistic task we loved him dearly, and with every justification – he was a very jolly man.

The gymnasium had been donated to the school by Henry Brocklehurst 'in grateful memory of his days at Loretto'. I'd be grateful if I could forget mine on the principle of 'Horas non numero sine serenas' ('I only value the beautiful times'). His generosity was no doubt inspired by the absurd inverted Victorian propaganda that 'your school days are the happiest days of your life'. If I'd thought that was true I'd have jumped into the stinking quicksands of the Esk the day I left.

The headmaster, Tim Colman, was a tall, swarthy, athletic Englishman who always wore brown plus-fours and a Cambridge tie. He inspired awe, but his warm spirit prevented it from turning into fear, except on the innumerable occasions when we had to report to his study at 10.30 for some baculine chastisement. Physical pain has never given me pleasure. Nevertheless the fear of such punishment had little corrective effect as may be seen from the following letter from my father to my mother: 'I called at school with Nicky's raincoat and Tim Colman took me up to his room. Although it was after "Lights-Out", they were all on the floor, with the exception of Nicky who, I am glad to say, was at any rate on the bed if not in it. I do not know what will happen to them tomorrow.' My mother always kept that letter in her cigarette case.

To Tim Colman I owe an immense debt. He was one of the best teachers that any boy could ever have met. He cared intensely in his lofty English way for the education and development of every one of us. His sarcasm and disdain were but the front of a shy and dedicated man. However roughly he may at times have been treated nobody ever left the Nippers but deeply grateful for Tim Colman's care and instruction, loving and revering this swarthy and aloof instructor. He believed instinctively in the wisdom of his compatriot Dr Johnson: 'Much may be made of a Scotchman if he be taught young.' He taught us manners, morals and the lore and stories of history. He never ceased swearing 'by the Duke and Duchess of Argyll', eating dry biscuits, smoking Craven A cigarettes and loving beautiful women. His memory I salute with honour. Mrs Colman – Pat Colman, his wife – was a woman of exceptional kindness and good cheer. She took a special interest in me because I was very small, and this interest she sustained with increasing affection until her untimely death at an early age not long after I left.

Such was the devotion that the Colmans inspired that Rachel the cook, Sarah and Rebecca, Nellie the maid and her sister Alice gave their lives to the service of Loretto and the Nippers.

On my first day, to my intense alarm, I was told that the matron's name was Miss Thompson but I was relieved to discover that she was not 'Sharp Tin' and had an entirely different and kindly nature. She was succeeded by Eileen Newton who was young, tall, blonde, had long and very beautiful legs, lovely skin and a great deal of sex appeal – none of which characteristics passed the notice of either myself, aged eight, or the headmaster, forty years my senior. She was the first girl to whom I felt physically attracted and very strongly. How appropriate the child's prayer of E.V. Cooke:

> The Woman tempted me – and tempts me still
> Lord God, I pray you, that she ever will.

It was always alleged by other boys that the feeling was mutual, since however much they messed up my hair, I was the only boy she never sent back upstairs at breakfast to brush it. At this stage, the facts of life were still probably unknown to me, but not for long, for in my fourth term in 1942, a Mr Mayhew joined the staff. He asked me to say and then spell 'any four-letter word beginning with F'. The universal Anglo-Saxon verb was suddenly whispered into my ear and in my complete innocence, I boldy announced it. The consternation of Mr Mayhew was complete; that afternoon, my informant explained the significance and meaning of the naughty word. Now my information was complete too.

One of the first experiences of our first term was a medical examination by the school doctor, Dr Cleland. He was all a doctor should be. He dressed in a black pin-striped suit, wore rimless glasses, was tall, big, cheerful, smelt of ether, and was almost bald. Though his gruff manner and liking for the lance frightened us as children, we quickly learnt he was composed almost entirely of a heart of gold. So far as I recall, this first inspection of my little frame was almost entirely devoted to assuring himself and me that the tiny gonads which were destined to be the source of such pleasure had descended in preparation for their busy life. Apparently they had. I am very grateful that Sandy Cleland put first things first.

In my second week I was introduced to another lifelong devotee of the school, Mrs – or as we called her, Hag – Tinsley. Hag Tinsley was the widow of the cricket professional, whose useful life was brought to a sudden stop when he was struck on the head while umpiring an

35

important cricket match by a golf ball fired by a little boy. Since this unfortunate occasion, Mrs Tinsley had run the school tuck-shop, but since there was now no tuck, she had no shop to run. She was very small and had a raucous Lancashire voice, twinkling humour and a brown straw-hat. Being better than her late husband at avoiding flying objects – perhaps because she was so short – she laughed her way into her nineties and was buried with the Loretto equivalent of full military honours. At that, our very first meeting, we took to each other immediately, perhaps because we were both about the same size.

We got up every day at seven o'clock and went along to the lower tub room, where we had a cold tub. The tubs were painted red – lest we forget – and since Loretto considered that the head played little part in a good Lorettonian boy, it was perhaps not surprising that sharp physical shocks were regarded as reasonable preparation for the day. Before I left, five thousand more cold baths were to be endured. Every day we had the same prayer which Tim Colman said nobly: 'Bestow upon us O God, that courage that thine own givest to meet serenely whatever comes.' It certainly had some meaning whenever we had to report to his study. Indeed, there was a lot more to come and serenity was in short supply. My early contribution to European painting in this world received commendations from our relentlessly tormented patron 'Groisy' Munro: 'Fairbairn has a fine sense of colour and a remarkable imagination.'

At night the sirens often wailed and we staggered sleepily down to the shelters which were damp and we were arranged in racks along the side and in the middle. Roll calls ensured that none of us had been picked off on the way down. On Saturdays after lunch we were allowed downtown to a few shops. In Woods you could buy crisps for twopence and raisins for a penny (real pennies) while Harly and Harper provided Ovaltine tablets and a malt bar which was in fact a laxative in disguise, and the Hayweights Dairy sold toffee cups for a penny which were too big to go into your mouth and, once in, too big to get out again; your teeth stuck in them if closed, and they took an hour or so to dissolve. At the end of my second term I was adjudged 'the same happy and polite little enthusiast'. Good manners and enthusiasm are two essential qualities of life; would that I still mastered both. In the summer we played cricket which postponed horrid rugger for another term, and provided one at least with a lesson in life – things are never so good that you can afford to presume that fortune will not turn, and never so bad that you can't win if you try hard enough. Never slacken and never despair – that is the lesson of cricket. Victory and defeat can be two balls apart in life as in cricket.

In the summer of 1942 we moved to another house in Gifford, Holyn Bank, a handsome Georgian house then on the Yester Estates. It was damp and faced due east so the sun never shone in public rooms unless you got up at worm-time, but it had many acres of ground, exciting woods, stables, a river, and a vast walled garden which was a cornucopia of fruit, including a vast variety of apples. Apples have a varied reputation, having caused *inter alia* the creation of sin, the Trojan War and thus the pleasures or pains (as you view) it of the *Aeneid*, the reputation of William Tell, and if taken daily the redundancy of doctors. No other fruit has achieved so much in league with men and women. It is a wonder costermongers are not richer merchants.

The village had only a few shops, but those it had were run by a community of most delightful and generous bawcocks. There was Toddy the postman, a tiny, grey-haired, French-looking man, with a face simultaneously twisted with the pain of his First World War wound, and wrinkled with his twinkling wit, whose words were always wise. Bert Tait was the butcher, a big cheerful bawdy stand-patter with a hoarse voice and always a joke under his grey moustache. As he indulged his liking for whisky, his humour and his habits betrayed his liking for girls. Mr and Mrs Hogg ran the newspaper shop – the quietness of their kind manner made it a treat to go in to see them. Then there was kind Mrs Gillies whose timidity caused her to blush at the mere mention of her name, and Mrs Riley who won every raffle and prize that was ever offered in the village – she was Irish. All these characters and many besides used to gather in the evening to play skittles and to drink whisky, when there was any, in the Goblin Ha'. It was a great game and I got good at it very young. I liked it because it didn't involve getting hurt like the games we played at school.

I spent many daytime hours in the holidays in the smiddy with Cowan the blacksmith; he was tall and grey. I was amazed by his skill and strength as I watched the genius of his craft and smelled the rich reasting odour of the horses' feet. Though almost without 'education' he had supremely good taste, a natural sense of proportion, a deep wisdom, and he was utterly satisfied by the full, skilled, simple life he lived. The whole community of Gifford had a contentment and a charm which was the product of the pace and satisfaction of their various lives: the strain and strangeness of town life, where so many people are never alone but always lonely, was unknown to them. Nor did they feel deprived of the false lures of city life. Each was a supreme individual; each was fulfilled; each gave and got the satisfaction of mattering.

The body and soul of Gifford was guarded by two worthy people. The Revd Cumming was in charge of our spirits and PC Angus MacDonald was in charge of the law. Mr Cumming, though scholarly, presented a dour doomladen front and a dry unsmiling misery which the Presbyterian Church in Scotland too often thinks is the appropriate face for Christianity to wear, while PC MacDonald, who was a Highlander and equally reserved, displayed the true Scottish character of a broad humour and a big heart. He also had a big fist and a big capacity for the craitur. Neither had much to do. Neither did much. Both did it well.

Village life was orientated towards and patronized by our shy, lofty feudal lord, the Marquis of Tweedale, who lived aloof in the beautiful mansion of Yester. Every New Year the whole village was invited to Yester to dance and drink in Adam's beautiful dining-room under the tutelage of the Master of Ceremonies, John Brown the gamekeeper. He was fat and ruddy. Cheerfulness burst out of him to every heart. It was all one big family, everyone danced, got merry, sang 'A Guid New Year to yin and a' 'and kissed passionately on the stroke of twelve – and the kissing didn't stop until every male had kissed every female and many more than once.

Here, as in Montrose, was a feudal or family community. Each had a different job, some had more than others. Some were rich and some were poor. Some went to Eton, most to the village school. Some drank beer, and some drank gin. Nobody cried 'It's not fair'. Nobody despised or envied those above for being who they were or for having what they had, or those below for being below. We were all privileged to belong. We all needed one another and loved one another for ourselves. There was no contempt for station in either direction. All preferred to enrich one another by sharing what they had to give by way of personality.

Life at Gifford and life at school continued in this fairly familar routine throughout the war years. I went through the traditional season of measles, chicken-pox, constipation and mumps. These times were spent in the sick house under the eagle eye and piping voice of a diminutive cagmag called Sister Brown. She had a quaint collection of febrifuges she fed to us by spoon, the most dreaded of which was a personally patented potion called 'Black Draught', akin to the Black Death, which acted as a lightning evacuant for small boys. It had similar properties to Croton Oil which was used to expurgate with half a drop Victorian lunatics and convicts. The great genius Francis Galton swallowed a teaspoonful during his alphabetical research into the effects

of the compounds recorded in the *British Pharmacopoeia*. He survived –
just. But he stopped at C. We enjoyed our times – 'Black Draught' aside
– under the care of this wizened Nightingale.

We had a period each week called 'News' under Tim Colman, which
encouraged us to take a genuine interest in the war and in politics. We
kept books of cuttings so that as the war progressed and we grew older
our interest deepened in politics and international affairs. Mine has
never flagged since. It was a very exciting war for children: Churchill,
Montgomery and Alexander were real heroes. And Hitler and 'his
grizzly gang' were huge and real too. The greatest excitement of the
impending approach of peace was the return of light and the
disappearance of the black-out. We went up, my brother and I, to the
village to see the first bus come in without blinds and faded lights. I have
never seen such a brilliant sight. No *son et lumière* has generated in me
such excitement and delight. I try to look with equal pleasure at buses at
night now, and have always wanted to floodlight the principal buildings
and spires and towers of all the best towns and cities in the country. The
wonder of light at night is magic.

The close interest which Tim Colman's news periods had instilled in
us throughout the war quickened as Europe gradually weaned her
patriotic strength and threw off the despotic grip of the Lilliputian
Huns. Churchill had expressed his immovable though little shared
foresight in his most defiant challenge on the fall of France. A century or
so before, Churchill's unfavourite historian, Macaulay, had expressed
uniquely that spirit of man which his oratory had kept aflame:

> Sovereigns may send their oppressors to dungeons; they may clear out
> a senate-house with soldiers; they may enlist armies of spies; they may
> have scores of disaffected in chains at every crossroad. But what
> power shall stand in that frightful time when rebellion hath become a
> less evil than endurance? Who shall dissolve that terrible tribunal
> which in the hearts of the oppressed denounces against the oppressor
> the doom of its wild injustice? Who shall repeal the laws of self-
> defence? What arms or discipline shall resist the strength of famine or
> despair?

Hutchie came and woke us to tell us France was free. On VE-Day we
cycled home for two days' break; flags and bonfires were everywhere
and there were endless celebrations all round. I recall, like a childhood
smell, the intenseness of the feeling of freedom and joy that peace
created. I recall nothing like it since. It comes back to me when I listen to

Churchill's triumphant and concise speech: 'The German war is therefore at an end . . . Advance Britannia! Long live the cause of freedom! God save the King!' The world had gained by war all it would have lost without it and had proved most painfully the truth of Hitler's most ironic boast, 'It is a national disgrace that a people should be ruled by a madman.' We paid our modest heartfelt tributes in church to the 'unbehoven dead who fed the guns' and cycled back to school and the unfamiliar life of peace.

CHAPTER 3

We returned to school to the divisive loyalties of politics. The gardener, Alec Hastie, was a staunch socialist and he had every right to be. He'd been a coal-miner of great courage until his health had been worn down by the loyal ardours of these splendid men. My father always told me that they were the finest and bravest and most diligent of his comrades in the First War. All miners have a very special spirit which Alec Hastie did not lack. However, his arguments imbued in me an antipathy to socialism. I did not resent those above me or those below me. Why should he? I did not know what class I was supposed to belong to and whichever it was I didn't choose it. I couldn't change it and I wasn't ashamed of it. I found his spite abhorrent and so did my friends. We therefore set out to frustrate the advance of such envy-lopers and each night after 'Lights Out', risking terrible penalties, we dressed and climbed out of the lavatory window in the upper tub room, descended three floors by drain-pipe and set off into the town to canvass against 'Pathetic Lawrence', as we called him, the Labour candidate; and thereafter to eat ices in the Mall Café. The risks were appalling, but our truancy proved in vain, though undetected. Alec Hastie greeted us one lunch-time with pride: 'The man own the wyreless is shooting hisself sick! Labour's in.'

Since democracy had failed, the methods of the 'maquis rouge' and Bolsheviks were all that were left to us. Armed with catapults we made our way to the roof of the air-raid shelter behind the school and put out every window in the Co-op bakery – the only symbol of the Left within our range. The crime discovered, those responsible owned up to their sabotage – not without pride. In the absence of the death penalty which did not apply at school, we were sentenced to the next best thing – six in whites (unlined trousers) which left a brutal baculine impression – or rather twelve of them – no sweets for the rest of term, and we were put in Coventry, except in class, for a period of seven days. That was nothing to the penalties and deprivation which Cripps, Dalton and the

41

rest of them imposed for the next six years on the country at large.

Since the Labour Government achieved restrictions on the supply of food which the German U-boats at their zenith had failed to do, school food and routine altered little. One benefit, however, of the close of hostilities was that the succession of vagrant French masters came to an end with the return from war service of Colin Mason. He was the brother of James Mason, the actor. His parents had only funds enough to educate one child, and they educated James as an architect. He abandoned his training and became very rich as an actor, but the prodigal son made no provision for a brother who rightly resented such thoughtlessness to the extent that he tore up any magazine which contained his brother's photograph. They made it up later. Colin, as a teacher, was all the better for not being trained, for very little that is worth learning can be taught. He returned from a rigorous war in the navy imbued with the disciplines and the pride of a man who had proved his quality at sea and in action. His blue eyes twinkled mischievously from his square, rather leathered face. He had a nasal, patronizing voice, suited to the pronunciation of French which was his subject. His boyishness endeared him to boys but estranged him from men and women. Like Hutchie and Tim Colman, he was devoted to education and interested in scholarship. These three took me far beyond the education and restrictions of my age and introduced me to the pleasures of literature, classics and thinking for oneself. Being encouraged in the things that were important to me, and thus fulfilled, I began to take an interest in things that previously were not and so I was absorbed unwisely into the rugger fifteen, became captain of hockey and the cricket eleven, and Head of School. I was worthy of none of them.

One climacteric occurred, however, just before I left my prep school which was to ensure the end of all this advance. After nineteen memorable years, the beloved headmaster of the Upper School, Dr Greenlees, retired. He had a character like Arnold of Rugby which commanded instant respect and lifelong affection from all. He had no educational qualification of any kind. No doubt that is why he was such a good headmaster.

Loretto was founded, essentially in 1862, by Dr H. H. Almond who was, in his day, far ahead of his time: his message was essentially, *mens sana in corpore sano*. Instituting 'boy government' at all levels he had a faith in the effect on character of organized games. He encouraged individuality of outlook, and regarded with contempt customs that were irrational or had lost their validity. 'I want Loretto,' he said on his death bed, 'to be the most rational school and the best.' His message had been rigidly adhered to, though his philosophy had been entirely undeveloped by successive headmasters, so that by the time I arrived it was as far behind the times as it had been in front of them at its foundation. The importance of organized games had swollen, *mens sana* had been forgotten and only *in corpore sano* had been retained. By slavishly adhering to his thoughts his successors had missed the purport of his message.

The successor to Dr Greenlees was Forbes Mackintosh and he had three Achillean heels. All the headmasters before him since Almond had been Lorettonians and he was an outsider. He was a scholar in mind and a cricketer in sport, in contrast to his belief or fear that the fame of Loretto had been created by decent fools on a rugger field. In his undeviating effort 'to do the right thing' he decided to ignore his natural inclinations in favour of those which he believed the ghost of Almond and living old Lorettonians would expect of him. With this spectre he had become obsessed.

He decided to instruct the first form in the Nippers for an hour a week in Greek. As a Greek scholar he could not understand why we, who had never seen, or in many cases heard of, the Greek alphabet, could not appeciate instantly the works of his beloved Homer in the original. We were compared unfavourably to circus clowns, mental pygmies and intellectual dwarfs. From all the many masters who had passed through our lives we had encountered and endured nothing like this fury before.

I won a scholarship to the Upper School, and left the loving and devoted care and instruction of my prep school for the topsy-turvydom that was in store. Tim Colman wrote: 'We shall all miss his polite friendliness and quiet sense of humour', a doubtful tribute but he was not to miss me nearly as much as I was to miss him. On no occasion did I miss him so greatly as when Forbes Mackintosh called all the new boys together and addressed us thus, and me in particular in front of them: 'I want you to look at this boy. He's just got a scholarship and he doesn't like rugger. That's exactly the sort of boy we don't want at Loretto.' His words were razors. What a reverse of the taunts of the Greek class so recently endured. And so for the next four years I endured the absurd priorities of this regime and reached in none of the subjects I had done at Loretto Nippers the standard I had been raised to when I was there.

On the occasion of the twenty-fifth wedding anniversary of King George and Queen Elizabeth my mother decided, with her generous heart, to take my brother and me to London. It was my first visit. I was thrilled, and have loved London ever since. We went through the routine, so boring to parents, of visiting St Paul's and Westminster, and Madame Tussaud's, and all the other exciting places for children. My brother and I obtained lunch for a shilling in a British restaurant in Northumberland Street, fed those scruffy pigeons in Trafalgar Square, and prepared for the great day. We watched the parade in the Mall and we were thrilled by all the panoply and the sight of the horses and the decorations. What a wonderful contribution of love and excitement the Royal Family makes to the lives of the British people. Imagine some dull old President like Harold Wilson or Lord George Brown getting anybody to turn out and watch them going along the Mall, or even for that matter President Mrs Lizzie Windsor, if she were only tenant of the throne for five years. It is the mystique, the permanency and the history of monarchy which anti-royalists seem most to resent. Our Jubilee visit was one of the most exciting moments of my life up to that time, but also very nearly the last for my uncle had booked us into the Onslow Court Hotel where Haigh, the notorious vampire, was the lounge-lizard of the cocktail bar. He might well have put my mother, my brother and myself in an acid bath along with Mrs Durand Deacon had the hotel been able to take us.

Though it was then criminally neglectful of the intellect, Loretto provided an excellent preparation for the art of life. It was very much a community and everyone respected one another as such. We were all equal but different and everyone knew everybody else. If Disraeli's description of the public school as a microcosm of the world is true then the Lorettonian world would be very contented, friendly and big-hearted if somewhat dim. In my boredom I learnt to read and to think for myself, and I formed a very close association with those masters who were interested in the culture of their subject. Reggie Smith shared his love of English literature with me and encouraged my love of him and it. Giggly, dribbly, and beaming with sprightliness and gaiety, smoking a pipe and wearing a cap which dwarfed his little sensitive face, he steadily pursued his own cultivation and imparted the depths and delights of English literature to those who were anxious to absorb them. Geoff Turner, a tall, kindly and fluent polyglot, encouraged my interest in languages. He had been a friend of my family for years and granted me the kindness of his home which was a refuge of civilization from school. His height and slow walk gave great dignity to a very dignified man. He was never in a hurry – except to help a friend – and his patience in the war of attrition which the headmaster and governors waged against him and his family inexorably but brutally till they drove him out, was the token of the serenity of a good man, though even his fortitude couldn't hide the pain of those treacherous wounds. Donny Reid was a different figure – small, Welsh and brash, his shock of white hair dominated a brown and congenial face. He was sensitive about the extent of his grasp of Classics and used aggression to disguise it. He was cheerful and he was fond of life, Classics and me. He wanted me to go on in Classics, but medicine required that I change to the colourless universals of Science after getting School Certificate with eight distinctions. For this I was awarded a red-and-white tie. There were six ways of getting it with your body but only one way you could get it with your brain – by getting five distinctions in School Certificate. That was then the scale of Loretto's values.

The lessons that I was not taught at Loretto were perhaps un-important; the lessons I learnt untaught undoubtedly were important: to respect each person without either deference or condescension, to be independent, to show goodwill and good manners to all people at all times unless you intend to be rude, to develop the individual and his idiosyncrasy to the utmost, to be yourself and being myself to be the creature and the servant of others. These were the themes of Lorettonian democracy.

When one is a boy at school, the masters – or some of them – seem giant men. As I grew up a sneaking suspicion overtook me that perhaps they are in fact only men among boys; on leaving I realized that most of them were only boys among men.

One of the compulsory duties was membership of the JTC – Loretto's army – later renamed at unnecessary expense by some egalitarian Leftie in the bureaucracy the CCF, because non-public schools had an ACF, and we must not be different. We were issued with a uniform by CSM MacLaren, or 'MacSporran' as we called him. How difficult it was to put on webbing and spats as a little boy, and what a weight a rifle was on a tiny shoulder. At the end of my first term we went to JTC camp at Barry Links in Angus, a sand-dune lying between the longest piece of straight railway line in Britain and the flattest piece of sea, and rejected by all but us, rainfall and clegs. Trying to find one's equipment to lay it out in the morning with ten in a tent was not easy. The straw palliasses were filthy and prickly and damp. We ate in a stinking cookhouse, like most camp cookhouses. We washed our greasy tin plates in cold, greasy water. To wash ourselves we had to cross the dunes to the bare, skeletal wash-stands with cold water. By day we did exercises in the sand, by night we drank filthy lemonade in the 'Soldier's Hole', and organized torment for suitable victims. It was a long, long week broken only by the joy of a visit to Mrs Hadden in Montrose in the course of which I visited by stealth Straton House, then sold but still unoccupied, and from the garden I stole some roots of the magnificent lily of the valley which grew there and which now grows to my delight at Fordell. Though it was a painful introduction, I came to love the military life.

At school, the routine of Spartan suffering was rigorously enforced. The bedrooms were unheated, windows open top and bottom, there were cold tubs, no fires and we wore open shirts and shorts and no underwear. To keep warm you had to run: double icing, not double glazing. The Governors must have had shares in oil, for it created in all of us a desire to spend the rest of our lives in warm houses.

From this routine of freezing torture, two hours a week provided light relief – Scripture and Art. The chaplain was now the Revd Lawrence Wright, an adiaphoristic divine. He was tall, friendly and outgoing, with a great heart and a lesser brain, completely unstuffy and a much better Christian for that. His ability to keep order in class over thirteen boys was as pronounced as the humour of St Paul. Nor was his ultrafidian mind ever able to discern whether we were pulling his leg or not. We directed at him a flow of naïve questions such as 'Is it true the disciples liked knitting?' and 'Did the five thousand take picnics to the Sermon on the Mount?' We enjoyed these periods of religious lullification.

The art class was also a weekly scene of unchecked idleness and irreverent mirth so we missed the token instruction in art which Loretto offered. Fortunately for me, in my last term, the young, virile, Scottish painter Douglas Baxter took over. Douglas Baxter differed from every schoolmaster and certainly every art master I had suffered or enjoyed. He was a man's man – and a woman's man too. He was virile and sturdy and had the face and haircut of a Greek head. Convention and orthodoxy were as strange to him as culture and taste were natural. He combined in his shrewd intellect a capacity for amazement and observation second to none which, with his natural intuition, formed the basis of his remarkable mind. Immediately he explained the mysteries of painting and conveyed to me, on the slenderest of evidence – which I can produce – the belief that I could paint. He inspired me with a faith with which nothing is impossible. He told me I could do it. He told me to do it my way and proved the wisdom of Oscar Wilde: 'The fine artist is the man who believes absolutely in himself, because he is absolutely himself.' I have been doing it ever since. He opened to me the boundless world of creation where nothing is impossible and everything is yours.

How sad for those who have to live in this world alone. No man was ever a better friend to me than Douglas Baxter for he gave me the greatest gift that I have enjoyed, and added unto it his friendship.

Friends rise and fade, but there are special people as well. In this world we collect special people though they play a vital role in only part of our lives. I think I have as valuable and exciting a collection as exists. One day I hope to have them all at once at a mighty party lasting a month. The dead will be represented by my memories of them, unless they care to come at whatever inconvenience. Immortality lives alone in our recollection and recounting of the wonders of those who touch us and whom we touch. Our fame endures only through the love of others.

In his judgment of the schools he had to endure Lord Cockburn wrote in 1840: 'The same powers that raise a boy in a good school make it probable he will rise high in life. But in bad schools it is nearly the reverse.' I hope he is right. I have had dreams since that I am back at school; it is my greatest fear. I would rather go to Hell; I'll have to anyway, no doubt. I pondered as I left the analysis of Henry Adams, that the chief wonder of education is that it doesn't ruin everyone concerned, teachers and taught alike.

Freedom! The definition of liberty – to be total, whole, independent, subject to no restriction and slave to no fool. That was the overwhelming emotion which burst out on the last day. I still celebrate my release from childhood and my release from school. The same impulse shared by emerging nations – to throw off the shackles of parents and quasi-parents and be yourself. Imago at last! Chrysalis no more. Now I was to discover the fears of freedom which are just as real as the torments of dependence and incarceration though infinitely less admitted or understood.

CHAPTER 4

I had arranged to set off on adult life in London investigating the world of finance which was a mystery to me. My father's first secretary, Elma Stewart, was now working in L. Messel and Company, the City stockbrokers, and she kindly arranged for me to do a job there at the princely salary of £9 a week for six weeks. The terrible oppression of rush and crush and the desperate attempt of millions of human beings to survive as souls in the maelstrom of city life made a deep impression on me. It confirmed all fears of insignificance and inadequacy.

The office was peopled with kind people of whose life, Mr Speller, the living image of Ernest Bevin, was typical. He rose at six, got the seven o'clock train, hung onto a strap-handle until he reached London and was disgorged with all the other peas in pods along the streets into the office. He said the same cheerful 'Good Morning' to the same cheerless crowd, had a rushed routine day interrupted by a rushed luncheon in a sandwich-bar on a stool, returned in a rush to the same boredom till he was released from it at 5.30 for the return crush home in time to gulp down some tinned food, fall into bed, set the alarm and rise with a start to start the rat race again next day. We are all mad.

Amongst the partners was one ancient master of feneration who came in about 11.30, read the *Financial Times*, signed the odd 'shaky' cheque with a shaky hand, bought thousands of Chinese Tea '27–'29, went for a rich lunch, port and cigar and returned to sell his shares and collect his inevitable profit. They might have been equally large losses and they required his genius to get it right. So I learned the fictions and practices of that strange world of money which surrounds the Bank of England, to which Lord Young, a noted wit on the Scots Bench in the nineteenth century, repaired with an English pound note. He handed it over to the dutiful clerk and demanded in his rasping Scotch voice, 'a poond sterling'. The clerk passed over a pound in change. 'Noo, laddie if ah'd bin seekin aifter change ah'd've asked fir it, would ah no?' he squeaked to the amazed consternation of the teller. 'Ah want a poond sterling which is definit in the statute as sae muckle weicht o' siller.' He was passed in ascending succession from horrified officer to officer of the Bank, each of whom shunned the responsibility of fulfilling a demand which would have caused such a fiscal earthquake. And so gradually he mounted the golden ladder of power until he was sitting in the Governor's room. 'And who are you, sir?' asked the suave Governor with deference to the craggy Scotch gentleman who was clearly a man of some elevation. 'Ah'm the bearer, sir,' Lord Young replied. Parliament forthwith changed the statutory definition of sterling to prevent lesser men getting rich and beggaring the Bank of England.

During my stay in London, there arrived from New Zealand the domineering personality of my father's cousin, Dr Elizabeth Gunn, who amongst other contributions to social welfare in New Zealand invented the health stamp system there. Knowing only sandwich-bars, I took her for lunch at the Great Eastern, a railway hotel recently nationalized. She grandly ordered game pie. The 'game' included rabbit. 'Vermin in my food!' she roared. Every flunky from top to bottom was summoned for a lecture on the iniquity of the state system which could sink to the practice of poisoning her with vermin. None was spared her cacophonous sermon. Meekly and wetly they accepted the strictures of this independent and worthy woman who had shown in her life and by her example how much more a man – and a woman – can do for themselves and for the welfare of one another than the State can achieve on their behalf. They bowed innocuously, as innocuous people do, as she swept out in a triumph of disapproval. I followed hopefully unseen. I was immensely thankful to return to the homeliness of beloved Scotland, after my first lonely venture into the big world.

I now had to prepare for the Medical Faculty of Edinburgh University. With typical generosity my father had sent me in London the news of my acceptance. The letter of acceptance was couched in terms of snide bureaucratic resentment. It made me feel unwelcome. But then as Bishop Creighton said, 'The universities are sort of lunatic asylums for keeping young men out of mischief.' I obtained digs at 10 Royal Circus – one of the great crescents of the New Town – with beloved Mrs Miller, the English widow of at least three husbands, the last of whom was a dentist. She was a hearty, buxom English woman with a manic laugh, yellow hair and glasses. She smoked endlessly, hence the colour of her sparse locks. She ran her house not for profit but for fun. She loved people in general and me as much as any – and whisky much more – and was faithfully supported by the hirpling Ruth, her faithful, bandy-legged English maid. Like all maids Ruth had a strong sense of wrong and a long sense of humour. She liked to be shocked, or pretending to be, but she loved life and people. I was installed in the first room I could truly call my own. I decorated it with all my pictures and possessions. Later I moved to a basement room where, to Mrs Miller's horror, I collected a large number of books and paintings and where I was, as she put it, quite a lad. On my first night before I embarked on my medical career I was filled with massive doubt. I knew in my heart that I did not want to be a doctor of any kind, I knew that I did not want to be a technician, but an artist, but I dismissed these doubts as fantasies and went up the next day to Teviot Place to be put through the tiresome authoritarian mill of university bureaucracy. Among other routines designed to humiliate the incoming student, the medicals had to act as guinea-pigs for a new technique being developed in inoculation against tuberculosis. A preliminary test called the Mantoux Test was done to see if you were immune already. So carefully and faithfully had I been protected from the risks of TB by TT milk and other precautions in my nursery that the test almost gave me the disease. As a committed funk, I hate being experimented on and I feel for those in wards who are demonstrated as models of illness for medical students.

On 6 February I walked as usual up to hated Physiology with my friend Billy Conn who, like his father, died of a cerebral tumour at a painfully early age. As we talked and walked we passed a newspaper hoarding which I half caught sight of. I thought it said 'Death of the King'. I returned to check but all it said was 'Latest Results'. On our journey home we were standing looking in a shop window in Frederick Street when Billy said to me, 'Is that newspaper man not shouting "Death of the King"?' I shrugged off the premonition I'd already had that morning, but sure enough the brave, noble and shy prince, George VI, had died and my earlier experience of the day had been a second sight.

Winston Churchill's tribute to that brave king (his last and perhaps his best ever) says all I could wish to express.

The last few months of King George's life with all the pain and physical stress that he endured – his life hanging by a thread from day to day – and he all the time cheerful and undaunted – stricken in body but quite undisturbed and unaffected in spirit – these have made a profound and an enduring impression and should be a help to all.

During these last months the King walked with death, as if death was a companion, an acquaintance whom he recognized and did not fear. In the end, death came as a friend, and after a happy day of sunshine and sport, and after 'goodnight' to those who loved him most, he fell asleep as any man or woman who strives to fear God and nothing else in this world may hope to do . . . every home . . . may draw comfort and strength for the future from his bearing and his fortitude . . . For fifteen years King George VI was king – never at any moment in all the perplexities at home and abroad, in public or in private did he fail in his duties – well does he deserve the farewell salute of all his Governments and Peoples.

At this time I was a passionate theatregoer and I went to every play and film I could afford. Opera I did not appreciate. Indeed, I hated it. I had been taken at the age of thirteen to a performance of *The Flying Dutchman* by my father who was a Wagner devotee. For the many hours it lasted, tears were but the first symptom of my boredom. The prima donna was large, fat, ugly, sang out of tune and smelt – even from the circle. Few experiences even in church as a child, lasted longer. Opera was hell. But later I was taken by my mother to a Festival performance of *Die Zauberflöte* performed by the Hamburg State Opera in which Liza de la Casa sang Pamina. I fell instantly in love with her and opera. All flying Dutchmen were forgiven. My mother was entranced by the performance. She was at her best. I never saw her again. It is a wonderful last memory.

Having passed my various boring medical exams I set off with my brother for a summer course in French at Strasbourg University. I had never been abroad before, and I still sense the delirium of excitement I felt that first time. Above all, the idiosyncrasy of French smells, French sign-writing, French habits, French transport, French food. It was a new world. The same feeling of excitement I had on my first visit to England, and on my first visit to London. The different personality of another nation delighted me. We stayed in Paris in a seedy hotel near the Etoile. It was full of characters. How much more exciting, how much more interesting than the concrete filing cabinets with their international cuisine and their obscene puff and extravagance which masquerade under the title of first-class hotels and succeed in eradicating the identity of anybody who enters. Our host in Paris was Graeme Murray (of Scottish gentlemen definition fame), son of Lord Murray who was a greatly beloved Lord Advocate and Scots judge, and Lady Murray, one of the kindest and wittiest old ladies I have known. In her lanquescent years over ninety she would write to me, apologizing for typing her letters due to failing sight. Tits and caps were beyond her understanding of the typewriter so her letters were almost in code. Graeme was a compulsive ex-patriot Francophile and Anglophobe. He was multi-lingual, had many crazy theories about life and religion, and loved music, women and food. The order changed as he got older. He was fascinated by coincidence and the absurd. His wife, Mairi, was Russian and they lived together very happily as many do provided they are apart.

Mairi had escaped from the Bolsheviks to Archangel with only her jewels. Unable to embark she had entrusted them to a Tommy in the British Expeditionary Force, asking him to put them in her bank in England, adding: 'Remember, this is all that stands between a proud woman and her destitution.' He did his duty. Hurrah for honour! Hurrah for pride! Hurrah for the decency of the British soldier!

After a gourmet's tour of Paris with Graeme, my brother and I departed overland for Strasbourg. I liked Strasbourg as a city. It bore alternating nameplates on each street, one below the other, which revealed the successive French and German occupations. The in-habitants spoke a language half-way between French and German, comprehensible to no one who spoke either, or even both. We took off one day to visit Germany. I was going to see, for the first time, those evil beasts who had been the bloody villains of my early life. They were only people after all.

And so we returned to Paris and Graeme Murray's delightful flat in the Avenue des Ternes – unpretentious, undecorated, not disingenuous, but not disinfected either. For our one night I slept on the floor in the sitting-room. I awoke suddenly and completely with a brilliant sun shining on my face, with the clear vision of my mother in the room – a *fata morgana* I thought. Next day we travelled to London, as planned, to be told 'Your mother is dead.' She had died the day before, at the very moment that I had my chimerical vision of her in Paris.

Her torments were at an end, thank God. 'She is at peace now,' my father said, in tears, as he touched her coffin lying in the side chapel of St Mary's Cathedral in Edinburgh. She was a wonderful, brilliant, racy woman. She was a true Episcopalian. A whole person. A friend to everyone. Uncompromising in the standards of her class and in her commitment to pride, taste and excellence. Single in her love of God, in her love of her beloved Angus, her beloved family, and her beloved Scotland, she was friend to all men and all women but tragically unable, as she was compelled to, to live life on her own. Loneliness was her companion. I wish I had met her when I had grown up when our conflicts might have been resolved by the equality my adulthood would have brought. Her torments were only exceeded by the devotion she attracted from her friends. What a waste! To my great regret she was buried in Edinburgh, where she had been so unhappy, and not at the Howff in Angus with her beloved More Gordons at Charlton. Now her body lies with my father's. But I am sure her soul rests at home in Angus. My slight talents are the leavings of her soul.

The death of my mother enabled me to emerge from the state of childhood to the equality of adulthood. I felt equal with my father in rank and no longer inferior because I was no longer in his thrall. He was no longer my protector since I had no maternal torment. More and more I found my mother's inclinations developing in me. I became more and more interested in painting, stimulated by the joy of the first exhibition of the works of Ann Redpath which I saw in Edinburgh in July 1953. She had been a friend of my mother's. Her painting, like her personality, was vibrating and effervescent. And that first exhibition made a lasting imprint on my visual imagination. With my love of painting, my love of music grew equally. I sang in St Mary's Cathedral choir in a concert with the band of the Salvation Army from Gorgie. What a joyous clatter of sound in that massive mausoleum it was! Bands, and particularly pipe bands, should play more in cathedrals. The echo magnifies the excitement of their din. In September I went to *La Cenerentola* and finally fell in love with opera for good. The story of Cinderella fascinates me. It is a sort of exercise in the principle of the Magnificat: 'He has filled the hungry with good things and the rich he has sent empty away,' and in the Beatitude: 'Blessed are the meek for they shall inherit the kingdom of heaven.' It is a sort of fantasy that the poor and the rich should join places, or at any rate that the poor should be made rich, unlike the socialist dogma that the rich should be made poor. All these fairy tales end with the assumption that Cinderella and her prince lived happily ever after. All marriages would be thoroughly successful if they ended as Cinderella's does before the honeymoon begins. I predict that had the story continued the prince would have come to speak the lines which Dryden puts in the mouth of Don Sebastian:

> Yet there you live demure with downcast eyes,
> And humble as your discipline requires;
> But when let loose from thence to live at large
> Your little tincture of devotion dies:
> Then luxury succeeds and, set agog
> With a new scene of yet untasted joys
> You fall with greedy hunger to the feast.

In modern times, the story of Cinderella would be different. The prince would have to sell his castle and his coach to pay wealth tax. He would then become a social worker and rescue Cinderella as a battered sister; then he would get a council house and have it off with her as a result, no doubt, of the intervention of the National Council for Civil Liberties. She would have an illegitimate child or two. He would leave and take to drink. All three would then live in the original miserable conditions of Cinderella on social security at the expense of her family and all other families, and social justice would thus be done.

In this year I also joined the Territorial Army as a gunner in the University Battery. Almost immediately I found myself in the guard of honour for the installation of the Duke of Edinburgh as Chancellor of the University. I don't think we were much of a guard to him, but it was a great honour for us. I did my ten years in the Territorial Army. The great benefit of army life is that it stretches you to find out for yourself your capabilities of endurance and achievement. The discipline hurts at first, but it forces you to improve, to be proud of yourself, to be better than you were, or thought you ever could be.

Life in the Medical Faculty was an endless drudge, learning more and more about less and less in the world of colourless universals. Two of the most kenspeckle characters whose excruciating instruction I had to endure were Professor Brash and Dr Jamieson. The name of Brash will for ever be associated with the conviction for uxoricide of Dr Ruxton, whose wife's dissected body Professor Brash methodically rebuilt. He had a tortuous expression and spoke in a glumpy, mumbling voice in which he rambled out his bumblings on anatomy. Though he was as laughless as the Weddas of Ceylon, he had one joke which was produced annually at his first lecture to cheers: 'Molluscs live on piles of piers – I do not refer to the haemorrhoids of the aristocracy.' So devoted was he to his macabre art that he daily consumed copious dyes and was injected with assorted chemicals, which the body retains, so that the progress of tissue changes in life could be measured on his death. On his death he bequeathed his corpse for the dissection to which he had submitted so many others in his lifetime. Dr Jamieson, his ancient assistant, had been in the anatomy department since the invention of death. He was sleek-headed like Cassius and had his lean and hungry look too. Upon his head he ever wore a black skull-cup. He was renowned for two things: his astonishing capacity to draw the most elaborate and masterly anatomical drawings which are immortalized in the manuals of anatomy, and his boasted misogyny, with which was coupled a distinct inclination to male students, though by the time I saw him he was too old to have a catamite. 'I would like to see a female member of the class to arrange tutorial instruction,' he would say in his piping voice. 'Any female will do.' He panted on to ninety.

In the summer I finally plucked up the courage to admit to myself that medicine was not for me. That was now quite obvious. But what was for me? That was entirely obscure. I thought of the army. But would it be such fun as a professional as I found it as an amateur, and anyway I had all the benefits of army life in the Territorial Army without having to exclude all else. I thought of architecture because I had always wanted to restore and convert good buildings, but nowadays architects are constructors not designers. The creative element has gone from the work. It is not function, nor art. What then, about the Law? 'What,' I asked my father naïvely one evening when we were driving to Gifford, 'do you call those people who wear wigs in court?' 'Advocates,' he said. I had seen a film with Eric Portman in the lead as a successful London criminal barrister – that, I thought, was the life for me. So, having allowed suffcent time to pass for my father to forget our conversation, I told him I was giving up, and with his everlasting tolerance, he wished me well. So I went back to my beloved Classics in the Faculty of Arts in September 1953, and left hated medicine and science for ever, though in mitigation I must admit that all I learned in my scientific years has been immensely useful. That is a very good argument against specialization. The generality and extent of my education, albeit fortuitous, has been of inestimable benefit and has given me so much enjoyment. How can a child understand his language if he knows no Latin or Greek, or the universe if he knows no science, or other people if he studies no languages, or human kind at all if he does not read stories of religion, history and myth. I deplore the restriction and aridness of modern curricula. After all, bad late Latin word as it is, 'education' means the drawing out of what is within you, not stuffing a skill into your brain. It is interesting to recall the words of Lord Cockburn on his entry to Edinburgh University in 1793: 'For all I have seen since, and all I felt even then [and he hated Classics at school] has satisfied me that there is no solid and graceful foundation for boys' minds like classical learning, grammatically learnt, and that all the modern substitutes of what is called useful knowledge breed little beyond conceit, vulgarity and general ignorance.' What would he say now, when Latin has been expunged from the learning of the law, and sociology is exalted as universal wisdom?

The Edinburgh Festival of 1954 provided many memorable events:

the Danish State Radio Orchestra under Eugene Ormandy and the Philharmonia Orchestra under Guido Cantelli and a particularly triumphant performance of *A Midsummer Night's Dream* with Moira Shearer as a feathery Titania in one of her last dancing roles. Those were the days when we had a theatre – the Empire – for ballet; a theatre – the King's – for opera; and a theatre – the Lyceum – for drama, and many more as well. How the arts have shrunk, despite the state's subsidy. One by one, the theatres disappeared and the Festival struggled to continue with increasing demands on the visiting performers on a hopelessly decreasing stage. Over this pandemonium presided the town council of Edinburgh, petty, wet and incompetent and quite oblivious of the great trust of which they were the guardians. For all the encouragement they gave the Festival they might have been burghers of Peru. For twenty years of procrastination they positively failed to build an opera house. In 1954 they rejected Mr Oppenheimer's offer to build an opera house, two theatres and a hotel for £750,000 of his own money. And the sole reward of the men of caution over the men of vision is a bill for one and a quarter million and a hole in the ground shuttered and padlocked lest it should escape. Well indeed did the Reverend Arsekine utter up the prayer in the Tron Kirk in 1706: 'O Lord, have mercy on all fools and idiots and especially the magistrates of Edinburgh.'

In the autumn I exhibited my first painting in a public exhibition at the Society of Scottish Artists. It was sold for ten guineas. I also had my second, and hitherto my last, premonition of death, my mother's being the first. I was invited to a party by Sir John and Lady Sommerville for their beautiful daughter Daphne. One of the guests had been at school with me, but I had not seen him since he had left. When I saw him I felt cold and tingling, because for a moment previously I had thought he was dead and I was seeing a vision. But he was very much alive and told me he was going the next day to Switzerland as a ski instructor. He did and was buried alive in an avalanche – poor man.

At this time I seem to have spent most Friday nights of my life at balls, where I mingled with sphinxes without secrets, and most Saturday afternoons at weddings. I dare say the balls led to the weddings. Week after week I watched the glistening eyes of many beautiful brides reflect the message of the lover's litany 'Love like ours can never die.' Later I nursed many of them through the painful tortures of escape from a dead marriage, kissing salt tears from the worn cheek of woe long before death had come to part them. On one occasion, I even went as far as Holland for a wedding. I was most impressed by the traditional Dutch custom whereby everybody whom the bride and bridegroom and their parents had ever met was invited to the wedding at the church. Afterwards they shook hands with the whole family in a line and congratulated each and all the family on concluding the contract. They then departed whence they came. Only those whom the bride and bridegroom wanted to meet again went to the reception which lasted all weekend. Much more civilized to pour select champagne down chosen throats than the cheapest down many. Instead of asking people, as often happens in this country, to the reception following the wedding we should make it a habit to ask one's acquaintances to the wedding only, and one's friends and families only to the reception. Wedding-goers would get less frequent drinks, but better ones. Moreover it is much more civilized to spend the first part of the honeymoon with your best friends. After all why ask them if only to say hello and goodbye?

While I was in Amsterdam, I stayed in the Prinsengracht and explored the city for many days on a bicycle, usually with an American on the carrier who was very impressed, literally, after each day. The glory of the Etruscans, the Rijksmuseum, Van Gogh – such are the classical wonders of the city: but the most fascinating discovery of all was an exhibition comparing primitive and modern art. They were very alike, but with important differences. The old forms were naïve, the new contrived; the old natural, the new artificial. The ancient artist was naturally primitive. His contemporary counterpart contrives to be naïve or abstruse. Critics today too often exalt what is void or abstruse in order to allege an intellectual superiority. Much non-art is exalted because of some pretended mystery. The cult of vacancy and vulgarity is hailed as major art. It is the cult of the absurd by the absurd – egotism and bogocity at its worst. It is time such charlatans were exposed.

CHAPTER 5

In the summer of 1954 I began my apprenticeship with Simpson and Marwick. My father was a friend of Roger Orr, the senior partner, whom I had known as a child at Gifford and whose son Patrick distinguished himself by swallowing a whole bottle of syrup of figs, because he liked the taste. He didn't, as they say, give a fig, but he evacuated plenty of syrup. Roger Orr had been a cripple in a wheelchair since his youth, having been a victim of polio. He was a cheerful, brash, brave and slapdash man with a long, wobbly face which was joined to his vast belly by a succession of chins which engulfed his collar and tie. The apprentices had to carry this elephantine form up and down stairs to his car which he drove with singular recklessness. His room, like his law, was chaotic, but he was much beloved by his clients and by me. I was assigned in my first year to the Accounts Department where I learnt the intricacies and mysteries of accounts charge and discharge.

Amongst the clients was a woman whose husband had been at school with my father and was, like him, a member of the Idlers' Club, formed by the six most brilliant swots in the school. In the course of his distinguished career he had secured a separate pension from each of three top imperial posts in addition to the considerable income he had already. His wife was one of three beneficiaries of two trusts. Despite their separate fortunes these two gerontic worthies in the evening of their lives practised a degree of parsimony which would have been worthy of the Abdals of Persia for whom it was at least a cult. They denied themselves heat in winter, relying solely on an electric fire the single bar of which glowed so dimly that its polished copper reflector could scarcely register its tepid warmth on their chilblains. And they ate as they dressed, most frugally. Whatever else money might be for, it was not for spending. Such habits are the foundations of the Scots' reputation for being canny. The legal advisers, by contrast, did not share their clients' aversion to the spending of their money. Legend has it that the writers to the signet never waste an estate on the beneficiaries. One should change all one's professional advisers annually, particularly if they ever have anything to do with your money.

I received for three years' work, £5 for my first year, £15 my second year and £25 my third. Simultaneously, Roger Orr had ordered for me a set of Session Cases which it was the practice of the firm to give to prospective advocates. On learning they had exceeded the bounds of generosity by giving me both books and money I was asked to return one or other, or both, but the demand was withdrawn.

In December 1955 I was elected a member of the Speculative Society, founded in 1764 for the purpose of improvement in literary composition and public speaking. In its heyday it had a very distinguished and illustrious roll of membership, and numbered very good minds among its members. Almost all the great names of the golden age of literature and the arts in Edinburgh are to be found among its former members and most of the great men of Scotland since, including many statesmen and Prime Ministers. Lord Cockburn, who joined in 1799, described it as 'an institution which has trained more young to public speaking and liberal thought than all other private institutions in Scotland'. I doubt if the claim holds now. It is interesting to read in the early sessions what were the subjects of debate some 220 years ago: 'Ought any crimes to be punished with death?'; 'Is capital punishment in any way lawful and expedient?'; 'Ought the city to be supported by fixed rates?'; 'Ought there to be any restraint upon luxury?'; 'Is the power of pardoning criminals advantageous to the state?'; 'Is a public debt advantageous or pernicious to the state?'; 'Would the happiness of the lower orders be increased in proportion to the diffusion of marriage among them?'; 'Ought divorces to be allowed to take place by mutual consent without the interference of law?' The subjects of public discussion have not changed much in two hundred years.

The Society meets by the light of a wooden Italian candelabra of great elegance in the old quadrangle of Edinburgh University in halls specially built by Robert Adam. Its customs are strange, unreasoned and eccentric, as are its members. The Society meets every Wednesday evening at a quarter to nine precisely and after hearing the reading of an essay and the calling of the first roll it is suspended for drinks at 9.45 which formerly were taken in the Captain's Bar. Alas! this good and traditional meeting of the two sets of Edinburgh characters –the one from the doss-houses, and the other from the posh houses – has ceased. After coffee the proceedings continue with a debate. Absence is fined. The debates are endless, and only professional bachelors and amateur husbands stay to the bitter end in order to avoid the last fine. I was lucky as there were some excellent minds in the Society in the three years of my ordinary membership. Peter Heath, a single and singularly scholarly philosopher was secretary. The librarian was Robert Maxtone Graham, who had devoted his talents to the cataloguing of the library of valuable pamphlets and other books. He was an advocate and a Scot, until lucre lured him into property and England. Of the ordinary members, Robin Lorimer was distinguished, learned, and far and away the most eccentric. He had a tatterdemalion appearance with prissling fair hair and maddened eyes which but for his glasses would have come out on stalks like a lobster's. Silence was a stranger to him and no tongue gave him more pleasure than his own as it did its best to keep pace with his mercurial mind. His publication of his father's great work *The New Testament in Scots* is an immortal tribute to his scholarship and his filial piety. His foil was usually Martin Mitchell, an abnormous advocate and bachelor whose pinguescent cheeks were so fat that it was a mystery how he could see out of his eyes. But his skill at all things naval and mechanical belied this impression. His sense of mischief and fun meant that his only expression was a smile, which was the reflection also of a singularly generous heart. This behemoth was a match for the brilliant Lorimer in the art of long-winded perissologies. He now dispenses justice with great sense and much mercy as a sheriff. The presidents, most of whom were also distinguished in intellect and have since become distinguished in life, presided over the affairs of the evening with a variety of tolerance, intolerance and eccentricity. If the Spec does not still match Cockburn's ideals it at any rate is a refuge and it is hoped a school for idiosyncrasy and eccentricity and the independence of mind of which both are but the reflection.

I had now added moral philosophy, civil law, constitutional law and Scots law to my completed enquiries. Moral philosophy was taught by Professor Murray, whose wizened and venerable face made it seem likely that he had known in person all those whose works he explained to us so lucidly from Plato on. Civil law was the estate of the atrabilious Professor Fisher. Everything about him had an air of mystery, his morbid voice, his drooping, bloodhound eyes, his slouching step. Even when he permitted a brumous smile to visit his expression it seemed to wrack him with intolerable pain. I have never met a drier man, but inside this presbyterian fortress lived a wise, kind tutor. We were privileged to be the first beneficiaries in the class of constitutional law of the instruction of Professor Mitchell, the extent of whose knowledge and the profundity of whose thought reflected the massive energy of his mind. His sense of humour was delightfully dry but unlike professor

Fisher that was all that was dry about him. All these distinguished luminaries entertained me on many occasions with their wisdom and their hospitality.

I was now due to sit my Master of Arts degree exam. Unfortunately I had long taken the view that I could read more quickly from a textbook than I could be read to out of one. Accordingly, I had frequently not been present at the nine o'clock lectures in Scots law given by Professor Montgomery, who solemnly copied out the texts of Gloag and Henderson's textbooks and read them to us, making such major changes from the original to put us off the scent, as 'in a case where X sued Y' where the original said 'A sued B'. Everything about this boring lusk was flameless. His speech was clipped and his presence was totally unvirile.

As a result of my regular absences from his gripping lectures I failed to enrol in time for my degree exams – I was a month late. The regulations state quite clearly that in very exceptional circumstances, and with an excuse of celestial originality, a student might be allowed to enrol up to seven days late, but in no circumstances whatsoever must he enrol thereafter. Believing that rules are made by petty officials to make life easier for themselves and to show their power I decided to try to discover the meaning of 'no circumstances whatsoever'. I went to my Director of Studies and explained that in a moment of mental aberration, I had entered the date of enrolment in the wrong month though on the right date. To prove it, I did so. He arranged that I would be allowed to meet the Dean of the Faculty of Arts, Professor Orr, but that would be the end of the indulgence. I can't say I thought a meeting with the professor was the same as sitting degree exams, but perhaps it was consolation and a necessary step to my goal. It was certainly not a consoling experience. The professor was tall and aloof. I was shown into his presence at the appointed hour. With studied bad manners he ignored me, though he knew I was there, thus hoping to increase his stature in my eyes and reduce mine in his. After tolerating this insult for a few minutes I turned and left. Immediately he got up: 'Where are you going?' he said. 'I am going,' I replied, 'to arrange an appointment with you at a time when you are free to see me.' This impertinence had the desired effect. He became humble, affable, and apologetic and threw in permission to sit the degree exams in mitigation of his embarrassment. It was a grim afternoon, but I had discovered the meaning of 'no circumstances whatsoever'.

I now had to go to the Matriculation Office and enrol. It was incomprehensible to Mr Jennings, the clerk, that an unbreakable rule had been broken, particularly a rule which would have broken a student. His normally amethystine complexion went so deep that it became almost black like a bramble. With a reluctance and contempt bordering on insanity he enrolled me. I sat the exams, passed them and forgot to enrol to be capped, and Mr Jennings had the ultimate indignity of having to ring me up to ask me if I was going to be there. On this occasion, such was his pain he almost laughed, much as he preferred misery to laughter. I had got past one more impossibilist.

The reason I was unable to enrol was that between sitting the exams and the graduation ceremony I went to South Uist to fire corporal rockets in the new rocket-range there. This was the latest thing and very exciting it was, particularly at night – like a giant roman candle setting off. It was great fun. We fished for mackerel and enjoyed ourselves in the Mess, which was under the genial eye of Major MacGregor, a most affable host. One year the tip of a wreck, which we took to be a Spanish galleon, appeared in the sands off the shore. Mac summoned up a naval diving-boat and we investigated the wreck. Finding nothing but wood and silt we set off to try to locate the wreck of the SS *Empire Politician*, which was the ship with a cargo of whisky on board which inspired that immortal classic *Whisky Galore* from the genius of Compton Mackenzie. We recovered from the wreck a lot of whisky, some drinkable which we drank, and some contaminated which we did not.

Whisky was important to the islanders. One worthy walked nightly from Loch Boisdale to Benbecula. He always drank nips and chasers, that is to say whisky and beer. On my enquiry he explained in his highland lilt, 'Well, if you just drink the beer, you get foo' before you're tight, and if you just drink the whisky, you get tight before you're foo', but if you drink the beer and the whisky together you get tight and foo' at the same time and so you know when to stop and go home.' I never knew how he did get home, wandering on the lonely road through the bogs. Luckily for him, he knew when to stop.

While on my annual army camp at Larkhill I went to a magical performance of Elgar's 'Dream of Gerontius' and Mozart's twenty-ninth symphony, played in Salisbury Cathedral under the engaging and egocentric genius of Sir Malcolm Sargent. I divide conductors into two groups: those who need the score and those who don't. Those who don't, act the music as they conduct it – they are true artists. Those who need the music are like a woman knitting from a pattern – the rhythm isn't there. After the concert I drove over Salisbury Plain in the moonlight without lights. It was an eternal sight.

One of the privileges given to members of the OTC was that one could do one's basic eight-week training for National Service in the vacation and go straight to OCTU or a unit when one joined up. So I went to Oswestry to undergo this grim ordeal. Strict and severe military training brings out the best. After the first day I didn't think I could possibly make it, as many others thought, though few admitted. By the end we took it easily in our stride and had become so fond of our persecutors, Sergeant McAfferty and Sergeant Smith, that we did our drill pass-out without a single order, counting silently to ourselves the hundred or more movements and drills. This was our tribute to those whom we had hated so much at the start and had come to admire so much by the end. Loyalty and leadership must be won.

The very first parade Sergeant McAfferty took contained a good example of that blend of banter and blasphemy for which British warrant officers are rightly renowned. 'All Jews, Catholics and other non-Christians,' he bawled unblinkingly, 'one pace forward, march. Church of England stand fast!' The faltering loon next to me took half a pace forward and paused. Puce with pretended rage and indignation Sergeant McAfferty advanced on his prey: 'And what is your religion may I ask?' 'Plymouth Brethren, Sergeant.' 'Your religion I said, not your bloody football team!' And so we were introduced to that splendid brand of military humour.

There was one officer by the name of Dacres-Manning who had achieved the unusual distinction of being disliked by cadets, NCOs and officers equally. He had earned the displeasure of the NCOs by making them get up when we did, and my displeasure by sending me back without lunch from the cook-house of the neighbouring camp over half a mile away. Now the IRA, early on in their evil intrigues, had raided the camp at Rhyl and stolen all the arms. Accordingly, all camps, and especially ours, which was not so far away, were put on a state of alert. The subalterns of the guard, who had just mastered the art of firing rifles, were issued with loaded revolvers; the cadets, who had mastered nothing, were issued with five rounds for their rifles, and the NCOs prowled about with loaded automatic weapons. I don't know if it was an unsafe place for the Irish, but it was pretty unsafe for everyone else.

One night when I was on guard, patrolling the gun square near the officer's mess, a thunderflash exploded on the square and in the light I saw the lanky figure of Lieutenant Dacres-Manning attempting to slink back to the mess. Now for revenge. I put out my rifle and he ran on to the end of it, losing wind. I turned him round with his hands high in the air and told him I would shoot him if he made a move and slowly opened and closed the bolt of my rifle to increase his scare of death, particularly as he assumed that I would not know how to use a rifle anyway. 'One more word from you and it will be your last,' I said, to add to his increasing expectation of impending death and thus I marched this gibbering prankster with his fingers touching heaven to the guardroom, to the amazement, horror and delight of all ranks who were gathered there. None of us had trouble from him again. Balloons easily deflate.

Days passed slowly. They were very long. We were paid four shillings a day, most of which went on Duraglit and blanco and polish for our bulled boots. The rest went on minor victuals in the NAAFI. I hated the sadistic PT instructors with their simple tortures like bunny hops and the bars, but we survived these perils to plan a disruptive departure. We entertained our beloved instructors in the local pub and set off for the concrete check-point on the hill on which all sights and instruments were calibrated. With herculean effort supplied by the alcohol we had consumed, we dug it up, moved it fifty yards, reinterred it, and returfed the place where it had been. Many a poor cadet must have been cursed and threatened for doing the sums wrong until the ruse was discovered.

I returned north to attend the funeral near Bingley of Stanley Platts, a cousin of my father. He was a bachelor and a mill-owner and smoked twenty Craven A a day, no more, no less. He was a precise, meticulous, kind little man, obsessional in his habits, and he had devoted his life to his beloved employees in the mill. He started with little, saved what he earned, and ended with much, which he distributed to his sister's grandchildren. He had never married because, when his sisters heard rumours that he in his prime was on friendly terms with his chosen housekeeper, they dashed north and replaced her with a hirsute gorgon, suitably named Miss Butler, who held out no such risk and upon whom, in his later years, *he* had to wait. In the General Strike and throughout the Depression, he kept on every man in his mill and paid them from his savings, though there was no work – such is the measure of a good employer. Ironically, during the Miners' Strike when his men got no strike pay, Arthur Scargill tried to buy Stanley's house. We buried Cousin Stanley on a beautiful, bitter, frosty day in the snow by the Druid circle overlooking the Brontes' house. He was a good man.

Having left Simpson and Marwick, I now began to devil to Willie McIlwraith. Like sorcerers, advocates have apprentices who are called 'devils'. I received great kindness from my devil master and his Norwegian wife, Karen, during the year, but he was, alas, a tortured man, though he gave no outward impression of being so. Rather he was cheerful, buoyant, confident, and apparently had a rock-solid practice and a clear run to the Bench on one level or another. But we never credit to others the doubts we harbour within ourselves, or realize that their confident fronts hide terrible fears and anguish. They, inwardly doubting and fearful, see all others as the confident masters of their fate. We, equally unsure, see them as the confident masters of theirs. Poor Willie was riddled with self-doubt and feelings of inadequacy. After making for the safe haven of the Shrival Bench, he took his life. If only I had appreciated his torment as much as I valued his helmage, I might have helped. If only I appreciated others' torment, I might be able to help them. None of us is a good enough neighbour.

In March 1957 the organist of St Mary's Cathedral during the time I was a chorister, Dr Robert Head, died. He was a formidable, musical eccentric, and if he didn't like what he heard, he either drowned it by pulling out all the organ stops, or frightened the choir by suddenly ceasing to play at all. He was wont to leave the organ and move a tiny treble – whose contribution was inaudible in any case – from one place to another, in order to improve the balance of the choir. For many years he was a bachelor, but he was stalked with unswerving and eventually victorious persistence by a spinster eldritch who arranged the cathedral flowers. Having netted her prey at the altar where she spent so much of her life, this single-minded cagmag never let him out of her sight and in my experience was to be found a yard to his rear and a yard to his right at the organ every day of the episcopal week. His death robbed Scotland of a worthy talent.

In April I went to a party for French models in the Caledonian Hotel in aid of some now forgotten charity. Some of the most exquisite models France could muster were there and all the most attractive girls Edinburgh could boast were there too. But what contrast – and this was the difference – the French girls and their clothes were a single work of art, a *unum quid*. Together the clothes and the model formed a whole. The Scottish girls, or some of them, wore pretty dresses, but girls and dress were quite separate, one simply inside the other. There was no union. The vanity was not there, nor the art.

I was to learn the same lesson from Françoise, whom I met and knew for a glorious year until August 1958. She was also French, very intelligent, rich and beautiful. She bought all her clothes in Paris and she wore very exotic and expensive underclothes. I asked her why, and she replied in her sexy French English – all girls should go to Paris to learn to speak English – 'When I am foolly draissed I look at myself in the mirreur and I am very beautifool; then I take off my dress and I look again, and again I see myself, and again I am verry beautifool, and I go on until I am undraissed and again I am very beautifool.' Such is the philosophy of the well-dressed woman and no doubt of the undressed woman too. I wept bitter tears when she returned to France. Happily, tears dry.

In the summer of 1957 I was due to take my LL B final exam. The only subject in law I had found difficult was conveyancing, which is the mystical and unnecessarily complex art of disposing of property in Scotland. The professor, Professor Henry, a partner in an exalted firm of Writers to the Signet, was an ascetic perfectionist to whom these mysteries were as clear as the constellations are to the masters of astrology. But to me they were meaningless and obfusc. I therefore did some work. I believed I had mastered the profundity of these abstruse absurdities. I wrote notes on postcards and reduced them to visiting cards as the mysteries sunk in. Nevertheless, lest I hadn't mastered them, I decided to do a double check. I arranged to sit the Bar exams as well as the degree exams. I thought I had done quite well in the Bar exams, but I scored only eight per cent (the pass mark was seventy per cent) and the degree exams were only a fortnight away. How could I master these mystical fantasies if I couldn't pass the only exam I ever did any work for? My calculations, in any event, had been a little premature and I had arranged to give a party with my friend, Kenny John Cameron, in the dungeons of Rosslyn Castle, attended by the tormentingly beautiful Alison Seebohm, so there was little time available for learning the science of conveyancing. ' A pennyweight of love seemed better than a pound of law.' Prospects for success at so dry a subject looked bleak indeed. I went to the first exam. The questions were incomprehensible, but then I thought 'The greatest fool can ask more questions than the wisest man can answer.' So I went into the second exam, strengthened by the morbid knowledge that nobody else could understand the first paper either. Baffled again, I waited in terror to see if I would even be granted an oral examination or whether I had failed already. I was granted an oral. Now the Almighty intervened on my side, as he has done from time to time in my life on critical occasions. As the lean ascetic professor strode omnisciently up the Mound to beat us at his game, he was suddenly struck down by a searing pain and transported, whence he came, by ambulance, to bed. That left the co-examiner, the visiting professor, to take the orals. Like me, he had no interest, or showed no interest, in conveyancing. He was a professor in Scots law, interested particularly in criminal law, as I was, so we discussed at length the theories of punishment and criminal procedure. We did not mention conveyancing at all. All day I hoped, but feared. I could stand it no longer. I decided to telephone the stricken professor in his bed. I recall his every Edinburgh word: 'You did two "shawking" papers, but the professor tells me you did a very impressive "awral" so we've decided to pass you.' I have never been more thankful in my life and to the professor, whose indulgence was due to the fact that as a member of the Bar I was unlikely ever to write the word conveyancing again, I extended my everlasting gratitude and my hopes for his continuing good health. It was as if the sentence of death had been removed from me. I was ecstatic, but one precaution had first to be taken. In those days, in order to pass one degree exam you had to pass two. I immediately and anxiously telephoned the lecturer in Evidence and Procedure to see if I had passed. To have climbed the Everest of Conveyancing and to be beaten by the molehill of Evidence would have been a tragedy indeed. I learned that I had conquered the molehill of legal procedure with a speechless swoon of joy. *Haud facile emergunt*! But I had emerged – just – with the degrees of M A and LL B. Once more the indescribable surge of freedom came to me as it had done when I left school. I was free of exams for ever and ever. Nobody could make me jump artificial fences again, except constituency selection committees.

I was now allegedly fit to practise, but I was to discover on the flinty anvil of the courts the truth of Wilde's wisdom: 'Education is a splendid thing, but it is as well to remember that nothing that is worth learning can be taught.' I graduated and was assigned my Latin thesis to write in order to enter the Faculty of Advocates. The despicable habit had grown up whereby advocates merely copied out the thesis of former and more educated members of the Bar, instead of writing their own. What ignorance and fudging. I wrote my own, no doubt in shocking Latin, and emblazoned the arms of the Faculty on the front. The public examinations for entry into the Faculty of Advocates was then a faint charade. Three members asked you questions in Latin and you replied in Latin. The questions and answers were pre-written by yourself. The members of Faculty must, at one time, have been educated men. Now Latin, incomprehensibly, has been banished totally from the degree in law whose foundation is the law of Rome. Classics, like all forms of self-discipline, are evidently out of date. Sociology and other bogus theories have supplanted them. Following the charade of the questions, the members voted with five knitted balls, but however many black balls or white balls were put in one was automatically elected. The officers of the Faculty congratulated us on our election, and proceeded in file to the court of Lord Migdale who administered the oath of allegiance whereafter Brown, the Faculty servant, put on our wigs and gowns. Immediately I was handed my first instruction by Simpson and Marwick to frame a summons for divorce. It was my first instruction and it was very welcome.

Here I must divert to describe the immortal personality of Brown. All the Browns I have ever known have been very good men – and women. He succeeded his father as the head servant of the Faculty of Advocates, and he spent his life, as his ancient father did before him, in the service of our legal brothers. I formed an immediate rapport with him and since he referred to me as 'God's gift to women', I assumed at his hand the title of 'God'. When I married he bestowed upon my wife the title of 'the Goddess', so God and the Goddess we have always been to him and he has always been 'Never Let You Down Brown' to us. His loyalty and his cheerfulness and optimism give hope and strength to the saddest heart. His open face, his huge eyes and his quivering eyebrows betray his love of life, fun, people and women. He epitomizes the pleasures and excellence of service, giving and taking the best. For him service and kindness are as they should be – their own reward.

CHAPTER 6

With a feeling of pride and nothingness, I paced the floor of Parliament House in my wig and gown. In the ensuing vacation I had the embarrassing experience of receiving my first instruction to appear in a criminal case in the High Court. Suddenly I realized I was alone. I had no experience and no understanding of the art of advocacy, which my degree and legal training had carefully omitted. With fear and trepidation, I went to my chambers in India Street in my ancient Wolsely to meet my instructing solicitor, Bill Dunlop. He was a big man in every sense and he had been a policeman before he became a lawyer and was impressive, confident and had a thorough and practical mastery of his cases. I was overawed. We discussed the case with my very limited ability to do so. He gave me advice, for which I was truly grateful. We emerged from my chambers and I offered to take him to the station if so great and large a man would accept a lift in so modest and restricted a carriage. In my nervous anxiety, I reversed into the car which was parked behind which unfortunately, and rather unusually, contained its owner. My confusion was total, not that my little car could have done much damage to anything, but the generosity of Bill Dunlop soon put me at ease, and at gin. Throughout my career thereafter he has been a consistent and generous friend – big in everything and in nothing bigger than his kindness to his friends.

The outcome of the case was rewarding. Lord Wheatley indulged a judge's newly enlarged rights to grant probation of which he, as Lord Advocate, had been the liberal author. He paid the traditional tribute to a virgin advocate, which sounded to my novice ear to be a genuine tribute to my shaky efforts. I emerged spangled with flattery; my client emerged too – equally unexpectedly.

My father had for many years had his eyes on a Georgian house in Duddingston Village called Lochside Cottage. Suddenly it came on the market. It was a house of great elegance suffering from neglect. His taste and sensitive nature restored it to a gem of Georgian excellence

71

and he filled it with the furniture which his father had collected in an age when such taste was unfashionable. The garden he filled with his favourite old-fashioned roses, and there he lived, contented and tormented for the rest of his fading days. It was a classic house, originally built in the eighteenth century by the Earl of Abercorn, and enlarged in the twentieth by a sympathetic addition. It lies under the whole weight and magnificence of Arthur's Seat which towered up to its full height from the bottom of the garden and seemed almost to possess it. To the south the rugged, simple shape of the twelfth-century kirk on its pinnacle rose to enclose the framed and magnificent vista over the busy, falling garden to the placid expanse of Duddingston loch with Prestonfield and the bird sanctuary beyond, the view being backed and stopped by the strong panoply of the Pentland Hills. In every light and at every time of day that view was tormentingly beautiful. At the bottom of the garden was a cottage even smaller than Lochside had been in its humility, which at one time had been one of the thirteen inns in the tiny village. The lower floor had been converted into a garage; the upper floor I converted into a studio and nest, where I spent my happiest and most ecstatic hours. 'Seduction is an emotional attraction,' wrote Bonnard of painting, 'an unreasoning surrender to an impulse to admire the fine beauties to possess: it is the first instant in the process of love.' 'Painting,' said Villon, 'is a form of *élan vital* – the vital impulse. It is one of the forms of love. I aim always to join the two, love and painting; they are Siamese twins.' In my studio I learned the wonder and the wisdom of his words. With St Augustine I devoutly prayed: 'Give me chastity and self-restraint, but do not give it to me yet.'

Although it was convenient to do so, I appreciate that it was a restricting mistake to move back at that time in my life under a parental roof, particularly since I had to share my father's affections increasingly, or rather decreasingly, with his secretary who became my stepmother. But I had the great benefit of a standard of comfort, society and civilization I would not have experienced in a flat on my own. The one fear of leaving our house at Gifford was the risk of losing our beloved Kate who had looked after each and all of us with devotion and loyalty since 1946. But her loyalty was total and she came daily by bus from Gifford to look after my father until his death, with a love and care which few families can ever have enjoyed. Kate was a joyful person. I first saw her serving in the bar of the Goblin Ha' Hotel at Gifford when I was twelve. She seemed very complete in her cheerfulness. I have never seen anybody who smiled and laughed so genuinely and so often. Whatever she got from life, she certainly gave everything to those who had the privilege of her love. She had many troubles of her own, but she spent her energies laughing away those of other people, and mine in particular. Her loyalty to us and to my mother and my father and my stepmother in that order and in succession was total. Conflicts of interest or attitude or personality made no inroads in her love for each of us. No family ever had a better or more cheerful friend.

My life began now to open up. I made many new friends and stayed at many beautiful houses, including Megginch Castle in Perthshire. Beloved Megginch! That house, with the possible exception of Straton House, played a more important part in my life and has a more romantic place in my heart than any other. I arrived awkward and uneasy on the first occasion to stay for a deb dance. Having no experience of such grandeur or such company, I was shown immediately by James, the diffident and faithful butler, into the drawing-room. There our host, John Drummond of Megginch, or J. D. as he was affectionately called, was addressing an amazed cackle of goluptious débutantes and their prospective knights-errant on the difficulties which had confronted him when a lady friend had died *in flagrante delicto*. He paid no attention whatever to me or my arrival, or to the reactions of his half-fascinated, half-shocked audience, but continued to dribble down his hand-knitted ten-foot tie and finished the story of how he returned his late lovely to her room, dragging her torso by the feet with her unfeeling head thumping down each bruising stair. I knew no one and no one spoke to me. Eventually we were offered a glass of Australian cooking sherry out of a china barrel and were sent to change for dinner. Had I had the power to make myself disappear, I would certainly have done so, but I had to reappear. The youngest and only unmarried daughter of the Drummond brood of three had elected to have me sit next to her at dinner. It was disastrous. She talked about her father buying Cézannes in a lane in Paris and I had nothing to add or subtract from her unbroken conversation. We went to the dance at Monzie Castle and I returned rejected, miserable and in waters whose depths were unfathomable. Somehow next day I came into my own and to terms with the assembled company. From then on for six years Megginch was to be my second home, and J. D. and Violet my dearest friends. I had more happy times at Megginch in those years than in the previous twenty-five of my life. Why so? The Drummonds all had the essence of good Scots and the quintessence of good fun. They had the highest of standards of entertainment and the widest of friends and tastes. Their status conflicted in no way with their humility or with their affection for their tenants or employees. J. D. was an eccentric *par excellence*, as his speeches in the House of Lords have confirmed since he successfully claimed the suitable title of Baron Strange. Behind his bantering buffoonery, there ticked a very sharp and observant brain. Fun is what he lived for and fun he dispensed to all around him. Violet, his wife, was a strange lady and became suitably Lady Strange. She was the jester's foil. If J. D. was the Mad Hatter, she played Alice in the Megginch fantasy, but without an ounce of naïvety. She was shrewd to the finger-tips, but she disguised her guile within a warm heart and presented herself to the world as a combination of absent-mindedness and surprise. She was neither absent-minded nor surprised. One of the best apophthegms J. D. ever told me was, 'People who live in stone houses should never throw glass.' He never did. Little did I know then of the enormous influence that Megginch would have on my thinking, and on the enlargement of my horizons. After many years of security, circumstances and taxation scattered this gay and hilarious family and J. D. took refuge with Violet in his caliphate in the Isle of Man.

In April 1958 I went to Glasgow to see the trial of Peter Thomas Anthony Manuel who was charged with six murders, each of which was punishable by his death. It was a dramatic case for many reasons, not least the number of his alleged victims. Furthermore three of the victims were relations of a Mr Watt, who had originally been charged with their murder and was named by Manuel as the killer during his trial and whose part in the plot seemed at least ambiguous. In the course of the trial Manuel dismissed his distinguished counsel and conducted the remainder of his defence with a tactic and fluency which displayed his brilliant, wasted mind. But Heaven had mismatched it. On the Bench in his scarlet robes with the red crosses denoting the descent of the High Court from its canonical forebear, was Lord Cameron, whose mind matched and in many ways echoed the acuity and cunning of Manuel. Manuel's ingenious and implausible tale, fertile with prodigies and lies, was dissected and discounted with matching ingenuity by the judge. The jury concurred with him and found Manuel guilty of a monstrous catalogue of carnivoracity. Only one sentence could be pronounced – the sentence of death. There is no other experience I have had which has the atmosphere and emotion of a capital murder trial in its final stages, whatever the result. Time and life seem suspended. All is unreal. One gazes at a man half-dead and yet alive. Manuel stood up to hear the sentence of death, which in Scotland 'was pronounced for doom' – a grim, firm-set, dark clerical man, his black hair sleek, his black piercing Jesuitical eyes fixed unblinking at his sentencer, hateful of the world in general and of his inquisitors in particular. His defiant stare was returned with equal calculation by the judge, each attempting to look the other down, neither succeeding. Power and cruelty gazed at each other in defiance, the one in superior and righteous triumph, the other in mortal and final defeat. We were in the presence of death and those who play with it. It was a massive scene and all who witnessed it stood in silence and shock at the final move in this mortal game of chess. For some moments the world stopped. Suddenly the whole court was struck back to life by the crack of the dock seat as it was swung back to remove the doomed murderer. Manuel turned in his own time and disappeared, doomed from that door unto death. Lord Cameron rose slowly to his full height and stood there immobile. The entire awestruck court hinged their knee. He bowed slowly and inscrutably and followed the macer through his door to power and freedom. It was an aweful experience, death and the law together have a dreadful majesty. Without death, however wrong or right, the law in every court is diminished. That is the real and only argument for the death penalty which, oddly, has never been advanced. When death and the law were synonymous, the authority of the feeblest magistrate in the lowest court was strengthened by the invisible noose which hung behind, if not in the power of, his Bench. The gravity of crime was that the ultimate crime attracted death. Now one is just playing with another life. The whole authority of the law in every court was tinged by its mystical power of death. Now villains take on the law, as a decadent inferior.

By contrast, Manuel's appeal on 24 June 1958 lacked all the drama and impartiality of the trial. It was pedestrian and offensive. As was the tradition, the Dean of Faculty had allotted a Silk to conduct the appeal, Mr R.H. MacDonald QC, now Lord MacDonald. He dutifully coughed his way through the points he had to make, unhindered and unheeded by the Bench. Presiding in the Appeal Court was Lord Clyde, a contemporary and rival of Lord Cameron at school at Edinburgh Academy and since. He had a most nimble brain and a deep but enslaved understanding of the law, bobbish movements and an unquenchable thirst for work which he despatched mercurially, running Parliament House on the back of an envelope, a task now fulfilled by cohorts of titled officials in the department of the Scottish Courts Administration and the Property Services Agency of the Department of the Environment. He had a total command of, and a defiant jealousy for the superiority of the law of Scotland, although unlike his great predecessor Lord Cooper, he added almost nothing of worth to it. His voice came in spurts and all his movements were agile and fidgety. His thin, angular, intelligent face was made to look thinner and smaller by his huge round spectacles which were fashioned for a head twice its width. Self-appointed Lord Justice General of Scotland, he was contemptuous of wrongdoers and intolerant of any argument in the Appeal Court which threatened a conviction. When Mr MacDonald finished his halting and plain argument, to which the court had impatiently listened, Lord Clyde drew out from under his red judge's book his prepared judgment. He congratulated Mr MacDonald on his excellent presentation of the appeal which he peremptorily dismissed, fidgeting about in his seat like a schoolboy caught short in class. He fixed a new date for the execution of Manuel and flitted off the Bench, as if he had been wrongly interrupted in the course of a game of snap. 'Judges,' said Oscar Wilde, 'like the criminal classes, have their lighter moments.' It was not so light for Manuel. He was duly hanged by the neck for his reeking villainies. Lord Clyde lived on another twenty years.

On 28 August I went with Françoise to the Stuttgart State Opera's production of *Die Entführung aus dem Serail*. It was a tormentuous performance. Next day Françoise departed for France for ever, taking that part of me which I had imprudently deposited with her. '*Il n'y a qu'une sorte d'amour,*' said La Rochefoucauld, '*mais il y en a mille différentes copies.*'

But the bee has no time to be sad, so I went for the weekend to Broughton House in Peeblesshire to dispense the bruised poisons of pain. My host was Andy Elliot, a cheerful, cultured agamist who lives in Lady Stair's Close with a happy red face and the sensitive and distinguished architect, James Dunbar-Nasmith, who has given so much of his tasteful time to the Edinburgh Festival. Broughton House was one of the first commissions of Sir Basil Spence. It is a vast, dead, pre-war reproduction of a sixteenth-century Scottish fortified house in 1930s dress, created by the same uninspired hand which misunderstood even more totally the inspiration of his own age. Nothing typifies his flameless style more than the building upon which his mystic reputation was founded after the war, the new Coventry Cathedral. It is a shed of a dull shape and coarse texture, without any sympathy for its gentle predecessor, containing in contrast the works of men who were inspired by the spirit of our time, Sutherland, Rentyans and the rest. But the emotion and the mystery of the renaissance of Coventry were lost on the boring author of this and so many other buildings. The dullness of Broughton House was in striking contrast to the magnificence and vitality of the gardens created by the genius of Mrs Elliot, whose green fingers have been inherited by her quizzical and genial son, Archie Elliot QC, now Lord Elliot. He has recreated the beautiful garden of Morton House in Edinburgh, until recently one of the great Trotter Estates, Mortonhall. With his mother's green fingers, he inherited the charm and enquiring surprise of his father, Professor Elliot. It was a joy to be in the company of this wise and twinkling old man. No one could witness his animated briskness or his enquiring benignity without feeling that they were the reflections of an ample and amiable heart. He obtained delight and surprise from every experience, every flower, every leaf, every light, every idea of people young or old. He was truly alive, though not for long after that. I returned on Sunday to hear Haydn's 'Creation' sung by the Royal Danish Chapel Choir, and pondered that I had never met a man that gloried more in God's creation. Indeed, in his garden he carved the words: 'Oh all ye green things on earth, bless ye the Lord.' I have had the same words carved on the chapel at Fordell.

I was introduced at this festival to Haydn's masses when I heard the Nelson Mass for the first time. These triumphant ecstasies of celebration were written one a year in honour of the name-day of Princess Marie Esterházy, the wife of Haydn's fourth royal Austrian patron, Prince Nicolaus II, who attracted him back from his second London triumph with the bait of free medical services and unlimited tokay for the rest of his day. Alas the National Health Service and supplementary benefit do not inspire such glittering returns or creations.

As was then my habit, I went to Perth races. My interest at race meetings, such as it is, is more in watching the fillies off the course compete with one another, rather than those on it. Hippolatry is not in my blood, gyniolatry is. My view of horse-racing rather coincides with that of the Shah of Persia, who on being invited by Her Majesty the Queen to attend the Derby Stakes, replied 'No thank you, Ma'am. It is already well known to me that one horse can run faster than another.' So can one filly, but frequently hoping to be overtaken. In the evening on Tuesday and Thursday were held the two Perth balls. The second of them was the grander. It took place in the magnificent ballroom of the Perth Courthouse, with its supreme sprung floor, amid diamonds and sashes and chandeliers, and a good blend of conviviality, sensuality, formality and champagne. Nowadays there is only one ball instead of two, and with crass insensitivity it has been banished from the room which was built for it, so that the bureaucracy can turn it into offices. If, in Burke's great words, 'the age of chivalry' died in 1789, then the age of romance joined it on a bureaucratic scaffold one hundred and eighty-five years later.

At Christmas, as usual, I went to Megginch where the atmosphere of continuing celebration dominated the house. There was the annual

Christmas pantomime, hurriedly written by J.D. and produced by the indomitable genius of Basil Dean. Basil's genius as a producer, which saw its height in the 1930s, when he found and launched so many stars and identified so much talent, was as infectious in the Megginch pantomine as it had been on the London stage, though fortunately for us who took part in it, the spice but not the steam had gone out of his direction. He was pernickety for detail and kept a host of imaginary infections at bay with a sea of TCP. Fortunately, unlike the Red Sea, it did not divide to allow the multitude of imagined microbes through. In a few days the pantomime, which the invited audience of friends and estate families at any rate said they thought was funny and professional, was concocted from nothing. It was certainly fun for all the performers and a tribute to the creative spirit of J.D. and Basil Dean. The second performance on Old Year's Day gave way to a glittering dinner. In order to exercise his uncharacteristic penchant for economy, J. D. had banned all spirits and other grogs from Megginch before dinner with the exception of sweet, warm Australian sherry, which was obtained from a china barrel in the library. As eels get used to skinning, I came, over the years, to get rather fond of it, but at New Year we had champagne, thank God, before dinner. After dinner, his Methuselah of brandy splashed its generous neck down our throats, and a tired, happy and contented company indulged the joy and goodwill and hope of a really happy house opening a brand new year. Of all the happy times at Megginch, none was more completely joyful than Old Year's Night.

In the cold of January we dispersed sadly – partings are always sad – to face the climb and toil of another year. In February I was instructed in my first murder case in Aberdeen. I was thrilled. I stayed at the Caledonian Hotel. The scene of the crime was on a trawler where a bad-tempered, unpopular and drunken mate had been silenced for ever by the accused in a fight on deck. He pled self-defence. The critical evidence was that when the mate fell after the fight, his arm was in his pullover, but when he was found, his arm was outside it. His suggillated corpse was found face up, drowned in his own blood, but what had caused the blood to flow and choke him? Was it the fists of the accused, or had he got up after the fight and in his drunkenness, staggering to take off his pullover, fallen and hit his head? The jury entertained a sufficient doubt and acquitted the accused of killing the mate. He was sentenced to six months for simple assault. So much for the bald facts of the case, but the events behind the scene and out of court were far less simple.

In those days Aberdeen was the last town to retain the glamour and trappings of circuit court. Outside the courthouse, the guard of honour of the Gordon Highlanders presented arms in respect to Her Majesty's Senator of the College of Justice who on this occasion was Lord Walker. Once robed in scarlet, he reappeared to inspect the guard of honour. As the portly judge shuffled into court he was preceded by two state trumpeters in the uniform of King Edward VII, blaring out a fanfare in discordant cacophony. At the 'forenoon' adjournment of the court which occurred, unsuitably, at one o'clock, the Lord Provost and magistrates gave a banquet for the Counsel and solicitors in the case, and the officer of the guard. This feast was also partaken by the clerk of court and the macer, neither of whom on this occasion were averse to potation. They could after all, as they did, sleep all afternoon. There were many toasts and speeches. One offensive republican-socialist councillor insultingly sat and refused to drink the Queen's health, which was particularly ungracious since the funds out of which he enjoyed and over-enjoyed his banquet were provided by her ancestor, King Robert the Bruce. We returned from gluttony to justice at about quarter to three. All this interesting panoply and ceremony which made the law more intimate for public and participants alike has been swept away in the name of bureaucracy and economy by the very bureaucrats who have doubled their army, their pay, their pensions and their empires. Grey people like a dull world.

Lord Walker came to the Bench very late, having been Vice Dean of Faculty for an unconscionable number of years. He was small and plump and had the air of a very old man looking after himself. In his robes he looked like a teapot in a red and white tea-cosy, with his puckish, round head crowned with his wig forming the bobble at the top. He had a habit of screwing up his face, which bore an appearance of venerable frailty. His chief relaxation on and off the Bench, apart from claret, was teasing and amongst the weapons he enlisted to his art was his habit of speaking so quietly that his victim had to ask him several times to repeat what he had said. It seemed as if it was an effort for him to speak at all and one wondered whether it was choice or age which made him speak so quietly. Many a time a witness, asked to repeat the inaudible words of the oath, would say 'Eh?' and be rebuked with the enquiry: 'Have you never heard of the great day of Judgment?' He never made an enemy in his life and was held in great affection. His remorseless sense of fun quickly showed in this case. A young police constable gave evidence that he had searched the trawler, but could find no trace of an offensive weapon. He had also been responsible for taking the photographs of the deceased's body in the mortuary. One photograph taken from the feet to the head of the naked corpse gave distortion to the male prowess of the late mate, which appeared to stretch from his crotch to his neck. 'Look at photograph C, constable,' said the chuckling Judge. 'Do you still say you saw no sign of an offensive weapon?'

On another occasion, in a case of assault, where the victim had had his teeth knocked out, Lord Walker enquired naïvely of the perplexed prosecutor whether they were the victim's own teeth or false teeth. 'I cannot see that it makes any difference m'Lord,' said the Advocate-Deputy curtly. 'Oh yes it does,' twinkled Lord Walker interstinctively, 'one is an assault on the person and the other is an assault on property and you haven't charged that.' Game, set and match to Lord Walker.

In the evening Lord Walker asked us all for a drink in his room in the Station Hotel – prosecutors and defence alike. 'Come in Nicky, do you like gin?' he asked in his inaudible muffled mumble. 'Yes, thank you sir,' I said shyly. He shuffled over to the basin, took a half-pint tooth glass from its rack, and filled it almost to the brim with what must have been nearly half a bottle of gin. 'Do you have anything in it?' he said with a look of sardonic innocence. 'Tonic,' I said hopefully. A bubble or two got in. After this vast bath of alcohol, there followed dinner with the Sheriff. Fearing I might not be too fit for the fray next day, the Professor of Scots Law at Aberdeen, Ronald Ireland, a noted agamist, who appreciated the good living which bachelorhood enabled him to afford, kindly took the Advocate-depute, Victor Skae, to his flat in Old Aberdeen to ensure that the handicap of our crapulence in the morning would be equal. On returning to my hotel there was a summons from the splendid clerk of justiciary, Stevenson, and the macer, Turnbull, to take the first of many nightcaps with them. Stevenson was a legendary and lonely figure. Though only titled assistant clerk of justiciary, he did the work of the clerk of justiciary which was then a sinecure, since properly abolished. It was then held by James Leechman QC, who received this handsome gift from Lord Wheatley when he was Lord Advocate. Untrained though he was, Stevenson knew more about the criminal law of Scotland and its procedures than any man living, and he was co-editor with Lord Walker of the fifth edition of Macdonald's work on the *Criminal Law of Scotland*, which was then the only textbook of its kind and the worst of any kind. He had a cadaverous face, like the corpse in Rembrandt's 'Anatomist', which suited him to the task of recording sentences of death, but it disguised his cautious loyalty and unalloyed kindness. He spent his laconic days reading the historical cases of Scotland's grim past in his room in the justiciary office surrounded by all the paraphernalia of a notary of the last century, now cast out and destroyed by some unimaginative loon in the Department of the Environment. Turnbull, the macer, was a hanging man. He belived in a world of good and bad, and the bad deserved verdicts of guilty and punishments by fire and brimstone, and one was always afraid when the jury retired that he might tell them that he would never let them out again unless they convicted. If his sense of justice was harsh, his sense of comradeship was anything but. These two excellent men, scribe and apparitor, were legendary bibulophiles when on circuit and their kindness, of which I was the frequent beneficiary over the years, was deepened by their potation. Their generosity on this occasion exceeded the experience of my yet unseasoned cask and I ended up back in my hotel in the arms of Margaret Lockwood, who was playing Jane Palmer in George Batson's thriller *Murder on Arrival*. Next day I had to be at my best – even if I wasn't – which I certainly didn't feel. It was a good introduction to the tests that defence counsel must withstand on circuit.

I visited for the first time the home of a Scottish eccentric and since a great friend, Sir Iain Moncrieffe of that Ilk. He was a member of the Scots Bar, a Queen's Counsel and one of the greatest genealogists of all time, having the inestimable advantage that he forgot nothing that he ever read, though his ebriosity often clouded the clarity of his recollection. He was a very brave soldier and a very loyal friend and a most amusing and original conversationalist. He was a Herald in the Court of Lord Lyon, to which I was appointed reporter the same month. The Lord Lyon was then Sir Thomas Innes of Learney, a hispid, gangling, whiskered figure of great charm and wisdom, with a squeaky voice. He disapproved of new-fangled things like razors, so his wife, Lady Lucy, clipped him with scissors in the drawing-room each evening, hence the whiskers. Inside his mummified head this post-diluvian genius had a vast knowledge of the families of Scotland and his appearance on public occasions was that of some lanky insect, struggling all arms and legs, to get out of his tabard. He was an excellent figure, a great scholar and one of many friends with whom I used to dine and lunch in Puffins' Club, which Iain Moncrieffe founded and which then had its residence in the little room at the entrance to L'Aperitif in Frederick Street. Iain Moncrieffe shared with Dr Johnson the view that 'high people are the best' and his resulting acquaintance with the heads of every royal or noble house meant that the membership of Puffins' was more glittering and assorted than the roll call of the dead after the Battle of Flodden. L'Aperitif was started just before the war by Donald Ross and designed by Basil Spence, one of the few successes from his pencil. Along the corridor through which you entered were discreet little nests, hardly lit, in which consenting adults feasted in hope of the warm scrum of love. 'We are all born for love,' said Disraeli in *Sybil*. 'It is the principle of existence and its only end.' It was certainly the end of many a night at L' Aperitif. There was an equally discreetly lit circular dining-room on the right for those who preferred to share the company they were keeping. At its end, the corridor opened up into an oyster bar where those with less romantic intentions or more convivial ones, ate and drank. It was Edinburgh's club: everyone went there for a chat on an instance and joined the company. The whole décor was out of keeping with the age it was built in, but reflected the instructions of the patron to the architect. The staff had the loyalty and character of a happy ship's team to the skipper who acted as *Maître d'hotel*, and was to them, as to me, as good a friend as anyone ever had. With Bill Younger, he batter-rammed me into the New Club against the establishment's fusillade of black balls. Shellfish was a feature of the menu as was good wine, and the remains of the excellent cellar found its way into mine, thanks to the thoughtfulness of the captain, on the unhappy closure of the restaurant. The walls were decorated with amorous mermaids practising the lascivious arts of venery to the delight of King Neptune and to the inspiration of those who were preparing to be imparadized in one another's arms; 'The sight of lovers feedeth those in love.' There was no more romantic place to have the hors d'oeuvres before 'the picnic of the body of a beautiful woman' and many a feasted stag left L'Aperitif with the glowing anticipation of Dryden's Antony:

> The sprightly bridegroom on his wedding night,
> More gladly enters not the lists of love.

A whole generation of Scotch lovers and Scots worthies have reason to be grateful for their several society to Donald Ross. Alas, L'Aperitif is no more and nothing has replaced it since its tragic demise.

I now set forth to found the Society for the Preservation of Duddingston Village. It is difficult in the wake of European Architectural Heritage Year and the devotion to conservation to recall and comprehend the hostility, contempt and resentment which the pursuit of preservation engendered in public and officials alike in those days. Very few espoused such old-fashioned and out-of-date causes, but enough rallied for the seed to grow into a respectable tree.

Duddingston Village lies under Arthur's Seat within the City of Edinburgh and is surrounded on two sides by the Royal Park of

Holyrood, once the hunting ground of kings of Scotland and now the sporting ground of lesser queens. On the south and west it is bounded by the expanse of Duddingston Loch, overlooked by the manse. The village is built in a square looking outwards, bounded by high walls. It has many very Scotch houses of various periods. It is unique in a big city. The Duke of Hamilton, as Keeper of Holyrood Palace, agreed to be patron of the new society. A goodly concourse of those genuinely interested in the culture of Scotland gathered to launch it. Lord Cameron, who had already done so much for the cause of conservation and the protection of Edinburgh by his robust championship of the Cockburn Society took the chair. Sir John Banks, a respected Lord Provost of Edinburgh, whose face was all spectacles and crooked teeth, was elected first chairman of the Society, and Sir Compton Mackenzie gave a moving appeal for funds. Fortunately, the Society had an immediate purpose – the restoration of the house where Bonnie Prince Charlie stayed before the Battle of Prestonpans. After months of negotiation I had eventually persuaded the owner of Bonnie Prince Charlie's house to sell it to me for £150. For years he had exercised the pithecoid selfishness of too many owners of dilapidated Scottish heritage. They prefer to allow it to fall into ruin in their hands rather than to see it restored by anyone else. The decline of Edinburgh has been due to the consent of its citizens and its leaders, who a century before had had such regard for its beautiful creation. The desecration of the town was fed by the indifference of the citizens who witnessed it, but now at last the battle is beginning to be won, though it is being fought far too late. The most warming letter I had was from little Miss Christie, who looked after the old folk in Holm House: 'Dear Sir, this is my mite towards the tidying up of Duddingston, P.S. excuse envelope.' It was all the more worth it for that. From those humble and fertile beginnings, the Society has gathered strength and power. Bonnie Prince Charlie's house is restored and occupied as a home. The ruined cottages are all remade. The twelfth-century church, of which Sir Walter Scott was an elder, is floodlit, and the village has been accorded the status of a special conservation area upon which the planning staff of Edinburgh did a splendid report in 1972. One last important building is in process of restoration – the Revd John Thomson's manse. The minister was a great amateur landscape artist. He called his studio 'Edinburgh' so that when he was there painting his servants could despatch callers at the manse, without dishonesty, by saying: 'Oh, the minister's in Edinburgh this morning, I'm afraid.' The private charity and effort of the community have achieved in Duddingston what could never be achieved and should never be attempted by officials of local authority, though they are now much more vigilant than they were before we began. But the State is no substitute for the individual, as it so hubristically attempts to be.

The fund for the restoration of Bonnie Prince Charlie's house quickly reached £500. I made the first of many applications to be a Conservative candidate, but, like good wine, I was rejected at all these tastings until I showed signs of mellowing maturity. There was an election pending in East Edinburgh, but I was beaten to the post by the worthy, brave Earl of Dalkeith, who, in his turn, was beaten by the socialists by only a handful of votes. But the Tories won handsomely in the country and for five more years the blessings of Conservative government were available to an ever-more prosperous, if ungrateful, people. Frustrated in my parliamentary ambition, I decided to fight Craigmillar ward in a local by-election. This was an area of east Edinburgh reputed to be so Red as to be too hot to enter. I increased the Progressive vote by 1,100 per cent – from forty-three that is to 477. I campaigned on the eternal theme of low rates and good cheap services which Edinburgh then enjoyed.

I now became engaged in a major row that was brewing in Edinburgh. In order to show its prowess as an academy of culture, the University of Edinburgh had conceived megalomaniac and avaricious plans to erase a vast chunk of southern Edinburgh, including many classic and excellent Scotch streets and buildings. This ambition was hatched under the edict of the philistine English principal, Sir Edward Appleton, a much honoured scientist concerned with the dull world of improvable universalities. Their first target was the brightest ornament and the first ornament of Georgian Edinburgh – George Square. It was built by James Brown, the architect, in 1784 and named after his brother George, the laird of Lindsey Lands and Elliestown. It is the first example of formal town planning in Edinburgh, and housed such men as the notorious Lord Braxfield, who said of the Radicals that they would be 'Muckle the better for being hung'; Admiral Viscount Duncan, hero of Camperdown and ancestor of my children and the Hendersons of Fordell; Dr John Jamieson, the great Scots lexicographer; and many others including the Honourable Henry Erskine, one of the great wits of the Scots Bar, who after being introduced to Dr Johnson gave Boswell a shilling for allowing him to see his English bear. Henry Erskine, the Whig Lord Advocate, was renowned not only for his wit, but for his self-effacing nature. In December 1804 he denied himself the office of Lord Justice Clerk, despite the pleadings of Charles Hope, in whose favour he declined it. That practice of judging yourself on your merits for office has only recently been resurrected with great pain, as we shall see. His judgment of himself was harsh but right. He pronounced the funeral oration at the death on 20 May 1811 of the imperious and glorious Lord President Blair. Lord Cockburn describes the contemporary tragedy of his obsequies and the poignancy of Erskine's threnody for the great Blair. 'The Faculty of Advocates, hastily called together, resolved to attend the late President to his grave. Henry tried to say something, and because he could only try it, it was as good a speech as he ever made. The emotion and the few broken sentences made his artless tribute by the greatest surviving member of the profession to the greatest dead one, striking and beautiful.' The remains of Blair were taken to the grave with all the civic pomp Edinburgh could supply, just as the remains of George Square were about to be committed to the dust with the cant of the city fathers in equal abundance.

Walter Scott's father built a house in George Square, and there Sir Walter lived in early manhood until he married in 1797. The list of eminent Scots who have lived in the square is long and impressive, but its history meant nothing to the ghouls of the University, who in common with the members of the town council were free citizens of Bohemia to a man. George Square stood in the way of their empire and thus was the empire building all for them. After endless debates and massive effort the graduands of the Alma Mater defeated the ruling cabal by a massive vote of 262 to fifty-eight at a meeting convened by the Chancellor, the Duke of Edinburgh. No intrigue or cunning was left out of the University's plot. They begged for time and leisure to consider their position, the very strategy which Goethe so wisely ascribed to all birds of prey:

> Ruhe und frieden! Ich Glaub's wohl!
> Den wunscht jeder raubvogel, die beute
> nach bequemlichkeit zu verzehren.
>
> (Peace and freedom! I thought as much!
> Every bird of prey requires them to
> devour their booty in comfort)

So George Square was destroyed and the hideous concrete mausolea the University erected in the place of these placid and historic houses is a monument to its barbarism: better that they had been buried in an unmarked grave. For miles around the square, noble Scottish streets and tenements lay empty, having been acquired for slaughter in fulfilment of the grandiose dream of the avaricious University planners. They laid the hand of death on the south side of the City of Edinburgh. Their incivism was unique. Nothing apparently civilized was safe at the hands or sacred in the hearts – if they had hearts – of the philistine kakistocracy who then ruled the policies of Edinburgh's college of learning. I was dismayed to the point of resignation by their victory.

> And work is the province of cattle,
> And rest's for a clam in a shell,
> So I'm thinking of throwing in the battle,
> Would you kindly direct me to Hell?

If in doubt try George Square.

The year ended, as usual, with a pantomime at Megginch and all the concomitant parties. On Friday, 29 January 1960 I listened for the first time to Edward Heath, then President of the Board of Trade, in the now defunct Conservative Club in Princes Street. His speech, as ever, was logical and authoritative, if not yet authoritarian. He proposed and argued the case for the abolition of resale price maintenance. No *cri de coeur* on behalf of the little shopkeeper, many of whom lived in Central Edinburgh, and whose existence and sensitivity, regardless of any electoral interest, I was anxious to protect, made the slightest dent in the frozen logic of his very own master plan, which turned the screw on, and turned away the loyalty of, our most devoted adherents and the best servants of the community. It should never be forgotten that the Conservatives lost the 1964 election by a few seats and I failed to win my seat by only a few votes.

The Speculative Society had a mutual agreement with Trinity College Historical Society for a debate which alternately occurred in Dublin and Edinburgh, and I was chosen in February to set off for Dublin. It was a very bibulous occasion. I was royally entertained with true Irish eccentricity and toured the splendours of that great civilized Georgian city which twentieth-century Irishmen have not yet had enough money to knock down and in which twentieth-century Englishmen have not yet sniffed sufficient money to make it worth knocking down. *Caveat Hibernia!* At one end of O'Connell Street stood the classic and beautiful Nelson's Pillar, now destroyed by blind Irishmen motivated by blind prejudice and fired by blind hatred. At the other stands a statue of Parnell, pointing to the Rotunda Maternity

Hospital, where prospective accoucheurs, as I once was, learn the art of obstetrics. On its base are written the words of Parnell's immortal speech:

> No man has a right to set a bound to the march of a nation;
> no man shall say to another man 'thus far and no further'.

The reproductive excesses of the Rotunda bore witness to the fact that the pill-less Irish men took him at his word.

My next battle was over Duddingston House, the splendid mansion built by Sir William Chambers for the Duke of Abercorn. The house was requisitioned in both wars and had been allowed to fall into a state of miserable neglect since the departure of the Abercorns for Ireland in 1914. It was an ideal house as a residence of the Secretary of State, or as a cultural centre such as Kenwood House in Hampstead had become. The new owner, Mr Gladstone, an hotelier, who had bought it for a song, proposed to turn it into a motel and have a caravan park in the grounds which were originally laid out by the great Capability Brown. The trustees of the Duke of Abercorn had offered the house to the Corporation for £10,000 but with predictable shortsightedness they had turned it down. The Government had just spent £100,000 on restoring Chiswick which was related to Duddingston in that both were inspired by Palladio's Villa Capra, and both display the beauties of the Villa's classic design. Experts are agreed that Duddingston House is a most important early landmark in British neo-classicism. I tried everything to no avail. I appealed personally to the deaf ears of the Secretary of State, then John Maclay, now Lord Muirshiel and head of the Scottish Civic Trust, only to learn that his successor tried to obtain the house too late for the very purpose I had suggested – the official home of the Secretary of State for Scotland. The house has been preserved, but what a miserable waste. It is like using the canvas of the *Mona Lisa* for a blackboard.

For the only time before he retired, I appeared before the timid judgment of Lord Blades. He was a man of most tender dolour who so shunned the brace of raw life that he had the appearance of a rabbit who had turned his fur inside out for fear of moths. He walked as if on eggs. His strict, simple habits and sheltered life in Edinburgh had made this peeping blinkard the archetype of the practice of judicial ignorance and this case was as good an example as any. It was a case of attempted rape in Glasgow. The accused had been drinking in a pub, as most Glaswegian accused have been, and there he had obtained the name and address of a reputed ramcat, preferring the simulated enthusiasm of a paid organ-grinder to the dignified acquiescence or rigid refusal of his wife. He was advised to knock on the rear window of the house of one Maggie, who he was assured would assuage his lusts. For this valuable information he paid to the pimp ten shillings. Unfortunately, in his libidinal haste, the client went to the house next door, where the astonished ancient who dwelt there, aged and alone, fought off his advances. The reply of the frustrated client to the charge of attempted rape was one of righteous indignation, couched in terms which were sharp, blunt and conclusive. 'Ah paid Johnnie McGonaghy ten bob tae git a ride on Maggie and ah got f . . . all.' The exact purport of his contrasuggestive reply was entirely lost on the tender Lord Blades. The blunt language of the accused's disappointment meant the exact opposite of what Lord Blades conceived it to mean. 'Does this mean,' he enquired querimoniously, 'that the accused is admitting having connection with this lady?' It took a long hour to disinvest him of that fallacy and instruct him in the Glaswegian vernacular.

In March, after some persuasion, I agreed to stand as the prospective candidate in the local election in Liberton. In the course of three or four weeks I visited every house of the 20,000 electors and for the second time in my life I was bitten by an alsatian. I do not, and never will, understand why anyone except policemen keep as pets these wolves, renowned as much for their treachery as for any other characteristic. At any rate, my suffering at the teeth of his faithless hound obtained the vote of its owner, and the consequent sympathy of the public and perhaps many other votes besides. When the result of the election was announced, I had reduced the Labour majority from over 3,000 to thirty. Thus by a whisker I was spared the tedium of many hours in the City Chambers of Edinburgh. Lady Corisande Bennet, daughter of the Earl of Tankerville, who assisted me in the election, wrote a suitable epitaph 'Haud facile emergunt'. I had very many kind letters, including one from a humble patient of my father. She encouraged me not to be disheartened and reminded me that the Fairbairn motto was 'Invictus maneo'. I have got frequent comfort out of both of these hopeful sayings.

In June I had a remarkable experience of 'knitting'. An American called to see me. He introduced himself thus: 'I just landed at the airport. I picked up a magazine about a guy whose name was Fairbairn. He's an artist and a lawyer. My name is Fairbairn and I'm an artist and a lawyer, and I guess we had to meet.' He then broke off and looked transfixed into my eyes. 'You've got them,' he yelled, 'you've got them! You've got golden eyes! I've searched the world and here they are.' Somewhat surprised by his inaccurate description of my muddy cornea, I accepted that I had golden eyes until Molly, now Dowager Duchess of Buccleuch, told me in a lift after a party that my eyes matched my tiepin, which was an olivine. I will settle for either or any description, provided it is accompanied by warmth or gold. I took my American on a tour of Edinburgh. He was most impressed. I proudly began by showing him the Castle. 'Gee, isn't that cute,' he sternly observed, 'but why did they build it so close to the railroad?' Thus he illustrated George Bernard Shaw's judgment of the Americans as the only race which has passed from a period of barbarism to a period of decadence without an intervening period of civilization. They're all *very* nice people. It's just a pity there are so few adults.

Side by side with these battles for civilization in which I was involved on the losing side, another anxiety was always on my mind – finance or rather the lack of it. My dwindling income and static, near non-existent practice at the Bar was a source of drilling concern. My daily drudge of five hours, tutoring the unteachable at Basil Paterson's earned me a pound a day – not quite enough. I found great difficulty, as I always have, in showing much interest in what bores me. The work which I really wanted to do was divorce and criminal work. Criminal work was then unpaid, for since the early days of the fifteenth century it was ordained by statute of James I of Scotland that every 'poor wretch should be assisted by a lele and wys advocate to follow sic pur creaturis caus'. Accordingly in my first three years at the Bar I earned ninety guineas, forty guineas and sixty guineas, some of which is still to be received from solicitors who do not waste fees on counsel. This necessarily caused a gradual but inexorable deterioration in my fiscal health, until one day I was summoned by the manager of my bank, then the Union Bank of Scotland, which has now been regrettably devoured by the Bank of Scotland in the process of the destruction of variety and choice in the name of efficiency. He was a clipped, neat man, addicted to blinkered views, precision, self-denial and golf, and he had learned his intolerance of the untidy – such as my overdraft was in his accounts – from his service in the Inland Revenue. He advised me that they were now banking with me to the immeasurable extent of £150. Nothing I told him about finance in general or my future potential cut the slightest ice in his mind. I pointed out that the National Debt was set up to borrow money at the same time as the Bank of England was set up to lend it, that the purpose of a bank was to invest and not divest. No arguments prevailed. He remained unmoved and unmelted, like a miserly and supercilious iceberg, though unlike icebergs our collison was his fault. In exasperation I turned the argument to threat. I warned him, without having obtained the Almighty's authority to do so, that if he was ever so obstinate and unaccommodating again, I would use my influence with God to have him removed from this earth. On that blasphemous and friendless note I took my leave. In the afternoon, having no more plans to forbid and no more clients to foreclose, he went out to play golf and collapsed on the first tee. He died that week at the age of forty-eight. I told his charming successor this frightful tale and have never been interviewed since by a bank manager, though the problem of penury still remains.

Not for the first time or the last, I was both skint and shent. At my age Alexander the Great had already conquered the whole of the known world and Kalixerna had taught him the avid passions expected of a Macedonian prince. I had achieved nothing. I was destitute. The future showed no break in the clouds, no hope, no advance. In my despair I had applied for the dullest of boring jobs for what then seemed the astronomic salary of £1,000 a year – Examination Secretary of the Institute of Bankers. Happily, as fate would have it, I was turned down without interview, for unknown to me the tide of fortune was about to turn, and the seeds were still sleeping in the soil.

Three events coincided. My clerk, who was ever hopeful for my downfall, and who had never liked me, a sentiment which was entirely reciprocated, had advised me to leave the Bar and get a job, hence my luckily rejected applications. An advocate's clerk helps you to get what is coming to him and since my clerk was rich enough not to need my help in this direction, I decided to sack him, despite the fact that it was not then the done thing to change your clerk. I therefore broke once more one of the divine rules of the Bar. I sacked my clerk, a procedure then unprecedented, and joined the stable of Gilbert McWhannell, whose generous, sunny and helpful nature was entirely in sympathy with me. He liked me, or if he didn't, he appeared to, and determined to help me, which he did. He was elegant and had a youthful air which denied his years, and he had a tall, neat well-dressed figure. His nature was sunny, carefree and calm. He just liked helping people, and help me he splendidly did. With his wife, Joyce, he bestowed on me endless kindness till he retired and departed to the refuge of Jersey.

The second strand in the chain of luck was occasioned by my penury. Whether or not my practice was to flourish, I needed money *subito* and *immediato*, for the practice of fee with instructions had foolishly been allowed to fall into desuetude by a weak Bar to the great benefit of solicitors who granted no such indulgence to their clients, and were thus able to obtain interest-free loans from those they instructed and those who instructed them. Two friends, who shared neither my sect of religion, nor my brand of politics, saw me financially through the summer and for two months I locked myself in my beloved den at the bottom of the garden in Duddingston and painted. I had always intended to set aside a continuous time to paint, for without continuity and contemplation one cannot explore the seas of conflict and the strains of joy which are concealed in the Aladdinian cave of the human mind below the resistant and hesitant surface of controlled personality. I had been bold enough to believe in Douglas Baxter's judgment that I could paint if I let my mind loose and myself go into the mysteries and torments of my soul. Armed therefore with time and confidence and stimulated by hope and necessity, I penetrated the secrets of my inner imaginings and expressed the libidinous urges of my poetic frenzy. A million ideas which had been locked tossing in my head now fought for release and supremacy in the resolutive flood of creation. The evocative curves of women's waists, the beauty of their breasts, and the torture of the wonder of their thighs; the prows and bows of boats; the rage of the sea; the ever-changing might of skies; the power of rocks; the haunt of water; the glance and glint of eyes; the tug of conflict, which the battles of cocks and beasts and men aroused in me; the call of colour; the ordered confusion of line which is nature's universal – all these echoed and incited my deep urges and compelled me on to recreate them in my own image. 'You will ask me', said Beethoven,

> where I get my ideas, but I cannot tell you with certainty. They come unsummoned, directly, indirectly. I could seize them with my hands out in the open air, in the woods while walking in the silence of the night, early in the morning. Incited by moods which are translated by the poet into words, by me into tones that sound and roar and storm about me until I have set them down in notes.

Such also is painting. The more I persisted the more the tortures and resolutions came and the wonder of the catharsis of painting took their place. And I learned, as I was beginning to learn in advocacy, that nature is the endless combination and repetition of very few laws. By the end of two months I knew I could paint. What triumph, what immodesty, but what reward. 'The artist's right,' said Gaugin, 'is to dare everything.' At last I had dared. With prodigious lack of judgment, but compelling financial need, I put the whole production of the summer on show at the

Lyceum Gallery. Many friends, knowing my plight, invested in an early Fairbairn.

Sydney Goodsir Smith wrote in the *Scotsman* '1960 has been an important year for him, for it has seen his liberation.' Liberated I was indeed. Both in spirit and from debt. The bag was more than seventy paintings, which made over £2,000. I felt like Croesus in multiple. What a relief. 'Wherefore,' I murmured from the book of Ecclesiastes, 'I perceive there is nothing better than a man should rejoice in his own works.' Sydney Goodsir Smith's generous review of my paintings continued thus:

> I think he is fundamentally an illustrator either of scene or mood. In his abstract he gets an idea, a subject, and pictorializes it emotionally. Though at first sight they may seem the usual abstracts playing with shape and very rich colours for their own sake, when you read the titles – which are purely descriptive – the picture takes on added interest beyond the simply aesthetic. Though no shapes are actually recognizable, the mood of the subject is very obvious indeed.

It was a very incisive description, for he hardly knew me then. Before his lamentably early death, I had the great privilege of frequently enjoying his company and conversation.

The third strand of my salvation occurred a month earlier. In September I was instructed by Keith Bovey in a case known as the 'Calton Murder'. There were four accused: two McAllister brothers and two Brown brothers. The charges were frightful, if typical in the lore of the Glaswegian *lex talionis*. There were two victims. One died and one lived, and for some reason the Crown had attributed the injuries of the dead man to the wounded man in the indictment and vice versa, presumably because the injuries to the man who survived were more ghastly than those to the one who succumbed. Being young and inexperienced, I read the medical records and had noticed this fundamental fallacy which the busy seniors had not had time to do. It was a lesson I never forgot – that medical records and indeed all the productions in a case hold endless secrets and conflicts which test the fancies and falsehoods of lay and expert witnesses alike. They always repay careful and total scrutiny. I learnt also in this case the second and third great rules of advocacy: never persist in trying to improve an answer if you get the least that will do, and never ask a critical question to which you do not know the witness's answer, unless all is already lost without it, and you have the talent to know when to risk it. My senior broke these two cardinal rules in one move. Having obtained a sufficient, if grudging, version of a conversation after the fight with her brother, our client, he continued to press our client's sister to give a more positive version of this innocent exchange. Eventually his persistence outstripped her patience and disarmed her loyalty to him, causing her to depart in irritation from the prepared version of her tale. She gave a dramatic description, in broad Glaswegian, of her brother's description of the victim's death. To the open question which she had been asked so many times: 'Are you sure he didn't say anything else?' she spat back the answer, 'Yais, John said he'd tae put his foot oan the man's neck tae git the axe oot of his heid.' That was fatal. Our client was convicted of murder and sentenced to life imprisonment.

Despite the result, this case was the foundation of my practice in the Glasgow High Court, and thus Keith Bovey, my instructing solicitor, described me in a letter to his wife:

> A young man turned up this morning wearing a lum-shaped bowler with twelve-inch walls, wing collar, bow-tie, fancy waistcoat and gold watch-chain, with a gold flat-iron pendant. He swung a silver-topped malacca in one hand and used the other to reveal why his hat had to be so tall to accommodate nine inches of melon-coloured fronds which he was wearing instead of hair. He proceeded to analyse the Calton murder with an ease which threw doubt on his QC's having been weaned, and topped this performance off at lunch by being as funny as Alistair [a reference to the celebrated Sheriff of the Shetlands, A.A. McDonald] and brilliant in many conversational gambits. I couldn't make this up could I? But it's true anyway.

It was a most generous encomium. Before the verdict was known, with his inimitable kindness, he wrote to me: 'Dear Nicholas, Very many thanks for all your efforts. Writing before the verdict I can say that my debt to you and that of the McAllisters is no less even if they go down. Yours sincerely, Keith.' Keith Bovey is a son of the manse. While his father's concern was for our peace in Heaven in the next life, Keith's is for our peace on earth in this life, of which he is more convinced. He is a passionate pacifist and a peaceful passionate besides. His views, his jokes, and his affections are expressed in a peenging voice, the like of which I have only ever heard from the tongue of himself and Helen, his partner in life and law.

Thus, then at one moment, all changed for the better in my fortunes and I heard the note of the eternal poem. The habitable world was full of bliss. The world was at my feet. The question was which way to kick it. Life was not easy, but my confidence was viable, henceforth I could do what I believed was possible and say what I believed was right. Now I could play upon the keyboard of a wider life. Without money, opportunity is restricted. Money is not necessary for a full life, but it helps. Without success, one's beliefs and one's confidence are unproved. For me there now began a period when the broad bright surges of life were in my tide, but this was not alone of my own creation. Luck and friendship played their generous parts.

I returned, and saw under the sun, that the race is not to the swift, nor the battle to the strong, neither yet bread to the wise, nor yet riches to men of understanding, nor yet favour to men of skill; but time and chance happeneth to them all.

CHAPTER 7

In the years that I had attended the Glasgow circuit, like a supplicant beggar, there was one solicitor who had caught my attention but who had always passed me by on the other side – Joseph Beltrami. From the outset of his independent career as a solicitor in the criminal law he had regularly, faithfully and wisely instructed Alistair McDonald, who suddenly and unpredictably forsook the Bar for the apolaustic life of Sheriff of the Shetlands. It was a terrible waste of his incicurable talent and a great loss for the Bar, but doubtless a generous gain for him and his supplicants. No tongue was more feared in or out of court, no man was more loved or hated and less ignored by his colleagues who waited on his impiteous wit with a sense of wonder or fear and a pretence of fawning assent. To his friends he was an everlasting friend; to those he held in contempt, he seemed a merchant of mischievous and comminatory insult. But none dared ignore him for he was a master of language and obtrectation and who could tell upon whose feckless head his whipping tongue would be turned next. Suddenly he announced his impending departure and the bequest of his practice to myself. I felt a most unworthy inheritor of the estate of so talented a tongue and so good a mind, and so generous a friend. So now Joseph Beltrami who had such justified trust in the departing McDonald, turned to his chosen but unproven heir. And so the Levi priest became the Good Samaritan and many a penny was given to the innkeeper for my benefit.

Joe Beltrami was even then confident. He was young, brusque and tall. So far as I can recall he instructed me for the first time in December 1960. He seemed totally in command of his practice and himself, but he was, like myself, certain yet uncertain and at the foot of the ladder, about to climb. I went to his dingy little office in Buchanan Street where I was barred from his important presence by the large brown eyes of his faithful secretary, Therese McBryan. I was ushered into the reserved presence. He had big, commanding eyes and spoke in a gruff bark which was an octave below the voice of anybody else, and he repeated most phrases two or three times. He smoked often, smiled rarely and had very definite views about the course he wished his case to take. His incisive talent was encased in the ample armour of a distant reserve. His strength and his sensitivity compelled him to keep people at a distance until he was sure that he could meet them on his own terms. He never laughed. Such flippancy interfered with his concentration. Nonsense scored nil. Indeed it was years before I first saw him laugh, though he laughs plenty now. He listened to nothing he did not want to hear, and said repeatedly and firmly what he wanted to say. The right to deafness was not accorded to his audience. This insistency and concentration was the bedrock of his mastery of the forensic art and the foundation of the legendary constellation of his successes. He kept his big, intelligent eyes on the ball of the case in hand. He was about to climb to the top, to supremacy, never outpacing his rank on the ladder until he could afford to do so. I was about to see why.

We had three clients to see and three murder cases to discuss. They came on the roll in the High Court one after another. We won them all in a hat-trick. It was the beginning of an incomparable partnership and a lifelong friendship which I have had the privilege of sharing with his delightful family and his various friends. Little did I guess on the occasion of that first awkward and stiff instruction what a remarkable partnership of success and understanding we would have together, and what a close friendship we would enjoy as the years went on. We shared what we had in common and enjoyed what distinguished us from each other. It was a potent and indestructible mix.

On 14 December 1960, in acknowledgement of the success of the first foray together I received a bottle of whisky inscribed thus: 'To N. H. Fairbairn, Esq., Advocate. A token of respect and congratulations from the police and officers of the High Court, Glasgow, on the occasion of the first hat-trick here ever.' It was typical of the generosity of heart of the Glasgow police, whom then I hardly knew, but with whom I have enjoyed a growing friendship and confidence and kindness over the years in practice, although I was always on the other side from them. I can say truthfully that there is no other police force in whose care I would rather be.

The New Year took me, for the first time, to the High Court in Dundee. I was instructed by the Nigerian High Commission to defend two Nigerian students who were charged with having 'on various occasions between the 1st and 15th November 1960 in a hotel in Dundee, and in a house in Dundee, penetrated the hinder part of the body of a 12-year-old schoolboy'. There were seven different charges including charges of unlawful carnal knowledge with each other. Both clients denied totally any truth at all in these accusations, a claim which was rendered convincing by the advice of my advisers that such activities were unknown to Nigerians, but which was rendered unconvincing by the facts that the boy in evidence never wavered in his account of events, and that he had undoubtedly paid many visits to their premises, and had been a frequent victim of or participant in sodomy.

This was the first case I had ever conducted before Lord Cameron. His massive figure and the mask of orgulous authority which he wore in front of his brilliant mind and behind his half-rimmed gold spectacles created a proper awe in court and reflected the omnipotence and authority of his presence. He rose to adminster the oath – a huge, domineering excelsitude in his scarlet robes; 'Repeat after me,' in a voice calculated to remind the witnesses of their comparative stations, 'I swear by Almighty God as I shall answer to God, at the Great Day of Judgment, that I will tell the truth, the whole truth and nothing but the truth.' He succeeded in transmitting to each witness the impression that whenever they would have to answer, he would be there in person in the next world to be sure that they did, and that by contrast God might be a somewhat less overwhelming figure. All morning the boy gave his detailed and fluent account. As his story progressed, it seemed less and less likely that he could possibly be making it up. After lunch it was my turn. I cross-examined him for three hours. As he got tired, he began to forget and alter the details of his various visits and the alleged assaults. I was convinced he was lying, but nothing would shift the allegations he made againt my charming and naïve clients. I therefore decided on a trick. I left the scene of our hitherto enquiry and asked him about his school life and his home. Quite quietly I asked a very simple question: 'I'm sorry, but I forget – what was the name of the boy who was assault-ing you again?' Without thinking or hesitating, he gave the name of a boy at his school. *Plus fait douceur que violence*. It was one of those very rare and glorious moments in an advocate's life and practice when he actually breaks a lying witness and compels him to tell the truth. It is a moment of supreme triumph, only equalled by the catharsis of love and painting. The boy was, in fact, telling two sets of truth and superimposing one on the other. He described in detail the many assaults committed on him and into him by a bully at school, and these he alleged that he had suffered on the occasion of his visits to the hotel and the digs of the two Nigerians, where he had in fact gone for friendship and refuge. He didn't have to make anything up which he had not experienced. He only had to alter the order of his recollections. Such witnesses are difficult to break. My clients were delighted and genuinely grateful for their acquittal and liberation. Usually expressions of everlasting gratitude and promises of rewards and letters to come which are uttered in the flush of acquittal are soon forgotten and never fulfilled. It is rare to be thanked again, but these two sent me a gold razor – the symbolism of the present was lost to me, but the genuiness of the letter was not:

> Dundee College of Education,
> Dundee, Scotland,
> 2.2.'61

Sir,

Admittedly, you should have been reduced to the conclusion that we are ungrateful by reason of our inability to express our thankfulness to you much earlier than now. Confessedly, we were so swept over by the great victory which you won for us that we clean forgot to get your address from you and on the other hand we could not get in touch with Mr Quinn who gave us your address until this morning hence the lateness of our letter! We are greatly indebted to you in life for the efficient way in which you handled our defence and for the resounding victory which you earned for us. We shall always remember you and all yours with the heartiest and sincerest appreciation for our liberty which you regained for us after our two months' ordeal.
We thank you a thousand times.
We remain,
Yours faithfully
A. Joshua
L.K. Olutim

By contrast the Nigerian High Commission who had instructed me and paid an English lawyer to come from England to watch their interest paid me no fee. Their letter had even less charm: 'I am directed by the High Commissioner from Nigeria to convey his thanks and appreciation for assistance you rendered in connection with these two citizens. Yours faithfully.'

My practice was now blossoming and so I was able to give up teaching at Basil Paterson's which had saved my life and my career. At four shillings an hour, through all those years, I had, I hoped, contributed to the life and careers of my many pupils as much as the shillings and experience had contributed to mine. Now in my twenty-seventh year I gave twenty-seven trees to the City of Edinburgh. I had been frustrated in my plan to replace elms in Elm Row by the chuckleheaded drumbles in the town council, which like most bureaucracies proved able to find a problem to any solution. These loons eventually gave me permission to plant only one tree, which I am happy to say is still growing, outside the gaunt Coal Board office in Lauriston Place which challenges the Castle from many views. The ancient Greeks had a word for the condition of such people as the planners of Edinburgh – *Apeirokalia*, which means the inability to see beauty or to distinguish ugliness. Trees find little favour with Scotch officials, but no building, excellent or frightful, is other than exalted by the visual mystery of surrounding trees. Indeed the majesty of the Gothic church itself owes its inspiration to the lofty lines of the tree. The child poet of France, Minou Drouet, now alas silent, precociously evoked the tree's tormenting qualities:

> Arbre, mon ami
> > mon pareil a moi,
> > > si lourd de musique
> > sous les doigts du vent
> > > qui te feuillettent
> > > > comme un conte de fees. . . .

There was a custom at the Scots Bar for judges to take their territorial name when they are elevated to the Bench. Indeed it was the custom of Scotch gents to refer to one another by their territorial title. In this century some judges have debauched the custom by taking titles to which they have no territorial claim. Judges were originally granted titles by King James V. Being badgered by the advocates, he irritably granted a title to the lieges but denied it to their 'quinies'. This excellent arrangement persisted until the late years of the nineteenth century when Lord Ardwell and his wife, Mrs Jamieson, were refused admission to the Ritz Hotel in Paris on account of the assumed adulterous nature of their association. So shocked was the Germanic purity of our venerable prim sovereign, Victoria, to hear that one of her own senators had been tainted with so ignoble and unjustified an aspersion that she extended the title to the spouses, which has proved a bait to which many an advocate's belligerent wife has been so attracted that she has manipulated her feeble husband's elevation to the Bench.

1961 marked the centenary of the death of Auguste Edouard, a genius in the art of silhouette, who immortalized a generation of Scots with his scissors. The word 'silhouette' came from the name of the Finance

Minister of France at the time of Madame Pompadour and merely meant 'a triviality'. (I can think of some other Finance Ministers who might bestow their names on trivialities.) Edouard fled from France to Edinburgh as a rabid republican and was promptly followed there by King Charles X of Navarre and France, who sought sanctuary from his debts at Holyrood. Under a socialist government Holyrood would be pretty full if the sanctuary still existed. The rabid republican became a firm friend of the exiled monarch, and did many striking silhouettes of his family. My interest in his work arose because my mother had a magnificent silhouette by Edouard of Sir Walter Scott writing at Abbotsford which had been given to my great-great-grandfather, Professor John Schank More, by Sir Walter Scott, along with signed first editions of all his works which were destroyed in the second fire at Charlton, my mother's home in Angus. In his life, Edouard completed 100,000 portraits, of which more than 5,000 were cut in Edinburgh. He cut a copy of each and kept them in his folios, but on his way back from America he was shipwrecked. His life was saved, but he lost his folios. He never, never, cut another silhouette again.

My divorce practice now took me into the appeal in a case which illustrates the profundity of the umbilical trauma in the relationship of man and woman. It was the first case in which I had appeared with Manuel Kissen QC as my senior. I appeared only once again with him, in Dundee Sheriff Court, on which occasion my wig and gown were pinched while I was sleeping on the train but left on the platform by a canny thief who shunned the taint of these legal clothes when he discovered what my bag contained. We won our impossible case in Dundee by a flick of fate – no case is ever so bad it cannot be won, or so good it cannot be lost. Not long afterwards Manuel Kissen was elevated to the Bench in double-quick time in acknowledgement of his treble-quick mind. Appearing with him was like travelling with a rattlesnake.

Mr and Mrs Waite began to live together as man and wife, as the report of the case discloses, in 1946, aged thirty-five and twenty, she being the child of unmarried parents. He was a commercial traveller and they lived together as man and wife in hostels as he moved about. It was one quintennial honeymoon of love and bliss. 'Great is their love who live in sin and fear.' Inexplicably, or inevitably, they decided for some reason to tie themselves together by marriage in 1951. It was fatal. The moment the umbilical cord was symbolically re-knotted, their need for each other transformed into resentment. The dilemma of the natal trauma is responsible for the love/hate alternation which transfers so many marriages from church to court. The choice of mistress or wife is more than a matter of morals. The urge to betroth and to possess is in conflict with the urge to be free; marriage repeats the conflict of birth and adolescence. The court refused to undo the knot, preferring rather to echo in their judgments Byron's couplet:

> But on the whole they were a happy pair,
> As happy as unlawful love could make them,
> The gentleman was fond: the lady fair,
> Their chains so slight, 'twas not worth while to break them.

I now decided that I had seen enough of worldly life for a bit, and that I would like a period of meditation. To escape from the pestilential assault of noise I was willing to forgo, for a strictly limited sentence, the balms of alcohol and to endure the searing tortures of amorous deprivation. When asked by Garrick, the supreme actor, what was the greatest pleasure he had enjoyed in his life, the ageing Dr Johnson surprisingly replied: 'Fucking sir, and the second is drinking. 'Tis a wonder there are not more drunkards since all can drink but all cannot fuck.' Those were the sentiments of that high and mighty Anglican on the experiences of his varied life.

At that time I spent my evenings in the company of a wise and rumbustious prelate of the Roman faith, Father Hamilton. His liking for port, and in its absence, lesser refreshments, had turned his beamy, bald face a deep amethystine hue but a cask so well seasoned was never affected by anything so feeble as intoxication. It was just one part of his bold Christian philosophy: all the gifts of God were there to be had, or not, as you pleased and port pleased him and women didn't. He was one of the many men wasted by being cast on an unworthy scene. Having tried to get me into the last remaining charter-house unsuccessfully, he arranged for me to go instead to Mount St Bernard Abbey. As I was submitted to the dumb gaze of my venerable hosts, I thought of John Dryden's wonderful lines in 'Don Sebastian':

> We know your thoughts of us are that laymen are
> Lag souls and rubbish of remaining clay,
> Which Heaven grown weary of more perfect work
> Set upright with a little puff of breath
> And bid us pass for men.

I enjoyed my first few weeks of silence and meditation.

'Tis the haunt,
Of every gentle wind, whose breath can teach
The wilds to love tranquillity.

Pythagoras was called the Son of Silence. Look what wisdom his meditation achieved. Could such insight have been conceived amidst the clatter of modern life? We would certainly never have allowed John the Baptist to go into the desert for forty days. Silence and solitude are jewels in a world of piped music and constant noise. *Dolce far niente!*

I came out of this monastery becalmed, and visited some of the glories of England, which hitherto, in my haste, I had missed as not worth stopping for. I visited Chatsworth where I admired the great head of Alexander the Great which was the focal point of the library. Years later I was walking in a corridor in the British Museum where I came upon it in an endless row of other heads, scorsed by the State in quittance of death duties from the room designed for it at Chatsworth and placed by some dullard in the row where it chronologically belonged. Museum people are essentially 'filers'; they like filling gaps. How ordered the world will be in the hands of the hated State lined up in logical rows by cohorts of headless drones for the people to gaze at in people's palaces. How equal that will be. How fair! And it will all be free, that is to say we'll all be made to pay for it whether we go or not.

October 1961 saw a most dramatic trial in Glasgow, that of Walter Scott Ellis, for the murder by shooting of John Morton Walkenshaw in his taxi in Tormusk Road, Castlemilk, on 23 July 1961. I was instructed by Joseph Beltrami to appear for the defence. Immediately, he and I went to see Ellis for consultation in the grim fortress of Barlinnie which comes brutally into the view as you drive into Glasgow over the hill from Stepps. We rang the bell on the great classical pediment which surrounded the studded door until recently, when some spendthrift capon of the Department of the Environment ordered its demolition so that he could spend a million and more pounds making an entrance which fulfilled the superfluous entreaties of the Mountbatten report. No. 13 Lee Avenue, it said naïvely on the pillar of the door. I imagine the others had all been knocked down. We passed through the yard to the medical block where C.C.S. (capital cases) were detained. Despite the abolition of capital punishment, the warders still hopefully refer to murder-accused as C.C.S. We were shown into the presence of Ellis in the little, bare interview cell. And some presence he had – an indelible presence I was to get to know very well. His face was ashen, as prison faces often are, particularly when they are in prospect of death. This pallor emphasized his sleek, black hair, but it was his hard black Jesuitical eyes which dominated his expressionless face. They were large black orbs with no discernible distinction between the iris and pupil and they seemed to pass through you like steel rods. His mouth was weak; his face was triangular and tapered to his chin. He was soft-spoken and good-mannered. He frequently licked his dry lips. He never blinked. We told him the worst and he said he knew we would do our best. We took our leave and passed back through the reasty smell of bad food and excessive floor polish which is the displeasing characteristic of all prisons and institutions. The evidence, we advised him, was grim but not fatal. The police took a less sanguine view. They 'found' some tell-tale spicules of glass in his shoe months after his arrest. That seemed to clinch their case. Not until the Crown produced their vitreous trump card did we return to see him. On that occasion his ruthless confidence was visibly shaken. He even blinked, or rather looked down, with the black eyes which had formerly seemed lidless. Pale though he was, he went even paler. His skin was almost pellucid and one felt one could almost see his skull. He had a very prominent Adam's apple in his slender neck and it oscillated up and down as he swallowed and fought to restore the oppugnant courage which was his nature. He was a wounded beast for he knew that the new evidence which was said to have been found was false, but he knew too that it was deadly and I could not help gazing at his neck and wondering whether he was shortly to be hanged by it and made dead. We left him in silence.

The penalty for the crime was death. Shortly before the trial, the Dean of Faculty insisted that a senior counsel be instructed since the Bar could not be seen in default in supplying of the best when life was at stake. Contrary to the wishes of the client, Mr Beltrami was therefore required to instruct a senior from the few who were still available and unbooked. Fortunately, he was able to engage R.A. Bennett QC, who now came into the case.

Ellis had taken a taxi in Mill Street, Bridgetown about 1.30 A.M. to go to his home in Ardencraig Road, but Tormusk Road, where the driver was shot, was not *en route*. Why not, if Ellis was the passenger? Or had he ordered the taxi to go to Tormusk Road after Mr Walkenshaw had radioed that he was going to Ardencraig Road, so that he could shoot him off route? But why should he want to kill a man he had never met? Just because he was a taxi-driver? Certainly whoever did it was carrying a loaded revolver for some reason and killed a taxi-driver with that weapon. Why did Mr Walkenshaw not radio his change of direction?

103

Was he ordered to change at gunpoint or did he go a long way round and pay with his life for doing so? All these imponderables were canvassed by both sides before the jury. Equally strange, Ellis was identified as having picked up another taxi being driven by a Mr McLeod in Stravanan Road not far from Tormusk Road and near Ellis's home. McLeod was in no doubt that it was Ellis who hired his taxi. He said Ellis gave him a ridiculously large tip and laughed in his face when he did so. If Ellis were the executioner, then he had crossed the glen from Tormusk Road to Stravanan Road, hailed another taxi, and shown himself to the driver, having paid one driver with mortal lead, and minutes later another in jocular and excessive silver. If he was not the killer how did he come to be looking for a taxi in Stravanan Road a few minutes from his home when he had left for home in a taxi twenty minutes earlier in Bridgeton? And why did he laugh in Mr McLeod's face? Was it the malice of the psychopath? Was it the arrogance of the power of a killer? Or was Mr McLeod's identification completely wrong or a false one?

Between Tormusk Road and Stravanar Road there lay a wooded glen in which a man had been seen running by Mr and Mrs Finlayson, who had been having a party in their house in Tormusk Road and had ordered a taxi to take some guests home. Was the man Ellis? Hearing an engine and two shots they had looked out and had seen an apparently sober man with something white in his hand running into the glen. It was no doubt the killer, but no weapon was ever found in the glen or elsewhere for that matter. If it was Ellis what did he do with the gun? No trace of it was ever found. It was known from forensic tests to have been a .22 revolver. The police said they had found .22 bullets in Ellis's home in a matchbox under some washing. Ellis and his wife said they were planted. True or false, the evidence exploded in the Crown's face because the police ballistics expert, Mr Souter, pointed out that neither type of bullet in the matchbox could have been responsible for the death; the long-nosed bullet would have had to be cut in order to be used in a .22 revolver, and that would have made a different wound in the skull, and the hollow-nosed bullet did not contain sufficient lead to account for the amount that was found in the dead man's head. Right or wrong, the evidence misfired. Fingerprints were found in the taxi, but not those of Ellis. Times, mileages and the fare clocked up in the taximeter all gave evidence for and against the Crown's allegations. The police had conducted massive house-to-house enquiries and Ellis's answers to these questionnaires were transpicuously false. He initially instructed a special defence of alibi to substantiate these statements, but after consultation the special defence was withdrawn at the start of the case.

A special defence of alibi tends to have a dangerous boomerang effect
– if a jury do not believe it or accept it, they assume, though they
should not, that it's falsehood and is in itself proof of guilt. No such risk
could be countenanced in a case with such a terrible and irreversible
penalty. It was the wish of the Procurator fiscal and the intention of the
Crown to bring in every taxi-driver in Glasgow and by elimination to
show that Mr Walkenshaw must have been the driver of the taxi which
had been picked up by Ellis. Shortly before the trial that plan was
rendered unnecessary by – or at least was abandoned as a result of – the
mysterious discovery of critical evidence. The police decided to have
another look at Ellis's shoes. To their amazement they discovered that
they had overlooked two spicules of glass, one green and one clear,
implanted in the sole of one shoe. These tiny fragments on analysis had,
severally and respectively, the same colour and density and refractive
index as, in the case of the green glass, a beer bottle found broken in the
gutter by the taxi and, in the case of the clear glass, the shattered
windscreen of the taxi. What luck for the police and for the Crown that
irrefutable evidence had miraculously come to light when their
prospects were so thin. The coincidence was, so they argued, fatal and
unanswerable. It certainly looked mighty clinching. On receipt of this
information from the solicitor, I immediately went to Pilkington's in
Lancashire and investigated the properties and characteristics of glass. I
learnt that at that time almost all glass was imported by them and
treated by them. I learned that the coincidence of an identical refractive
index and density was likely, that the characteristics of beer-bottle glass
were too common for any inference to be drawn, but, most important of
all, that for the refractive index and density to be significant, it would
have been necessary to take the reading to a figure which the police
experts in the case did not have an instrument capable of measuring,
despite their claim that they did. Ronald Bennett, brought late into the
case, asked me to take these crucial witnesses. The destruction or at any
rate the ambiguity of this evidence, as of the bullet evidence, introduced
considerable scepticism in the minds of the jury towards the
prosecution's case. Strange it was that they had managed a reading
without an instrument that could make it. Equally strange that the
glass had been found at such a late and critical moment in the
preparation of the Crown case: it stuck with an acrid taste in the
jury's throat. On our advice Ellis did not give evidence. The
Crown, in our submission, had not established their case beyond
reasonable doubt and nothing that he could add would subtract from it.
Indeed, any attempt to explain his false answers to the initial

questionnaire would only have done him harm and given them a heightened significance.

Norman Wylie QC, who was prosecuting for the Crown, made a curt and cogent summary of the Crown case to the jury. 'The murderer,' he said, 'got out of Mr Walkenshaw's taxi, entered the top end of the wood wearing neither hat nor coat, and fifteen minutes later – the time it took to run from one end to the other – Walter Scott Ellis was standing in the road hailing another taxi' – even though he left Mill Street in a taxi half an hour earlier. The facts seemed to fit chillingly. Ronald Bennett QC addressed the jury for the defence and enunciated quietly the many tested contradictions: the taxi was off route if Ellis was the passenger; the fingerprints on the taxi were not his; the bullet in the brain was not of the same type found in Ellis's house; the man who had been seen running away from the taxi was in a light suit, while Ellis was in a dark suit; and finally the times given by witnesses established that Ellis could not have been there. 'Please remember,' he said, 'that the police are not infallible . . . You will remember that a Mr William Watt was arrested for the murder of his wife and child and held for sixty-one days until the real murderer, Peter Manuel, was arrested.'

Now it was time for the charge by Lord Patrick, a judge of scrupulous fairness, unruffable patience, remote dignity and beautiful manners. He had an air of hyaline delicacy about him which gave him a look of great age and much wisdom. His aloof courtesy was guarded by an impenetrable reserve, which was a bar to almost all intimacy. His was a solitary heart. He had a total and profound grasp of the law. He was a taintless and grim man for whom a departure from impartiality would have been abhorrent and unthinkable for he truly loved and guarded justice. He was the living expression of the profession of judge at its proper best. His excellence was so great that it is a luxury to recall it. His charge to the Ellis jury was classically explicit, simple and impartial. The jury of eleven women and four men retired to their tormenting responsibility. It was for them to pronounce death if they would on the living creature they had gazed on during the previous few days.

It is difficult to describe the atmosphere of a capital murder trial. Counsel and solicitors have to meet and talk with a man who is quasi-alive and quasi-dead. The angel of death hovers in the court buildings. The public shy away and fall quiet as defence counsel pass. The police and court officers approach one with whispering deference, lest for a moment you might be distracted from saving a life which has, to a great extent, been committed to your hands and depends on your capabilities and concentration. We had tea while the jury was out: it wasn't real tea.

The suspension of reality was total, but nothing more could be done now. Had we done enough? Had we left anything undone? The thoughts hurt. At last the awful buzzer went to announce that the jury had come to their fateful and painful verdict. I have only had one superstition in my life and that is that I will not enter the court until everyone but the Judge is seated. It began at that trial. The court was packed. The magistrates had come down to listen to the verdict and sat bechained on the left. The jury, grim and inscrutable, sat opposite. The senior detective officers in charge of the case filled the front rows on either side of the dock, conscious of the awful result of doing their duty. In front of them sat the press, more indifferent to the result than anyone else in court, for any news is good news and a dramatic acquittal is as good as a mortal conviction, each determined to exclude their colleagues from the exclusive story they were all identically recording. Such is the amorality of the press. They are neutral between good and evil, help and harm. The public thronged the gallery upstair for in court they are to be seen but not touched. I took my place beside my nervous senior and next to Joseph Beltrami, in black coat and striped trousers out of deference to the High Court, inscrutable and apparently calm and confident but displaying his anxiety by writing his name repetitively on a blank sheet of court paper. Opposite sat Stevenson, the clerk of the court, his sheet-white, bloodless, melancholy face, reflecting the thought of death that haunted all of us. All were silent. Hush was universal. Suddenly, Turnbull, the macer, strode through the door of the Bench with pavonian pride, the iron mace on his shoulder in one hand, the black cap in the other. 'Court,' he bayed long and loudly. We stood as one man. Behind him came the frail, sad, gentle figure of Lord Patrick, his head shaking slightly from age, his lipless mouth tense and pursed, demonstrating the anguish which his judicial duties imposed on so upright and sensitive a man. He slowly took his seat and put on his simple glasses. Opposite him in the railed dock, flanked by two stout, grim policemen with batons drawn, their massive forms dwarfing their charge, sat Ellis, gazing ahead with those black eyes, still swallowing and with that same vacant, hopeless look on his ashen face, which I had last seen in Barlinnie. Was he alive or was he dead? We would soon know. Not a member of the jury glanced towards him. Was that because they regretted imposing death upon him and dared not face him as they did, or was it because they grudged granting him his life?

'Would you call the Diet, Mr Stevenson,' Lord Patrick said with impeccable politeness. Ellis stood. The Diet was moanfully called.

Stevenson turned to the jury. 'Ladies and gentlemen, who speaks for you?'

'I do,' said a haggard man in the front. He stood.

'What is your verdict?'

He paused for what seemed an eternity, for it was after all a matter of eternity. 'We find the charge not proven by a majority.'

Time and life resumed. Lord Patrick ordered the verdict to be recorded. Turnbull put the black hat on one side and Ellis walked free from the dock. He came to counsel's room to say thank you. This was a case which aroused passionate interest, interested passion and just outrage since an innocent and good man had been executed in public without apparent reason. Outside wild scenes occurred, of both glee and hostility. Ellis was punched and punched back. PC Cochrane, the genial court officer, had his finger broken in the mêlée. The hatred of the taxi fraternity mingled with the joy of Ellis's friends and the competing ardours of the press, for in Pope's words:

> All look with reverential awe,
> At crimes which scape or triumph over law.

That evening, after a few drinks with Joseph Beltrami to mull over our success, I had dinner with Nina, the Danish singer. I hailed a taxi to take me to the restaurant. The taxi-driver, seeing who I was, refused. Fair enough.

It was a horrendous case. Ellis claimed that he had a razor blade in his cell to commit suicide if he were convicted. I hope he used it to shave. Perhaps he didn't need to, he'd just had a very close one.

CHAPTER 8

In March 1962 the High Court circuit in Glasgow ended in a disturbing result. Of thirty-four different charges brought, in the North and South Courts, only four resulted in verdicts of guilty. I myself defended two brothers each on two charges, three other brothers each on three charges, and many besides in the South Court. The Crown obtained only one conviction in that court. This apparent imbalance between the success of the Crown and the defence had for long been noted with resentment by the police. They could contain their impatience and frustration no longer. A storm was brewing.

Some clients have recurred throughout my practice. One such, Arthur Thomson, regarded by the police as a sort of Glaswegian Godfather, I defended more than once for reset, theft, assault and robbery. He is a short, thick-set man, with clipped hair, impeccable manners and bulbous eyes like a cod. His lips stick together and slap apart when he speaks, which is rarely, and when he does, it is in a voice so soft as to be little beyond a whisper. Certainly he has no objection to silence. He is known by his deeds, not by his words. In all my dealings with him, he received me with old-world courtesy. Perhaps that is the God-paternal manner. His quiet charm was not lost on the jury either – they acquitted him.

On 27 July 1962 I held my second one-man exhibition of paintings, this time in the Outlook Tower in Edinburgh. Sydney Goodsir Smith reviewed the exhibition, describing me as 'an expressionistic impressionist'. A title I am content to retain and live up to if I can.

In the weeks that led up to marriage – my first – to Elizabeth, daughter of chief of the Clan MacKay, we spent some time looking for somewhere to live, though not, we hoped, in Edinburgh. The week before we were to be married I received an advertisement by post for a thirteenth-century castle in Fife. It sounded, as sellers' descriptions tend to, ideal and romantic. We crossed the Queen's ferry and went to the house, finding it with difficulty in the depths of the woods. I knocked on the locked door of this impressive fortress, surrounded by neglected grounds. A dyed-blonde female head appeared from a window and said 'No viewings without an appointment' in markedly brusque and markedly slurred terms. I insisted and used the fact that we were to be married in a week to soften, or swim through to, the custodienne's heart. With suspicious and mellow reluctance, the inebriated chatelaine allowed us into this great fortress. She showed us round. It was like a stone maze, half-constructed, half-dilapidated, but I fell for its possibilities and before we left I had bought Fordell Castle, having made out and signed the missives on the dining-room table, where the owner was still immersed and submersed in lunch at 5 P.M. Now I had found our rhubarb tree.

Elizabeth and I were married in St Giles Cathedral on 29 September 1962 at 2.45 P.M. With most unchristian spirit, Dr Whitley had refused to allow the Very Reverend Charles Warr, Dean of the Thistle and Chapel Royal, who had married Elizabeth's parents, to conduct the service. The press naturally concentrated their stories on the fact that the Lord President, Lord Clyde, and four other judges, had attended our wedding in St Giles, having refused to attend the kirking of the courts when Dr Whitley had similarly refused to allow Dr Warr to take that service. It was a mean act, unjustified by any scruple or charity.

Elizabeth wore a white Tudor dress and carried at my request a single red rose on her mother's ivory prayer-book. I hate bouquets, but if they have to be presented to concert pianists and singers, couldn't the cellophane be taken off first? The pages and bridesmaids were dressed like Mary, Queen of Scots. The theme colours were the dark-blue and white of Scotland. Each of the girls wore a cross which we gave them, each of the boys bore an ivory cane made for me by the whiskered pipe-maker in the Lawn Market. Kenny John Cameron, cool and calming as ever, was best man – he is now an even better man: as Lord Cameron of Loch Broom, he is the Lord Advocate. Having gathered together all our friends for the only time in our life, we departed without having any real meeting with any of them. Wedding receptions are a farce. I am sure it would be much wiser if the guests departed and the couple stayed with their close friends and family whom at vast expense they have collected together rather than insist on saying goodbye and dashing off to the solitude and comparative loneliness of the honeymoon.

On 11 November, Armistice Day 1962, three weeks after our return, we entered into occupation of Fordell. I took part in the morning, as an officer, in the military parade before the cenotaph of Edinburgh University. At lunch-time we crossed the Forth and moved into Fordell with a bottle of gin and some packing-cases. The packing-cases were still full in the evening, the bottle of gin was empty – like Fordell. Its resurrection seemed a daunting task. It was snowing, and we were not to see the grass for four months. For six years, I worked away at the restoration of the house and the creation of the garden. We moved into one habitable room on the top floor and with the rude essentials of life, chairs, tables, beds, warmth and happiness, we gradually fought our way out of it, demolishing and restoring as we worked. We had the enormous benefit of being near Rosyth Dockyard from where we obtained a talented source of good craftsmen and good friends who offered their amazing and enthusiastic skills to the restoration of the house. I must record our debt to the panguric friends who out of loyalty and pride over the years resurrected the dignity and drama of Fordell – to our Fifish maid, Isa, whom we inherited; to John McCluskey, who did the electrical work and played professional football for Dunfermline; to David Moir, our first hand and his successor, David Sharp; and to our sturdy, loyal, talented, proud and excellent naval colleague, Ian Millband whose fabricant craft and ingenuity helped to create so much of the interior character of the house. And to Ian Ward, for whom everything was a challenge and nothing was too much effort or too hard work and whose pencil-thin sister, Ray, became for three years the gentle nanny to our children. With this occasional team we restored the inside and outside of this humble but glorious Scottish fortified house. We were fortunate – though it was unfortunate – that Fordell House, into which the Hendersons had moved in the eighteenth century, and which the Victorian Hendersons so enlarged in the nineteenth that it became impractical in the twentieth, was demolished pitilessly. From it we obtained the shutters and doors, the library and woodwork, bits of the magnificent wrought-iron staircase and masses of stone with which to build walls and make up the house and garden. As in families, the old became the source of the vitality of the young.

In their classic work *The Castellated and Domestic Architecture of Scotland from the 12th to the 18th century*, in which they describe and illustrate most of the antiquarian buildings of Scotland, David McGibbon and Thomas Ross, the talented Victorian architects, took a special fancy to Fordell Castle and indeed a drawing of the iron dragon on the front of the castle forms the frontispiece of the first two volumes. They go so far as to suggest that 'the private grounds of the castle are probably unsurpassed in Scotland'. When we arrived they were certainly unsurpassed for neglect and devastation. In the nineteenth century, after 100 years of vacancy, the castle was turned into a romantic fantasie by George William Mercer Henderson. He erected the magnificent cast-iron gates at its entrance on the east, transformed the interior into his concept of a medieval keep and castellated the surrounding wall which had previously been defensive with a dry moat. The castle stands on a rocky promontory, containing a coal seam of two feet, and is surrounded on three sides by the Keithing Burn. On the north side there is a sheer drop to the river of some eighty feet. The garden, which was created at the same time by the sensitive George, was oppressively elaborate with topiary yew trees and box in immaculate abundance. A prominent and original feature was the peacock garden which was laid out every winter in parterre with pieces of coloured glass, of which I have found quite a lot, round a pottery statue of a peacock, so that even in the deadest months there was colour near the house. The precise form of the garden came to my knowledge through the devotion and perspicacity of Oscar Wood, who graces the minds of students of philosophy at Christ Church, Oxford, with self-abnegating wisdom, just as he graces the tongues of the dons of the same house with his exquisite taste for good wine. Snuffing about silently in an antiquarian shelf in Oxford he discovered a plan of the garden of Fordell dated 1890 and with typical love he sent it to me. For some reason which I have yet to learn, but which I assume was because of the war, the entire garden was ploughed up and uprooted at the start of the Second World War and the castle was allowed to fall to the mercy of crows and cattle at about the same time.

After twenty years of neglect Fordell was sold in 1952 for £100 to a local business man who began to resurrect it. Ten years later his money, his interest and his gin exhausted, he sold the rectified shell to me. Had I known the extent of the task of the resurrection on which I was embarking, I would perhaps never have undertaken it at all, but is that not true of all in life? Over the years I gradually recovered and restored the garden – its basic structure and many of its principal features still being present, chief of which is the ancient cedar of Fordell which was brought back from the Crusades in 1210 by the gallant Hugh de Camera, to whom the lands were granted for his religious chivalry. From that date a chapel has existed at Fordell Castle which may well originally have been a religious house, but the present chapel, dedicated to St Theriot, a saint of somewhat obscure renown, dates only from 1650.

The chapel contains the remains of every Henderson of Fordell from that date, and in their devotion the family equipped the windows with sixteenth- and fifteenth-century German glass. Alas, the previous owner who came to restore it stayed to plunder it and, as funds ran short, he sold off many features of the property, including this valuable glass. Much was broken in the process and I picked up some breathtakingly beautiful fragments of Dürer scenes which told what the best had been like. I salvaged what I could of the glass and restored it in two windows. But the west window and the four south windows were beyond recall and so we cut the plain glass of the library doors of Fordell House to fit them, and these I had engraved by Jean Murray, wife of our best man, depicting various scenes of vice and virtue and other biblical allusions. These allegorical engravings she executed with great skill, verve and imagination and they have been a source of pleasure and inspiration to all those who have gazed at and through them. There is something very rewarding about being able to see out of a church, and I wish that the beauty of nature was visible from more churches. Stained glass windows should be reserved for windows which are too high to see out of, like the rose windows of Notre-Dame and Chartres. They were never intended to separate God from the Nature he created or to make religion secret. So I resurrected the chapel and fulfilled the words of James the Apostle: 'Even so, faith if it have not works is dead being alone.' And so the great work continued, sometimes fast and sometimes slowly. The final event was the pointing of the outside. We erected scaffolding – in a high wind I remember – and pointed the whole exterior. It was a daunting task, but it had its reward in completion; I never want to erect scaffolding again, and I pay my tribute to those who erect and work on it. In 1967, the work almost completed, we were able to have a party to celebrate the fourth century of the present building though it contains much that is older, including the tower in which Mary, Queen of Scots stayed for the marriage of one of her maids of honour, Marion Scott, to George Henderson, Laird of Fordell, and to which she also came on her escape from the keep on the island of Loch Leven. When we bought the house, there was some late and poor panelling, which was rotten, in her little room, so I ripped it out and replaced it with panelling made out of the shutters of Fordell house, fashioned by the eye and hand of the barbigerous fabricant, Peter Nicholson, who has contributed so much to the restoration and adoration of Scots houses, of which Ochtertool House in Fife and Edinample Castle in Perthshire are but two examples of his tempered concern and devoted and skilled dedication.

During his time as Director of the Edinburgh Festival, Robert Ponsonby discovered in Norway a portrait of Margaret, Countess of Lennox, who was the mother-in-law of Mary, Queen of Scots (being Darnley's mother). He bought it and asked me when I was still a student if I could find a place for it in Scotland. I took possession of the portrait but was dilatory in finding a home for it, and in his anger Robert Ponsonby wrote to me from New York, whence he had fled, expressing his dismay that I had not carried out his wishes. In my guilt, and in my poverty, I felt that the only course of honour was to buy it, which I duly did, so now it is in its rightful place in the panelling in the bedroom of Mary, Queen of Scots. You should always have a portrait of your mother-in-law in your bedroom.

The castle grounds were divided on the north and south of the house by a vast yew hedge forty feet high, out of control, like a regiment of green brushes at a funeral. I was torn between reverence for its antiquity as one of the few remaining features of the great garden and my resentment at its overweening lugubrity. I decided that the part to the north of the house must go. Fixing a tractor behind one of the three great limes which complement the house, Jimmy Gold, a doughty borderer, eradicated these vast cemeterial bushes one by one. At last the house began to take on its own proportions. The removal of the southern hedge in 1972 completed the operation. To celebrate and mark the four hundredth anniversary of the house, I decided to build a wall in place of the northern hedge. The New Club in Princes Street, a building of great distinction, had been demolished at the behest of its members to illustrate that they not only had bad judgement, but bad taste. 'No crime is vulgar,' wrote Oscar Wilde, a member of the New Club, 'but all vulgarity is a crime.' This crime had the taint of vulgarity. On the top of the building there were nine magnificent urns which stood some five feet high. I had long admired them when I came down the Mound in my university days, and on my daily walks from Parliament House. When I saw that the building was being demolished, I went to the demolishers and asked if I could buy these grand pots. They readily allowed me to buy four, and these are now in the garden at Fordell. I had constructed long formal ponds with fountains between the two parallel hedges that remained south of the house and there I erected pillars for two of the great pots. Their siblings crown the decorative wall which Lex Balfour, our ploughman, and I built in a week to commemorate the quarter-centenary. The wall bears a date-stone, 1967, carved by Stephen Lawson and the initials of all those who gave their help to its construction. This success generated a new energy, which resulted in the creation of other walls and ponds and rockeries, a children's maze and boxwood clock standing, like the church clock in Grantchester, perpetually at ten to three.

Thus Fordell was restored with great pain and much love for the second time in its history. So the great fortress had become alive again, a great and glorious stone womb in which to collect and worship beautiful and amusing things, to give joy and delight to all who visit the ancient fortalice. Every man's home is his castle. For me my castle is my home but more it is the very expression of my soul within and without. And every year we extend and enlarge the idyllic nature of the house and garden for all to enjoy. There are hundreds of other Scottish houses of similar date and type which could be equally restored to the inestimable benefit of our culture and of our environment. Far better that they be restored rather than frozen as expensive ruins by the Department of the Environment and surrounded by neat and inappropriate little lawns boasting iron notices telling you to keep off them. Just when I had completed the restoration, Harley Williams, the distinguished barrister, psychoanalyst and heart specialist, came to stay. His lyrical words describe the fruits of our labours:

> You are used to the reaction of complete astonishment which overcomes your visitors! Elizabeth and I were entranced by the rococo atmosphere you have made at Fordell, each room different, each room part of a general design. How you managed to carry all this out, you untrained in architecture and burdened with other duties is a mystery to me, but it clearly proves another aspect of your talent. It was very kind of you to have us and we were delighted to see your little daughters cuddling in their panelled turret, and obviously so happy and pleased with life. As for the chapel – this was a surprise. I admired the windows, the lettering of the newer memorials and the feeling of reverence and life which you are bringing back into these old stones. As for the fountains playing below the keep – I am sure that very soon you will arrange that concealed spout which, in response to an innocent movement from your guests, will cause them to be sprayed from above – a game, I believe, which Alphonso XIII loved to play in the gardens of the Alcazar. We were delighted with everything, but, of course, there was not early enough time to talk.

In this glorious nest of age and peace and nature our three daughters, the little women – as I call them – were nurtured and brought up amidst the glory of flowers, trees and butterflies, amidst the songs of birds and amongst the animals and values of the countryside. Each was a quite different personality, but all with charm, wit, good manners and humour; each with quite different and even unrelated appearance, but each beautiful in her own right. As children they were always very

115

neatly and delightfully dressed. Charlotte, the eldest, was meticulous in her neatness. Her deep brown eyes contained a look of responsibility, which elder sisters feel. From her earliest age, she showed a creative and intuitive intelligence. For two and a half years, she ruled the nursery and our hearts until the birth of Anna-Karina, whose blond hair emphasized her huge cornflower eyes like twinkling sapphires. Anna-Karina, as befits second daughters, was naughtier but good. Her favourite outfit was a pair of little scarlet wellington boots and a little blue raincoat, which emphasized the glory of her eyes. These two little women, so different and so striking, were inseparable and still are and they were unceasingly enchanting to all who met them. When I was living in my studio at the farm, for the weeks when I was painting, these two little women brought me my breakfast from the Castle every morning in their dolls' pram and then spent the day painting or writing poems for my delight. Another two and a half years later, Francesca completed the trio. At birth, she had hair like the wings of a moth, so she was called 'Moth' for some years before other nicknames were attached to her like 'Fortissimo' (FF) which were her initials, when she began to talk all the time; or 'Flower Frilly' as FF became when she dressed and behaved with exotic attraction, or 'Valkyrie' which reflected in its way a different manifestation of the development of her character. Day after day, these dear little women climbed the long steep circular stairs to and from the nursery on the top floor to play in the Castle or the garden. We had the good fortune to obtain the services of an ancient Scottish dominie, Miss MacKenzie, who was steeped in Christian values, manners, nature and learning. She spoke with a rasping Scottish voice and all three little women had the inestimable advantage and benefit of her wise principled Christian instruction at Broomhall, where Lady Elgin provided the children with a little schoolroom. And so was fused on to the remarkable personalities of these three good different little women, a love of nature, a concern for humanity, and above all the fundamental anchor of good manners and good breeding and con- sideration and concern for others, which is the bedrock of Scotch civilisation. Alas, but with different joys, they grew up into bigger women, always enriching Fordell and their friends with their talk and their sense of fun, as they do wherever they go. But I believe that Fordell proved a foundation of civilisation for them, which however long they live or old they grow will ensure that each gives to all they meet much more than they would ever take from them, and most of all kindness, humanity, understanding and fun.

At the beginning of April 1963 Aeneas, Lord Reay, Elizabeth's father, died suddenly and tragically whilst on safari in Kenya. He was fifty-eight. Immediately we were the object of a piece of characteristic kindness at the hands of Harry Keith, now Lord Keith, and a Lord of Appeal in the House of Lords like his most distinguished father, Lord Keith of Avonholm. His natural expression is glump, laconic, torvous and sour. He has the forbidding defences of a Scots thistle, but within these ramparts lives one of the bravest and brightest men Scotland has given to law, flushed with a kindness and humour he does not publicly display. Knowing of this sadness, he thought that both of us would be the better for a holiday, and in any case he had only met Elizabeth at our wedding and wished to get to know us better. Accordingly, he arranged for us, together with Alison, his loving and lovely wife, and himself to go to St Wolffgang and Vienna. There was no refusing so kind an offer, or so insistent a host, and he showed us the splendour of the former capital of the Austro-Hungarian Empire which he knew intimately. I was depressed by the obsession of the late Emperor Franz-Josef with crimson, for everything in his palace was that colour; I told him so to his dead face in the Kaisergruft where one could walk about amongst the actual coffins and sarcophagi of the emperors. He did not reply. It was strange to feel one was an inch or two from the remains of so many dominant and tragic figures. We had a feast of treasures at Schonbrunn, music at dinner and good food.

On 19 August 1963 I defended for the first of many times William Smith for 'assault to severe injury'. His plea of self-defence was upheld by the jury. On this occasion, his victim was not a member, as it usually was, of the Herrity family. I called him 'Whispering Smith' because he had a strange *sotto voce*, hairy Glasgow voice, which was almost inaudible. I was to hear many more whispers from him.

In June the University army set off on a brave adventure to Norway which was the brain-child of Charles Campbell, the Commanding Officer. I first met CSA when he was CRA and came to visit the University battery at Otterburn. He seemed at first sight a withdrawn and harmless sort of person. We had our annual battery dinner the night before we fired the guns. This was an unfortunate order of events. Knowing that our heads might not be too clear next morning, we determined to ensure that whosoever had a clear head it wouldn't be him. Thinking wrongly that he was probably suffering from senility we indulged in doctoring his milk and singing him, as we thought, to sleep. In fact he was bored and awake with his eyes shut. Every drink he was given was larger than he asked for, and we sang songs which we hoped would make him sleep. After dinner, long after he had passed, as we

117

thought, comatose into his comfortable bed, we all went to our drunken and drowsy palliasses in the reluctant knowledge that we had to fire guns in the morning, but in the confident fantasy that we would have two hours respite before the fragile CRA arrived shakily on the scene. No judgement of a man could ever have been so mistaken. This seasoned cask was unaffected by the dribble we had poured into it and in any event was too proud to be affected by anything so feeble as inebriation. Long before we arrived late on the gun position, he was there prancing about in the cold and lonely air of Otterburn Moors – short, stumpy and aggressive, like a mole in a bate. In the mists of the moor and the mists of our minds, he railed and harried us, even forcing us to run with ammunition, which I had been brought up in the artillery to understand was a cardinal sin. And so I learned, which I have had so many reasons to confirm since, with gratitude and with grace that Charles Campbell was a man of grit – if grumpy grit – a mixture of top brass and brass tack with a steel spine and a gold heart. As a lawyer and a soldier he was the most wonderful combination of red flannel and red tape.

We landed in the north of Norway at Andelsnes and marched south on the route taken by General George Sinclair, one of the great Scots mercenary soldiers who went to the aid and defence of King Gustavus Apolphus of Sweden and died on 26 August 1612 in battle. We paid tribute at his grave when we reached it. Every village gave us a rapturous and affectionate welcome. It was so hot by day that we had to march by night, but whenever we arrived, children were always there to greet us. Like animals, children in Scandinavia practise the wise arts of hibernation and aestivation, never sleeping in summer when it's not dark, and never getting up in winter when it is. We ourselves rarely slept when we were not marching, for two reasons: one was because it was never night, and the other was that there was such goluptious entertainment wherever we went, that sleep was subsidiary to enjoyment. One night, Colonel Charles suggested that we should scale Norway's highest mountain. No such mad plan could have been conceived in sobriety and so armed with the fortitude of our native nectar, we set out with his two loyal, and lovely, WRAC drivers and piper to scale this mighty mountain. It was cold, beautiful, mad, steep and exhilarating. Though it could not be said we were sober on our departure, we were certainly sober on our return at dawn, or rather at the time that dawn would have been if there had been one at that time of year in Norway. From there we departed to Oslo to a tumultuous reception, for the progress of the Skottetoget had been eagerly reported in the Press. It was like being a member of the Liberation Army: the streets were filled with a quarter of a million people to greet us as we marched in our kilts headed by the pipes and drums to the barracks of the Royal Norwegian Guards. Here we relaxed and enjoyed ourselves and all the salacious pleasures of Oslo, and of the Bluebell girls in town. Next morning we marched to a very special and frightful ceremony in the castle to lay a wreath at the wall where the heroes of Norway who had resisted torture in defence of freedom and friends were shot on the orders of the Gestapo when those mephitic sadists had failed to make them break. Only in capital murder trials has the angel of death touched me so painfully, hauntingly and closely as did that mournful ceremony at that vacant wall. I trembled with awe as Krateros trembled when he saw Lysippus' statue of Alexander the Great in the sacred way at Delphi. Death and pain screamed silently from that simple wall.

The contingent departed by sea, on a minesweeper, leaving us, the Colonel and his staff behind to clear up, or rather mop up. As it sailed down the Oslo fjord on a sea of glass, the pipe band played our signature tune, 'The Bonnie Lass of Fyvie', at about five o'clock in the morning. The sound echoed round the mountains, and doors and windows opened in amazement and pleasure. The Colonel and I returned to all that was left to drink and eat – gin and Smarties. We flew home to meet the returning sea-borne heroes. Having left them flushed and happy, they returned grey and green. I was thankful to have come back by plane.

At the Edinburgh Festival in September a drama conference had been arranged in the course of which there was a variety of what were then called 'happenings'. This involved the somewhat trivial concept that surprise was art, being a misunderstanding of the fact that art should be surprise. In the course of the conference, various surprises of most trivial conception were arranged to demonstrate that people reacted to surprise or shock – hardly a phenomenal discovery, but nevertheless hailed as such by the intellectual equivalent of the *nouveau riche* – the *nouveau pauvre*. One of the happenings involved a naked, though static, girl being wheeled across the stage on a trolley while a speaker was lecturing on a subject that had nothing to do with her or much else. Edinburgh was horrified or electrified by the sight of God's most noble creation. The statue of John Knox wobbled on its base, breathed hellfire and spoke forth its rage like the statue of Il Commendatore in *Don Giovanni*, in which opera, however, Donna Anna's tauntings went unprosecuted. To think that the monstrous regiment of women should have a representative on full view! Horror shuddered down the puritan spine of Auld Reekie. Flesh had appeared in the very temple of respectability, the devil incarnate had appeared carnate and, what was worse, he was a woman! No crime more capital had ever shaken the capitals of the capital city. Pornocracy was but a whiff away. Both the girl and the authur of the conference were instantly arrested and charged.

The girl was Anna Kesselar, a twenty-year-old model who lived modestly in Portobello. It fell to the *Daily Express* to sum up the duplicity of the emotions of the press in general and hypocrisy of those who threw up their hands and raised up their voices in horror in particular. Their banner headline read: 'Shocking Nude Incident – Picture Inside'. For indeed, it would clearly be a pity if those who weren't horrified by seeing it for themselves missed the opportunity of being appalled second-hand. This monstrous obscenity must be broadcast to show how shocking it was. I was instructed by Lawrence Dowdall on behalf of both accused. Lawrence Dowdall had for years been a legendary name, in the households alike of the wicked and good. I think this was the first time I had the privilege of his instructions. As ever they were meticulous. He had built up a phenomenal and worthy reputation as a defence solictor in Glasgow which was founded not only on his professional cunning and the penetrancy of his mind, but his pellucid mastery of epigram and wit. He had the habit while addressing a jury, of putting one foot on a chair and holding out his hand, and one could watch as the members of the jury one by one grew feathers and a beak and with passerine naïvety flew to guzzle the morsels this tongue fashioned for their digestion. They were charmed by his flair. Years later I had the privilege of entertaining him at the House of Commons on the occasion of his most deservedly receiving the insignia of the Order of the British Empire.

The trial was attended by a cosmopolitian corps of Press, appropriate to a matter of such international and intellectual importance – it was after all an international festival on trial. Baillie Tom McGregor gave a sane and earthy judgment. He found Anna Kesselar not guilty, and in issuing his judgment had some wise words to say:

> I am not concerned with whether a happening is good theatre or an art form. I am content to leave argument of this subject to those better equipped to do so. What concerns me is the publicity given to the incident by certain sections of the press, which to say the least was not only sensational, but bordering on the hypocritical. Also, in my opinion, certain members of the public – some prominent, some not so – wittingly or unwittingly made statements which would have been much better left unsaid.

Left: Nicholas Fairbairn's mother

Below: l. to r. Robin More Gordon, Cosmo Fairbairn, Nicholas Fairbairn, Grandmother More Gordon, Harry More Gordon and Elinor Fairbairn, standing

Right: Nicholas Fairbairn with his father

Below: The launching of the Society for the Preservation of Duddingston Village *l. to r.* Nicholas Fairbairn, Lord Cameron, Sir John Banks, Sir Compton Mackenzie

By kind permission of SCOTTISH DAILY RECORD & SUNDAY MAIL LTD

Above: Joseph Beltrami with Nicholas Fairbairn

Left: Walter Scott Ellis

By kind permission of GLASGOW HERALD/EVENING TIMES

Above: Patrick Meehan

Right: Jimmy Boyle

Below: Fordell Castle

Nicholas Fairbairn at Fordell

Nicholas Fairbairn and Margaret Thatcher at Mrs Hadden's 100th birthday party

How wise were the words of this good, earthy man. The trial in a way had a very influential effect. The restrictive and compulsive ethic was on the wane. The forgivers took over where the forbidders had failed. In the words of Horace: '*Quid leges sine moribus vanae proficiunt?*' Edinburgh had been liberated. In the course of the trial I met a great number of people who were interested in the arts and in modern theatre with whom I became increasingly intervolved, amongst them Jim Haines who had recently developed the Traverse Theatre in the Lawnmarket. This meeting was the beginning of momentous events for me.

On 22 December 1963 Elizabeth gave birth to twin daughters. She went, parturient, into Simpson Maternity Memorial Pavilion (to give the ghastly concrete place its ghastly concrete name) on the 21st, and after leaving her I spent the evening in the company of her uncle, Bill Younger, on the eve (though we didn't know the secret) of becoming Sir William McEwan Younger Bart, and Sir Compton McKenzie and his highland wife, Lily, at their home in 31 Drummond Place, which had been the home of my father's parents at the time of my grandfather's death. About 4 A.M. I was awoken by the news that twins had arrived. Their delivery was skilfully achieved by the tender skills of John Sturrock, nearing his retirement, whose same skill had brought me into this world almost thirty years before. I went immediately to the hospital and spent most of Christmas there with Elizabeth and the children. Birth is a wonderful and moving event, and to be surrounded by nativity and all that it involves at the time of Christmas, with the nurses singing carols and joy all around, was amost intimate experience and celebration. The matron, Miss Collett, in the tradition of matrons, was forbidding and stern. For a good reason: she had high standards and cared for everyone, and she did not believe, and was right not to believe, that compromise was a sign of affection. We got to know and love Eve Collett very much. In view of their intimate association with the birth, Bill Younger and Monty Mackenzie agreed to be a godfather to each twin.

In April, Dr Charles Warr, who had been so cruelly prevented from marrying us by the wicked spite of Dr Whitley, baptized Charlotte and Micheline in the chapel at Fordell, filled with daffodils and now fully restored. As promised on the day, Compton Mackenzie and Bill Younger were among the eight godparents. It was a beautiful and happy occasion. Five weeks later, inexplicably, Micheline was dead. The peaks of joy and the troughs of grief are the pattern of life. We cannot deserve one and not suffer the other. We buried our darling child in her little feretory on the floor of the chapel where so recently she had been christened, and we made a prayer for her:

> Dear God, help us to love all we see – as Micheline did;
> To love all who see us – as Micheline did;
> To be loving, gentle, good and beautiful in all things
> And ever to stand closer to Thee. Amen.

I now represented a poor girl who had attempted to end her mother's life by adding codeine to the forty-two tablets and ten different drugs she was taking to relieve the suffering of angina and arthritis, and alleviate the effects of her third cerebral haemorrhage. My senior was Harold Leslie QC – afterwards Lord Birsay – upon whom the dignity and honour of Knighthood of the Thistle was rightly bestowed for his outstanding services to the Church and the community and the culture of Scotland. I never saw him without a smile on his face, a twinkle in his eye, a joke on his tongue and a kilt on his backside. He was a 'verray parfit gentil Knight'. After consultation we advised a plea of guilty. With characteristic modesty he then withdrew and I appeared alone with a plea in mitigation. Almost inexplicably her mother recovered from this ultrafatal dose, and upon her recovery she wrote a letter of touching devotion and love to her child in prison:

> My most beloved darling child: I do hope you are keeping a brave spirit and we will soon be together again. You know and I know, that you are my own darling daughter, and the best and most unselfish person I have ever known. Your ever loving and absolutely understanding mother.

Such is the true spirit of a Christian heart.

The Sherriff Principal, the late Sir Ross McLean, a man of outstanding compassion and also of great maritime skill and bibulous habit, gave her a sentence which in effect meant her immediate release. Perhaps the acid test of what is right or wrong is its motivation – what is done for love is good. Those whose emotional pressures do not break them should pity and suffer those whose do.

> Let thy soul lend its ear to every cry of pain,
> As the lotus bares its heart to drink in the morning.

This case raised in my mind the increasing difficulty of the medical profession as science advanced, to decide when it is right, artificially, to sustain a life, be it young or old. For that power may soon be available indefinitely and we must resolve the morality of the decision. Let us not forget, as we become more and more sentimental and less and less resolved in our confidence, that it is life and birth, and not death, which threatens the values of the future and the survival of mankind. In the age of elegance and the age of reason, they enjoyed life no less, but they lacked our contemporary obsession with and horror of pain and death. When Dr Henry, the great Scots historian, was told he was mortally ill in 1790, he wrote forthwith a message to Henry (then Sir Harry) Moncrieff: 'Come out here directly. I have something to do this week; I have got to die.' So do we all. Not enough of us practise the habit any more.

Following on his defeat in the Festival nude case, the Burgh prosecutor in Edinburgh was determined to recover the purity – or rather the puritanity – for which Edinburgh had previously been infamous, or renowned. 'Virtue would not go so far if vanity did not bear it company.' Accordingly, in May 1964, he branded *Fanny Hill* indecent. He no doubt chose her as she had recently been approved as decent by the magistrates in England. To emphasize the difference in the morals of Coventry and Edinburgh, it was the expurgated edition which he prosecuted while it was the unexpurgated edition in England which had been found pure. My senior was Ewan Stewart QC – now Lord Stewart – a Senator of the College of Justice, the stature of whose nimble mind was in inverse proportion to his modest height and against whom I was often to appear when he was Solicitor-General in days to come. The longest cut in the expurgated edition was a mere eleven pages. He quoted the great dictum of Lord Sands in the case of *McGowan v. Langmuir* in 1930: 'A picture of Mrs Brown, to which only the very straitlaced might take exception if displayed as a work of art in a remote city, might be grossly indecent if displayed in Brown's drawing-room in Edinburgh.' Despite his many excellent skills and a doughty defence, poor Fanny was found indecent and banned from Edinburgh for ever. As a result of which judgment the literary citizens have been compelled to read the unexpurgated edition in full. I recommend it; it is written in excellent English. I have never believed in the efficacy of censorship. It advertises the forbidden fruit and the desire for it is heightened by its forbiddance. Rather did I hold with Seneca that shame will restrain what law does not prohibit. The public take no interest in a fetid work of art until it is forbidden.

In October 1964, Sir Alec Douglas Home necessarily called the General Election. It was the last moment of the Conservatives' five-year term. I tried to visit every house. My campaign in Central Edinburgh makes strange reading now: in thirteen (wasted) years the Tories had brought to Scotland the car industry, the Ravenscraig Steel strip mill, the Forth Road Bridge, and they had doubled the standard of living and halved taxation. We were freer and better off than we had ever been. And the major beneficiary was the wage-earner, which was achieved by making those above him correspondingly prosperous. All these benefits subsequent Labour Governments in each year removed again. Let us all learn the wise words of Abraham Lincoln:

> You cannot bring about prosperity by discouraging thrift. You cannot strengthen the weak by weakening the strong. You cannot help the poor by destroying the rich. You cannot establish sound security on borrowed money. You cannot keep out trouble by spending more than you earn. You cannot build up character and courage by taking away man's initiative and independence. You cannot help men permanently by doing more for them than they can do for themselves.

That tersely is the answer to socialism on the head of a very wise pin.

With socialist envy, the Labour campaign in Central Edinburgh was personal. They used the word 'castle', which means a fortified residence, to impute to me grandeur, riches, exclusion, and all the legendary wickedness of the baron towards his vassals. I lived in luxury they alleged; the voters all lived in slums. I was a wicked, privileged oppressor. Envy is their creed, prejudice their doctrine, reason and truth their enemy. Little did they know the slum which I had bought and taken over. They prepared a pamphlet containing a picture of my house, when it was a ruin, though they didn't appreciate that, and compared it with five sordid pictures which they deliberately falsified and manufactured portraying children in mucky basements and a pensioner in a slovenly home. All these situations were concocted for the photographer, such was their dishonour and such is their dishonesty. My programme promised the abolition of slum conditions by 1973 as was our commitment. My opponent promised a brighter future; the immediate demolition of the houses in the photographs, and lower rates. Ten years later, every house which was photographed stands as it did. And I have reduced my house, with much pain and effort with my own and other hands from the slum I bought to its habitable condition, and thus saved part of our national heritage and also a great deal of public money. So much for the politics of envy. The silent member, by his treacherous tactic, was returned, as was a Labour Government, thanks more than anything to Edward Heath's maniacal dismantling of resale price maintenance and with it the traditional loyalty of the independent shopkeeper to the Conservative Party. Let us learn the lesson. Harold Wilson became Prime Minister: he and a few of his beknighted and bebaronned friends alone profited from the ensuing decade. He deserves to be remembered in the annals of the absurd as the man who reintroduced naked patronage, forsaken a hundred years before, into the life of the country.

On 8 December I appeared for James Steele who was charged with a contravention of the Coinage Offences Act of 1936, to wit 'that he counterfeited 14,144 two-shilling pieces at his dwelling house at 13 Caledonian Road, Edinburgh'. James Steele was eighty. He was caught red-handed, so there was no alternative but to plead guilty. But the manner of his apprehension was amazing. At Tullieallan Police College, a senior officer was lecturing to prospective policemen on the criminal code in Scotland. When he reached the crime of counterfeiting, he said, 'I need not dwell on this offence, since there has only ever been one case in Scotland which occurred in 1930 when a man, Steele, was found guilty of counterfeiting half-crowns in Gorgie Road, Edinburgh.' Up shot the hand of a teenage cadet. 'How old would he be now?' he asked. 'Well, if he's still alive, which I doubt, he'd be over eighty. Why?' asked the lecturer. 'Because there have been complaints of thumping coming from a house on my beat where an old man called Steele lives.' Youthful curiosity was rewarded. The police investigated and true enough, there was James Steele stamping out his florins – as he had in fact been doing probably ever since his last conviction – but as he melted down his waste and used it again, he could only be charged with the 14,144 of the current bake. The metallic constituents and their proportion in the coinage are public knowledge and are published in the annual books of reference, so James Steele ordered strips of metal of appropriate thickness, width and consistency from Imperial Chemical Industries. His requirement in changing from making half crowns to florins was occasioned by the fact that ICI sharply narrowed the strips, rather than increase the price and perhaps lose a sale. They were entitled to – *caveat emptor* is the law. Feeling it imprudent to complain that the strips were not wide enough to make half-crowns, he turned his art to florins. The great difficulty of counterfeiting is to obtain sufficient pressure to create the milling which is internal to the rim on the face and the reverse of the coin. Many hundreds of tons of pressure per square inch are required to achieve it. James Steele obtained this effect hydraulically with his water-tap, and it was the thump of the water-tap which in fact led to his exposure and the second conviction. Disposing of coins and florins in such abundance presents its difficulties, so he wisely obtained an amoretto, who happened to be a bus conductress, as his main outlet. Inlet and outlet in one – what economy! After all, he was a gifted economist. Though her inlet sufficed, her outlet didn't. He therefore enlisted the help of a young boy who, for a modest consideration (paid in florins) exchanged the excess output for postal orders at the local post office. With the acicular acuity for which public corporations are renowned, the sleuths of the post office security noticed after eighteen months of this daily practice the regularity and peculiarity of these monotonous transactions, without however noticing that all the florins were always of the same date. He was challenged by two Post office detectives. James Steele's youthful accomplice was more than a match for these sceptical genii; 'Where do you get all these florins?' they asked with brutal perspicuity. 'Well,' he said honestly. 'There's an old man up the road called Mr Steele. He changes all his money into florins and sends me to the post office to get postal orders, and then he changes them all back into money again.' The sleuths accepted this absurd, if quasi-truthful tale. What the expertise of the Post Office missed, the ingenuity of the police cadet uncovered. James Steele was sentenced to two years' imprisonment, no account being taken of his age and health, and no account being given to his genius and enterprise. Even at Christmas the Appeal Court, after the briefest moment of interjudicial consultation turned its conglaciate heart against my plea for clemency for a sick, but talented, old man. 'We can't decide cases on the basis of goodwill for Christmas,' japed Lord Clyde, adopting the lead part in Dickens's *Christmas Carol*, and determined to lose no opportunity to demonstrate that clemency and mercy were foreign to his heart and to keep the ghost of Lord Braxfield content – a code of honour at least beautiful in his own sight.

The Crown announced in court that a spokesman at the Royal Mint – for even mints have spokesmen these days – had opined that they had experienced no counterfeiting of coinage of such skill and precision. But that was not quite the end of the tale: I was informed by the police, on enquiry, that so good were the counterfeit florins that the Mint were only able to tell that they were forgeries because they had an extra milling on the rim. This information, which I gave to the court hoping that they would reward perfection as a mitigating claim, was read by one of that brand of fanatical enthusiasts who collect useless objects and pointless information of the narrowest and most abstruse kind, and who all appear to live in the southern fifth of England. This blate gook set about counting the millings of tens of thousands of florins, shillings, sixpences and half-crowns, and found that the number of millings varied. He confronted the Royal Mint, spokesman and all, with his information, which was no doubt a breach of the Official Secrets Act. They refused to comment. He flew north and cornered me, and such was his insistence that the Mint finally conceded that every milling was put in with a hammer and chisel by hand. He was content with the explanation. The Royal Mint should send for James Steele. He emerged from jail in time to vote for me at my second General Election, but God has called him to the task of lining clouds since.

For many months my father had been in decline. I formed the view as I watched the wretched process of deterioration into infantility and decay, that throughout our lives under stress we have a series of tiny cerebral leakages which affect more or less, gradually or dramatically, our personalities, our temper and our powers. It was a repulsive and difficult experience to watch so wise and kind and vigorous a man totter into disintegration and death. At what age, I thought, do we enter eternity, for I had lost an infant child and a decrepit father? He entered it in the dying hours of 1964. This was his obituary in *The Times*:

Dr Ronald Fairbairn, the distinguished psychoanalyst, died on Thursday in an Edinburgh nursing home at the age of 75. His profound contribution to psychoanalytic thought has been increasingly recognized in recent years in Britain and abroad. He was born in 1889. From Merchiston Castle School he went to Edinburgh University where he graduated in 1911 with Honours in Philosophy, a training which led him to change his intention of becoming a lawyer and which left a characteristic clarity and rigour in all his future thinking. His first postgraduate studies conducted in Germany and in England were Divinity and Hellenistic Greek. During the war he served in the Palestinian Campaign under Allenby. By the time of demobilization he decided to train as a psychoanalyst and he returned to Edinburgh University to qualify in Medicine in 1923. After a year's psychiatric experience he began in private practice as a psychoanalyst in 1924 and three years later his MD Thesis on Freud's Theory of Oppression was highly commended. In the early part of his career Fairbairn shared with Freud much of the professional isolation which a dedication to psychoanalysis then entailed. But as with Freud too, his integrity and independence kept him steadfast to his purpose of understanding and treating human conflict as he found it with no flight from all its disturbing depths and complexities. He contributed a succession of papers which commanded respect, both because of their thoughtful inferences from his clinical data and because of the elegant and concise style in which he presented them. Struck by the restrictions which he saw in his patients' capacities to make satisfying human relationships, in spite of desperate longing to do so, he began in 1940 a series of papers which marked the full maturity and originality of his thought. For him the divorce between energy and structure in Freud's theories and the dominant position given to impulse and the satisfaction of desires were not adequate explanations for the tragic failures in human relationships that he encountered. He therefore fashioned a radically new theory of personality in terms of dynamic structures developed from experience within the first personal relationship between the infant and his mother. Though treated by psychoanalysts with reserve at first, his views made a more immediate appeal to many social scientists engaged in the application of psychoanalytical principles to social tasks because of the way they permitted the individual to be understood in terms of the social experiences which had shaped the personality.

Dr Harley Williams, his and my friend, the author, lawyer and doctor, paid a more personal tribute:

I remember the first time I got to know your father. We were in Paris studying midwifery and he took gravely ill and was for a time in the British Hospital. I remember the impression of his warm-hearted charm very well. He was older than most of us and gave an image of smiling distinction and intellectual authority. I don't think your father had any mediocrity in his make-up; and in dealing with the world, mediocrity is an advantage. He chose the most difficult branch of medicine and you, Nicky, have no idea how psychoanalysis was execrated when he began it. He took his own independent line and even in that jealous circle of men who were waiting to see his individuality come to grief, he carried his point and established his theories in a very difficult medium. Did he count himself a success in life? No one can tell, but I think he made for himself the kind of life he wished. He took great and secret pride in your career, but I believe you puzzled him. He always expected you to do great things, and he was big enough to wish them to be different from his own style of achievement. Ronald was a cavalier from the sixteenth century with a smiling assurance and a certain scorn for the present age. Psychoanalysts live apart, in separate dimension, but in his case I believe the aloofness was natural. I deeply regret that I did not make notes of his talk and wisdom about literature and art and the way things are made, and how human beings work. Scientists will turn to his writings and they will find them to be the main road and not a side road. You have a lot of him. His understanding lies at your disposal. You should not be unduly sad at his parting, but be grateful for the rich mental qualities he gave you. I did not fully understand him but I shall always admire him, for intellectual distinction is rare. Psychoanalysis does not make men tolerant. Your father had his polemics, but I don't think he ever hated his enemies. You have his wisdom – accept it. Not the acquired part that comes from a good education but that innate quality of an exceptional man.

But his closest professional colleague was Jock Sutherland who did such sterling work at the Tavistock Clinic and has now returned to Edinburgh. In these words he paid his tribute:

I first met Fairbairn in 1928 when I had become an assistant in the Psychology Department in Edinburgh University. When I took up psychoanalysis I then got more directly to know the kind of hostility he had to endure for years. Thus I received from the Professor, following a talk I had given, a note which said: 'While you are a member of the staff of the Department I shall expect you to abstain from any public advocacy of psychoanalytic views. I cannot have the department identified in any way with these views.' I mention this, not to dramatize the professional adversity in which Fairbairn had to live, but bring out something of what he had to contend with, and how the qualities in his character emerged in the situation. It was characteristic of him that he never told me, until many years later, of that treatment which he had received in regard to his post and of many attempts to make his life difficult or impossible. He was of course disappointed and regretful about his isolation and the obstructive attitudes he encountered, but his great inner strength and reliance was such that he went on doing highly creative work independently and virtually alone for the next 25 years. In all of the years I knew him, I never heard him make a malicious remark about anyone, nor do I think he ever bore a grudge against those whose hostilities to psychoanalysis were at times more vindictive. His convictions about his own work gave him a great toleration and understanding of the limitations of others. There were three qualities, his kindness, his courtesy and his humility, which were very prominent in his make-up. I do not think I have ever known anyone who took what one might say such a responsible attitude to others. I always felt, no matter who he was dealing with, they were always deeply respected as individuals. This concern for others and care for others, and for the dignity of the individual were deeply spontaneous in him, and he combined them with a marked feeling of enjoyment and a good sense of humour. Art and religion for him were profound expressions of man's needs for which he felt a deep respect.

He was a great man, dedicated to the dignity and salvation of the individual, and we laid him to rest in the Dean Cemetry beside my mother. I pray he is contented at last. John Donne provides my farewell salute:

> Yea, I must do him right; he was a man
> Above men's height; even towering to divinity
> Brave, pious, generous, great, and liberal
> Just, as the scales of Heaven weigh the seasons.

A few days later, the other great father-figure in my life joined him in death – my mighty hero, Winston Churchill. Shakespeare's Brutus, in paying his tribute to the corpse of Julius Caesar, voiced my feelings:

> Why, man, he doth bestride the narrow world
> Like a Colossus, and we petty men
> Walk under his huge legs and peep about
> To find ourselves dishonourable graves.

With Charles Campbell, my Colonel, I went to London to pay homage to Churchill's supremacy. Throughout my life he had enlarged the scale of human conduct and the size of the men around him. With his departure, all public men were diminished and shrunk. We are in an age of pygmies; there are no big men left to make us walk tall. The old glory of politics has faded; it is now a lower description of men who are tempted to enlist in political service, and no words expressed better the shrinking scale of public life in Britain which Churchill's death dramatically occasioned than the articulate pen of Bernard Levin: 'To partake of everything, to drink from every cup and stir every pot, to travel and to see, to talk and to cherish. To read and to ask and never give up doing these things – that is what marks out the dwarfs who remain.'

We queued from the other side of the Thames at St Thomas's Hospital and slowly, after hours, we came to Westminster Hall and there, in its rugged splendour, under the proud magnificence of the Union Jack and the Garter Collar, were his mortal remains. Like my father, he too had tottered into death. His funeral, so much in contrast to the bizarre and vulgar replica in the United States of America soon after for General Eisenhower, was glorious and overwhelming. It had everything of taste and dignity and excellence, worthy of that mighty man. Shelley's haunting words, which were inscribed as the preface to the magnificent book which Parliament gave him on his eightieth birthday, are the total summary of his singular and triumphant worth:

> To suffer ills which hope thinks infinite,
> To forgive wrongs blacker than death or might,
> To defy power which seems omnipotent
> To love and bear; to hope till hope creates
> Of its own wreck the thing it contemplates
> Never to change nor falter nor repent;
> This, like thy glory, Titan, is to be
> Good, great, and joyous, beautiful and free
> This is alone life, joy, empire and victory.

On 22 February 1965, I appeared on behalf of Walter Scott Ellis for the third and last time. He was charged with writing threatening letters to Sheriff Lionel Daiches QC, who had presided, and the Procurator Fiscal, James Tudhope, who had prosecuted, at a recent trial at which Ellis had been convicted – wrongly according to him – of attempted housebreaking by kicking a bakery door. The matter was remitted for sentence to the High Court and he was sentenced by Lord Grant to four years' imprisonment. The sentence was out of all proportion to the offence or even to his record, though not perhaps to his list of previous acquittals. Ellis felt particularly aggrieved since some of the eyewitnesses were taxi-drivers, and he had been not long acquitted of the capital murder of the Glasgow taxi-driver. The trial for this crime was transferred to the High Court in Edinburgh in order to prevent prejudice by members of a Glasgow jury. The letters, all of which were printed, were of the most dangerous and threatening kind. They could only be taken seriously.

This was the first of several cases in which the Crown was represented by the Solicitor-General, Mr Ewan Stewart QC. I appeared for the defence and the Lord Justice Clerk, Lord Grant, was the presiding judge. The verdict in all these cases was one of acquittal except for the last, which was the case of Her Majesty's Advocate against Patrick Meehan who was wrongly convicted, served seven years and received the Queen's Pardon. The result in this and the succeeding cases with this triumvirate on the forensic stage had a huge bearing on the conduct of the Meehan trial.

In the Ellis case the police experts gave evidence that the handwriting was the same as the writing on cuttings on the back of the door of Ellis's cell, but there was no evidence which could directly connect him with the authorship of the letters.

In order to contradict the evidence, I travelled to Cardiff to learn the secrets of handwriting from the Home Office expert, Harrison K. Harrison. I went by aeroplane with Joseph Beltrami's assistant, William McGlynn. He had never flown before and was reluctant to do so. After we had been sitting in the plane only a few minutes he asked if we were nearly there. I pointed out to him that the door was still open and that we hadn't even left. When it was announced that we were being diverted to Manchester from Birmingham I nonchalantly commented that we wouldn't have enough fuel to get there. He went berserk! He returned by train and I returned by 'plane full of insight into the science of graphology.

When Ellis was giving evidence the Lord Justice Clerk made the following blunt enquiry: 'Did it never occur to you that if you had supplied a sample of your own handwriting you could have cleared yourself?' Without a flicker of his hard, black eyes or a moment's hesitation Ellis replied: 'It is not for me to prove my innocence, My Lord.' From then on the Lord Justice Clerk, chop-fallen, kept quiet.

The jury unanimously found the charge against Ellis 'not proven'. My service to Ellis was three out of three. On the next occasion he instructed another counsel. The Lord Justice Clerk complimented the defence on presenting the best-prepared case he had ever heard. He was to hear in the Meehan case a much better preparation from the same defence team but by then his health had deteriorated and his attitude had soured.

On 8 May 1965 Elizabeth gave birth to our only son. On the 9th, having been baptized by Basil Miller – an old family friend – Edward Nicholas died and we buried him beside his sister, Micheline, in the chapel at Fordell.

In July I appeared for two men who had been members of the City of Glasgow Police but who had emigrated to Canada to join the Mounties. They were charged in Canada with robbery of the sum of $1,200,000. The stolen notes had been cancelled with three puncture holes to make them invalid but for the purposes of the Crown they were held to be valid. Working for some weeks they managed to replace the missing bits from some notes with parts of other notes, thus prospectively halving their take. But tedium overtook greed and they decided to settle for the reward and a fraction of the sum of their booty. Having informed the insurance company where the notes could be found in a garage, they flew into London at the Company's suggestion to collect their reward of £35,000. The solicitor who handed it over took it upon himself, rightly or wrongly, to inform the police. The two were arrested in June, quite improperly, for they were on bail in Canada, due for trial in September and were perfectly entitled to travel wherever they wished. Their £35,000 was seized. The Sheriff Principal in Edinburgh found that there was 'a strong and probable presumption' that they had committed the offence in question. A request for the extradition on the personally signed petition of the Governor-General of Canada was duly submitted and the extradition order was granted by the Sheriff. The two men appealed against the Sheriff's findings. To their intense displeasure the Appeal Court had to convene during the vacation, until then an unexperienced phenomenon. I submitted my case that there was no evidence to establish a strong and probable presumption of guilt. In any event, the accused were on bail and could do what they liked, and wherever they cared to do it, until the date of their trial arrived. 'Do you mean to say you've brought us all in from our vacation just to hear that?' Lord Clyde enquired with irritation on the conclusion of my argument. 'We find that there was more than sufficient evidence for the Sheriff Principal to reach the conclusion he did,' said Lord Clyde, and strutted out with giggling glee to resume his holiday. A month later in Canada, the accused were acquitted. Lord Clyde was therefore more easily convinced of guilt by hearsay evidence than the courts of Canada were by the evidence itself. Free again, they returned to Scotland to stake their claim to the reward money in an action in Edinburgh Sheriff Court. I pondered Hamlet's words:

> In the corrupted currents of the world
> Offence's gilded hand may shove by justice,
> And oft 'tis seen the wicked prize itself
> Buys out the law.

Over the years I became extremely concerned with the alarming increase in the population of the world and much later, in 1979, I was elected to the Board of the World Population Crisis, which was the Scottish branch of the Family Planning International Campaign. Since in industrial countries a ten per cent increase in the population requires a hundred per cent increase in the infrastructure of towns, roads, airports, universities and the like, and all countries aspire to the Western image, I see no chance of salvation unless philoprogenitiveness is brought under control. Even nuclear war in thirty years' time would probably leave more on earth surviving than there are now. It is a thought which all should ponder with an unsentimental eye. Many couples leave many children unborn and we do not mourn the denial of their existence. If each family conceived as many as they wanted and intended there would be no crisis – we could all have as many as we chose.

Once again I appeared for Arthur Thompson in November 1965 on a charge of assault and severe injury. He was found not guilty. The following month, December, I appeared once more for 'Whispering Smith' on a charge of murder for the second time in seven weeks of a member of the Herrity family who plainly and proudly were not on friendly terms with Smith. On this occasion Smith was charged with killing Joseph Herrity and stabbing James Herrity. He was found not guilty of both charges on the grounds of self-defence, which is not surprising in view of the evidence of the surviving Herritys that they intended to kill Smith that night and would do so again given a chance, and of their description in court by witnesses as 'the fighting Herritys from Hell'. When the jury was out I went to see Smith in his cell. Unlike most clients he actually said thank you, and in a most endearing way. 'Thank you very much sir, thank you very much,' he rasped. 'When yi' were addressin' the jury there I thocht for a moment I hadnae done it masel'.'

From one death I passed to another of a different kind; Jim Haines, Director of the Traverse Theatre, asked me to play the part of the judge in Tita Weiss's play *The Investigation* – which is a dramatic presentation of the trial of twenty-two guards from Auschwitz who were tried in 1964 for the murder of several million Jews. The production was directed by Mike Ockrent, then a member of Edinburgh University Dramatic Society and later, in 1974, to become a Director of the Traverse himself. I quote from *The Scotsman* review by Alan Wright:

A monstrous ritual was performed last night in an Edinburgh church.

It is surely the most devastating court-room drama that has ever been written. Not even the descriptions of obscenities committed in the course of duty are as alarming as the protest of defending counsel that only the killing of a few hundred thousand can be proved conclusively. The presentation on a stage of such a theme and in such a manner has no precedent. The passion of the oratorio lies in the words: 'The boy stood there with his apple.'

> Bogar went to the child and picked him up by the feet and dashed his head against the barracks wall. Then he picked up the apple and called me out and said 'Wipe this off the wall' and later, as I sat at an interrogation I saw him eating an apple. We came to the camp in such great numbers – there are so many who brought us there that what happened ought to be comprehensible even today.

Despite the enormity of the crime there is no place for hysteria in this trial. Only a few of the murderers were passionate in the killings – we are told – and the victims never struggled because every one of them believed that he could survive.

How many deaths do we condone or overlook today within the dictatorships that hold such widespread sway in the world, provided they are committed by men of dusky appearance or Marxist views? Who wept for the Cambodians, the Laotians, the Vietnamese, killed in their millions in cold blood when Western guilt signed the Treaty of Paris by the hand of Henry Kissinger? If any weep they weep in silence.

There had been so many acquittals in the High Court in Glasgow that the Assistant Chief Constable had reached the limit of his discretion and his tether. He made a public announcement that the Crown was represented by wet-eared juniors while the defence always had the best brains of the Bar. Inaccurate as this picture was the Crown nevertheless reacted and sent through the energetic and talented Advocate-depute, Mr Ewan Stewart QC, who had in his defence days been a formidable, successful and devious adversary of the Crown. What is more, he knew the law. He had the appearance and about the height of an erect mole and his mind contained all of the mole's cunning and industry and much else besides. With him and his gentle wife Sheila I had previously enjoyed a close friendship which was interrupted by his departure for New Zealand as the first Ombudsman – a post he took in the hope that the mild climate would cure his wife's asthmatic health. But the experiment obtained neither her improvement nor his fulfilment and so, luckily for Scotland and the law, his singular and particular talent and his dear wife returned. His arrival in Glasgow as Solicitor-General was prompted by a proper intention of reassuring the police and he came to conduct three cases for murder in the North court on behalf of the Crown. I had been instructed in all three.

The first of the three was remarkable in two respects: it was the first trial of a murder in a Scottish prison; secondly, it was the first time that a witness in Scotland confessed to murder in the course of a trial. Frederick Joseph Cairns, a prisoner in Barlinnie, was charged with the murder of Alexander Malcolmson, another prisoner, by stabbing him in the back. The crown witness, James Lindley, then a convict in England, refused to take the oath or to give evidence on the grounds that he did not wish to incriminate himself. Eventually, after explanation by the judge, Lord Johnston, that a Crown witness who gave evidence could not be prosecuted, he took it – baselessly. But he refused to say who had stabbed Malcolmson although he claimed to have seen the stabbing. Other prisoners had given evidence for the Crown that he had ordered them, under threat, to name Cairns as the assassin. Eventually, examined by Lord Johnston with stupefacient guile, he said: 'I stabbed Malcolmson, sir.' This false claim was sufficient to disturb the jury's equanimity. They returned a majority verdict of 'not proven' in favour of Cairns. He was freed. Twenty days later Cairns went to the office of the *Scottish Daily Express* and said: 'I got away with murder. I killed Malcolmson.' In this instance the *Scottish Daily Express* acted with commendable responsibility. The Press generally have no motive to distinguish between good and bad. For them bad is usually better. They are neutrals in the moral world. They kill friends and foes alike, normally with arrows tipped with the drug of hypocrisy. Cairns was warned that what he said would be reported to the Crown office and Ian Brown, then news editor and afterwards editor, responsibly examined and re-examined his story in detail. The Crown proposed to try him again for perjury and perverting the course of justice. But cancer imposed the death penalty on the youthful Cairns before the Crown could achieve any lesser sentence.

I have often been asked how counsel can appear for a client whom they believe to be guilty. No case better illustrates the principle that counsel must act on his instructions – if they are reasonable – and not form judgements or hunches as to their truth or accuracy, than Her Majesty's Advocate against Devoy. In this case his counsel would have convicted him with confidence and without doubt and wrongly as it turned out. Kenneth Devoy was a quiet, modest man of thirty-four years who, on Saturdays, worked as a scribbler in the betting-shop of Andrew McLaren, a belluine, hot-tempered man of forty-seven who made a practice of ill-treating his wife, who was thirty-three. She left him and, at McLaren's request, Devoy arranged a holiday for her at a hotel in Largs, a town whose ghastly name belies its character. In August Devoy and Mrs McLaren not surprisingly commenced their concumbency, Devoy's wife having left him in 1964, after four years of marriage, for another man, Henry Masson, whom she apparently preferred.

Ad interim McLaren had made numerous and real threats on Devoy's life and Mrs McLaren decided to return to her husband and to tell him the brutal truth that they had been living together. McLaren asked Devoy pacifically to come round and see him and settle the matter on decent terms. Devoy went. There was a mighty fight. McLaren's body was found at 10 P.M. by Detective-Inspector Elphinstone Dalglish lying in the snow in the grounds of McLaren's bungalow. Beside it was an axe and under it a knife, both McLaren's property. He had eighteen axe wounds in his head and eight stab wounds in his back: with some other minor injuries thirty-two wounds in all. Devoy gave himself up to the police. He was charged with murder. He replied 'No'. His solicitor, John Reilly, lodged a plea of self-defence on his instructions. That much is beyond controversy.

His instructions to me were clear. He had taken Mr. McLaren to the house of Masson and his estranged wife, and then, as arranged by telephone, had gone to see McLaren at his bungalow. McLaren had run at him from the house with an axe in one hand and a knife in the other. Devoy managed to get the axe from him and struck McLaren four times until McLaren relaxed his virile grip. Then Devoy ran off. He made his troubled way to the house of his estranged wife, as previously arranged, to report to Mrs McLaren but she had gone. He stayed the night and gave himself up the next day. His account left many questions and twenty-eight wounds unaccounted for, inflicted by an unknown hand. I did not believe his account: I took the view, and I believed the jury would too, that he was merely unwilling to admit losing his self-control and making a reckless and frenzied attack which went far beyond the act of self-defence. He would not be moved from his account. Despite advice that if the jury took the view he was lying they might convict him of murder rather than culpable homicide he stuck to his story. On those instructions I conducted his unlikely defence.

In the course of the trial many witnesses spoke of McLaren's frequent and determined threats and plans to kill Devoy. They testified that he ran out into the street with a revolver or went hunting for Devoy with a kukri or tried to run him down with a car. All the witnesses opined that McLaren was in earnest. Dr Walter Pollock Weir, the eminent pathologist, who divides his time between the slab and the green, gave evidence that all but four of the axe injuries were light as if inflicted by a man in a state of frenzied fear, or by someone of lesser strength, such as a woman. The judge, haughtily sceptical of what proved to be a most percipient observation, asked Dr Weir on what grounds he based so unlikely an assessment and if he had ever conducted a post mortem before. Dr Weir modestly admitted that he had done several hundred post mortems a year for over twenty years or more. The judge accepted his opinion, which was in fact superlatively discerning, and the reader should note it. In evidence, Devoy said he had no recollection of inflicting any but the four wounds and that he had never struck McLaren on the ground. I confidently and hopefully expected a verdict of culpable homicide at best but after sixty-five minutes the jury returned a verdict of 'not guilty' and he was discharged from the dock by Lord Johnston, amazed but thankful. Typically, he paid tribute to Mrs McLaren in the Press. 'I feel she has gone through a lot because of me. She risked everything and came to see me in prison. I can only thank her for that.' She did indeed visit him every day until the special defence was lodged and then never again. In contrast, she said in the press: 'I can never forgive him for what he has done. He made a terrible mess of all our lives.'

In those days the minions of the media entertained acquitted men and wrote their story after much champagne and a slap-up meal. At the expense of the *Scottish Daily Express* in a hotel – hauntingly in Largs – Devoy revealed to them the whole truth. Alas I cannot reveal it to the reader except to say that his instructions to me were the truth, so far as they went, if not the whole truth. He had only struck four blows. I had misjudged him. Another had delivered the rest. No case ever better illustrated the supreme and just rule that a counsel must act on his instructions whatever his judgement of the truth may be.

In the next and third murder trial, a pub brawl, John Logan Kennedy was charged, 'along with Alexander Massey, with the murder, on Christmas Day, of Thomas Henry Spence, by stabbing. It is a strange and frightening fact that Christmas Day and New Year's Day, which are intended to be moments of goodwill and renewal, attract a very high rate of murders and stabbings in Glasgow, owing no doubt to the fact that excess celebrations and libation take the brake off the fiery hibernian tempers of those concerned. Massey was convicted of murder by a majority. Kennedy was found not guilty by a majority as well. I had achieved my second hat-trick, and on this occasion I received a whole bottle of whisky, not from the Glasgow police, but from the generosity of my instructing lawyer in the third case, Mr Len Murray, with whom I was to have a much more important association in the final release of Patrick Meehan. Despite the formidable genius of Ewan Stewart, the defence had triumphed again. What the police had failed to understand was that no counsel for the prosecution or for the defence can win unless he has a good and honest case to plead or is faced with a false and bad one.

CHAPTER 9

The 1966 General Election was now upon us. Immediately the election was announced, I received a verse of Oliver Wendell Holmes in Lilian Crichton's dying hand:

> God give us men. A time like this demands
> Clear minds, pure hearts, true faith and ready hands;
> Men who possess opinion and a will;
> Men whose desire for office does not kill;
> Men who have honour; men who will not lie;
> Tall men, sun-crowned, who live above the fog
> In public duty and in private thinking.

No ideal could have been more forsaken by the parvanimity of the Labour Party who indulged in a campaign of personal abuse and tail-nipping. Once more John Calder, the diminutive and controversial publisher, and my friend, though at that time a socialist, came to my defence. He has since adopted the multiple schizophrenia of the Liberal Party. This was what he said of my opponent:

Any man who goes in for personal smear campaigns against a political opponent, making charges that he knows are not true but which he believes may arouse emotional prejudices in his hearers, is not only lowering the whole British tradition of fair play in politics, but is assuming his audience is stupid. Such a man is Mr Oswald who has chosen to attack Mr Fairbairn because of his professional defence to myself in a minor court case, and because he is one of three thousand Edinburgh citizens who belong to the Traverse Theatre Club. The Traverse is internationally famous as a theatre which discovers new playwrights, often Scottish, and starts them on their careers. It has been visited and enjoyed by all classes of people, including members of the Royal Family. Mr Oswald is not, in any case, qualified to attack the Traverse Theatre as he has never been there. In appealing to his constituents' prejudices, as he imagines them to be, and not to their reason, and in assuming he can blacken his opponent for having a greater culture than his own, and thus attract votes, he is showing his basic contempt for politics. I believe that most Edinburgh citizens are fair-minded and reasonable people with a respect for honesty and principle, qualities which Mr Fairbairn has in abundance, and that they would be well served in Parliament by him if they elected him. I make this statement in spite of the fact that I myself am a member of the Labour Party, and shall be voting Labour in another constituency.

It was a most loyal riposte to the general perfidy and hypocrisy of socialism.

My chief ally and help in the campaign was Victor Symes, a trade union branch secretary, whose life was tragically cut short not long afterwards by cancer. There is an absurd fallacy that wage-earners have a duty to vote Labour and that they obtain benefit by doing so. No myth has ever so overwhelmingly smothered the truth. Victor, in common with many million other trade unionists, recognized the fallacy of this traditional and base assumption while not for one moment contesting the benefit of trade unions themselves, with which I wholly agree when they are true to their purpose. For do they not set out to obtain the very objects of conservatives: the familial safety of their members and advancement and enrichment of their children? Victor recognized that I understood this basic thought and believed that I could vibrate it. He insisted that we fight for a positive Member of Parliament, working for the interest of the working man, for in fifteen years my ex-tram-driving opponent had never spoken in the House of Commons at all. Alas, the promise of action over silence was not enough to disturb blind party loyalties and the silent, kindly member was returned again. My defeat was made the more poignant by the death soon afterwards from cancer of Lilian Crichton, who had put her faith in me with the same vigour that she put her heart and work into the Conservative Party and who had lovingly set me on the course of a life in politics in the first place. She penned me one last message in her failing moribund hand: '*Durate et vosmet rebus servate secundis*'. I determined to be worthy of her trust. Victor's death came soon after. He was the epitome of a great working man – blunt, sharp, proud, industrious and generous – the source of the nation's wealth.

For some time the Traverse Theatre in the Lawnmarket which promoted contemporary theatre in Edinburgh had been in a state of eternal war between Jim Haines, the gifted entrepreneur who conceived it, and the committee under Andrew Elliott who, with some colleagues, paid for and ran it. Jim Haines's capacity for spending other people's money was equal to his capacity for creation. Neither knew bounds or wanted to. He didn't believe in bounds – not bounds on him that is. Like all socialists and egoists – for socialists are egoists and, despite their protestations of community interest, are really only interested in their own – he took the view that money should be free and superabundant like air. He therefore believed and practised the belief that he had a right to absorb it or disburse it as he chose. My name had been suggested as a possible chairman who could be acceptable to both sides and thus resolve the conflict. I agreed very reluctantly on conditions which the *Scotsman* fortunately published; namely that I got complete co-operation from all concerned and that Jim Haines was prepared to fulfil whatever conditions the new committee of the Traverse and the committee of the Arts Council might impose. At the tormented annual meeting, the whole previous committee resigned and I was elected chairman *in absentia*. I was in fact in London, *inter alia* arresting an escaped prisoner in Montpelier Mews. I had a very kind letter of acknowledgement of my minor contribution to this act from the Assistant Commissioner of Police, Mr P.E. Brodie, who is one of the best and least acknowledged Scots the English ever had in the Metropolitan force:

17th June 1966

Dear Mr Fairbairn,

My attention has been drawn to the arrest and subsequent conviction for a large number of serious offences of an escaped prisoner. I see from the police report that the arrest of this man was achieved largely as the result of your prompt and public-spirited action when, with another citizen, you assisted the officers in restraining and controlling the prisoner until the arrival of a police vehicle. I was very pleased to read that you were commended by the Magistrate at the Lower Court and also by the chairman of the Sessions. There is a strong possibility that, but for your timely intervention, the prisoner might have escaped and the police officer would have been seriously injured, and I would like to thank you for your very valuable help and to tell you that it is warmly appreciated by the Police.

Such gratitude and appeciation is warming, though I felt in my case unmerited. What is more urgent than to do one's duty when a good man

143

– and our police are such good men – needs help at the hands of a desperate assailant in a mood of infernal wrath? He was, as it turned out, armed with a loaded gun and two knives, and was high on pills. There is a view constantly urged upon us that the police are not on the same side as the public. If they can be successfully branded as 'pigs' and made to appear as the brutal centurions of the state and oppressors of the people the way will be clear for the type of 'people's' tyranny their detractors fervently favour. The British police are citizens in uniform and we are all policemen in mufti; that is the best guarantee of our free society.

The new committee of the Traverse set urgently about its task, for the theatre was in a critical state of debt. It was not long before Jim Haines predictably decided that nothing would bind him, and certainly whatever else might, not his word. He refused to believe that financial discipline or self-discipline were the necessary ingredients of life in society, and certainly not in the sort of society he presaged, in which he was the most important beneficiary, if also the most generous user, of funds collected by others. After a course of contrived plots and counterplots and appeals for friendship and attempts to set one part of the committee against another, all of which fell well within his amorphous ethic, he offered to resign. We lost his genius and saved his theatre, whose existence stands witness yet to him and his imagination. It was one of the most painful decisions that I have ever had to take. He never believed for a moment that the treacherous acceptance of the resignation of so exceptional a person fell within our ethic. But it did. Our loyalty to contemporary theatre and this theatre which was his creation, and to one another, far outstripped and outweighed our loyalty to his selfishness. To his uncomprehending dismay, we accepted his resignation with genuine regret, reluctance and thus remorse.

My pain was eased by the birth of our daughter, Anna Karina, on 13 May 1966. Charles Warr christened this delicate and beautiful child in the chapel in July, surrounded by the wonder of the summer's best roses. From the moment of her birth she was distinguished by two enormous blue eyes.

July also saw the next instalment of the war between 'Whispering Smith' and the Herrity family. This time Smith was charged with assaulting John Herrity to his severe injury with a knife, and firing a gun at John Herrity to his severe injury, and also firing a gun at James Herrity and cutting him with a knife. The Herritys again admitted that they had been out on a mission of vengeance on Smith. He was acquitted thereby once more, and proved his capacity as a warrior and funambulist at last. So far as I know, that is the last instalment in the war of attrition. After all, there weren't many Herritys left to carry it on, and they always seemed to lose anyway, so they were wise to sue for peace. If they had had the advantage of reading Pliny's account of Hannibal's invasion of Italy over the Alps, they might never have embarked on their original adventure.

July saw the termination too of another legal relationship; Walter Scott Ellis, now thirty-four, was charged with armed bank robbery on a massive and frightening scale. He was bravely arrested by the police. So far as I know, he did not instruct me to defend him, or if he did I was unable to do so. After a very long trial, he was convicted with three others unanimously, and Lord Hunter jailed him for twenty-one years, the longest sentence imposed at that time in Scotland. Despite his many acquittals, he had already succeeded in accumulating nineteen previous convictions.

Lord Hunter was one of several giants at the head of the Bar at the time of my calling. As a silk, his effective oppugnancy in court was as renowned as his belluine bombast and raucous ribaldry were outside. No prophet would have anticipated the judicial supremacy and the impeccable judgement which have distinguished his career on the Bench, of a counsel so given to blunt bias and mocking partiality before he got there. He is a supreme arbiter, with a huge frame and a distinguishing caruncle above his ample nose, like a bell-push for his formidable brain, huge in dimensions as in character. Passing sentence on the maniacal quartet before him, he gave proof of his sagacity:

The evidence led in the present case, coupled with previous records of the accused, demonstrates, in my opinion, that while these men are at large, the safety and perhaps the lives of innocent members of the public are at risk. I trust what I have said will be carefully noted by any person or authority who might in future undertake the responsibility of considering a premature release of any of these accused men, and I trust that if the question of premature release should ever come up, the responsibility of making that decision will be exercised with extreme caution and with due regard to the safety of innocent members of the public.

Nothing is easier or regrettably more common than to accord martyrdom to convicts in jail. The sadistic sinner is too often accorded the veil of the presented saint. Those who bayed for the release of 'Poor old Hess' were paradoxically the same who demand the return of the death penalty for domestic murderers. Psychopaths, rendered impotent and neutral in confinement easily attract sentimental sympathy. The chances of their release should be as remote as the likelihood of their repentance.

The case had been masterminded by Detective-Superintendent Elphinstone Dalglish, a cunning and friendly officer with a knob head, and Lord Hunter paid fulsome tribute to the bravery of him and the other detectives who arrested Ellis in the lonely cottage at Newton Mearns. He congratulated Mr John McCluskey, the Advocate-depute, who had conducted the Crown case so brilliantly and methodically on achieving a just result.

Although Ellis had deserted me for other advisers, Arthur Thompson had not. He was charged with killing Patrick Welsh and another by deliberately forcing Welsh's car off the road with his Jaguar and into a lamp-post. Two policemen, brothers, one a detective and one a uniformed constable, claimed to have seen the event personally and described it as an act of deliberate murder but they could not explain why, if they had witnessed this crime, they did not stop and arrest the accused and render such services as they might to the victims. They gave the rather limp excuse that they had their wives to take home first. One of them would surely have been enough to do that. I did not believe that they had seen what they claimed to have seen and neither did the jury for they unanimously found Arthur Thompson not guilty. On the principle that each man in his time plays many parts Thompson appeared that afternoon as a witness in the North Court in the trial of Patrick Welsh's brother who was charged with murdering Thompson's mother and trying to murder Thompson by blowing up his car in revenge. He was acquitted for lack of evidence. One all.

For the first time but not the last I made the professional acquaintance of John Ramsay, better known as Ramenski, a Pole by origin and a man of great charm and considerable age for a thief. He was charged with breaking into and stealing from the National Commercial Bank in Rutherglen. He was affectionately known to the police as 'Gentle Johnny', for he never indulged in violence. He had a distinguished record of meritorious service in the war for cracking German safes behind enemy lines, having been let off jail to join the commando unit set up by Major-General Laycock. He was a compulsive criminal even until death – which is rare – breaking out of anything he was inside and into anything he was outside. He escaped five times from Peterhead and often from Barlinnie. He wanted at his age to make a final coup and retire from crime. The Royal Bank of Scotland at Rutherglen was therefore his chosen victim. The bank contained two safes, one of which was empty, the other of which contained £84,000. Ramenski, cat-like and agile, although over sixty, entered the bank by a sky-light and proceeded to open a cashier's drawer. He removed the petty cash and left only a key in the drawer which he insouciantly overlooked. He then wired the safe with high explosives, retired to the roof and fired a charge. He used enough explosives to blow up Rutherglen itself and two diligent young constables making their morning patrol were knocked down flat by the blast half a mile away. They made haste to the bank and found Johnny Ramenski climbing out, smoke-charred and empty-handed. He had blown the empty safe. The key he left in the cashier's drawer was the key to the full safe accidentally left behind by an imprudent teller. Poor Johnny: another four years to add to the forty-five of his sixty-two he had already served! He was as amateur at crime as he was professional at escape.

Now a new experience entered my life: serious broadcasting on television. Although I had frequently appeared on the box I had not previously been recruited to undertake a series. I did a pilot broadcast of the series 'Your Witness' on television which was chaired by Ludovic Kennedy and my advisers were the barbigerous Matthew Spicer and the seductive and goluptious Esther Rantzen, whose hypersensual voice has been such a balm and stimulant to television audiences. All three have been friends ever since. Returning to Edinburgh from the programme, I played the part, at the Traverse Theatre, of John Profumo in a dramatic production of the Denning Report, directed by Gordon MacDougall, who had quietly succeeded Jim Haines as the theatre director. His gentle and unruffable character had enabled the traumas of Haines's departure to be passed over and the wounds to heal. I inserted into the script the apt words from the *Rape of Lucrece*:

> Why should the private pleasure of someone
> Become the public plague of many more?
> For one's offence why should so many fall
> To plague a private sin in general?

Those who mightily condemn the slightest carnal venery of those who undertake the responsibility and deprivations and strain of public political life, whatever its possible rewards, would be the first to indulge in such venery themselves given the chance and the last to accept the traumatic disruption of family life which such service entails. Is it not ironic that in the allegedly prim, controlled and 'moral' age of Victorian

147

rectitude, when there was a morbid preoccupation with the sense of shame, the heir to the throne and the revered and martial Prime Minister, the Duke of Wellington, could sleep with whomsoever and how many ever they wished almost with public acclaim and certainly with public amusement? Yet in our immoral and unprincipled age, the concumbency of a parliamentary or a royal figure is regarded as a fatal flaw and an unforgivable sin. Charlemagne, though not encouraging his daughters to marry, expected them to have affairs with his officers and officials. During the red years of the French Revolution, Bonnard the apostle was in love which greatly mitigated his bloodlust and cruelty. Private passion is a good antidote to public frenzy.

On 25 May I was invited by Joe Beltrami to go with him to Lisbon to see the final of the European Cup between Celtic and Inter-Milan. Although no devotee of football, I enjoy any game played at its best and I was, in any event, a devotee of Joe. So I went, and we watched a wonderful game in the sun in the beautiful National Stadium near Lisbon, like an amphitheatre near the sea. While I was there I placed a bet – which I rarely do – with one of the party who was a bookmaker as to what the result would be: I got it right. I won my bet and it paid for my trip. In the evening we went with the team to a night-club. It was interesting to see Jimmy Johnstone, whose tortuplicated and cursitating genius on the field was so remarkable, reading a comic, oblivious to the blandishments of the donnas of Lisbon. Unfortunately, despite the fact that this magnificent achievement of winning the European Cup by a British club was the work and achievement of that rugged, brawny tough, blunt and worthy manager, Jock Stein, he received no honour in recognition of his sevices to football, whereas a knighthood was immediately forthcoming for Alf Ramsay when England won the World Cup. That is the sort of slight which creates resentment in the Scottish mind and breeds nationalist sentiments with the speed of dry rot.

Spying does not play a very large part in the life of Scotland, so far anyway. It would if we became, which God forbid, an independent, oil-fired, tartan ruritanian tax-haven. I next appeared for one Peter Dorschel, a German, who was charged that 'he tried to solicit and induce and endeavour to persuade another person to commit an offence under the Official Secrets Act 1911 for a purpose prejudicial to the safety and interest of the State'. He did indeed obtain certain documents which were an engineer's plans of the lay-out of the lavatory in a Polaris submarine. I hope the Russians found them useful. Would that that was all the plans they ever got. Lord Grant rightly and brusquely imprisoned him for seven years.

James Boyle now came up for trial on his third murder charge. I had defended him for murder twice in seven months in 1956. Now I defended his co-accused, William Wilson. I was instructed by James Latta, an immund Glasgow solicitor of strange associations, as we shall see. There were three charges of assault of a minor degree and a major charge which ran as follows: 'You, James Boyle and William Wilson did, on the 14th or 15th July 1967 in the house occupied by William Rooney at 35 Cornwall Street, Glasgow, assault said William Rooney and strike him on the face, neck and body with knives and did you murder him.' It is not uncommon in the underworld for members of it to be money-lenders, and it is ordained by them to be an unforgivable offence to fall down on the payment of the exorbitant interest demanded. Rooney was one such lazzarone, having borrowed money unwisely from Boyle. He had committed the capital offence of failing to repay on time, a crime for which in their world there is no mitigation or relief. About midnight, Boyle, with Wilson in his company, called on Rooney. The door was opened by Rooney's girl-friend, Margaret. 'Is Willie in?' Boyle enquired, 'Willie, it's Jimmy,' she said, unaware of the fatality of her command. Rooney, naked to the waist, ready for bed and slightly inebriated, came to the door. Boyle immediately plunged a knife into his abdomen causing an unfatal wound. Margaret instantly became hysterical. 'Hoo could you dae that tae Willie, Jimmy; hoo could you dae that in front o' me?' Margaret screamed in her grief and excitement and fear. 'Ah'll show yi hoo I could dae it,' Boyle riposted coolly. With deliberate and innate viciousness, he went over to the prostrate but vital body of Rooney, and in front of the hysterical Margaret nonchalanty cut the throat of her wounded lover, for which he was convicted.

Boyle became the problem prisoner, so uncomfortable to contain by human prison officers that the special unit was set up at Barlinnie where he was allowed to sculpt and write. He became the hero of, amongst others, Richard Demarco, the director of the Richard Demarco Gallery, and himself. He wrote a book, *A Sense of Freedom*, which justifies himself or rather seeks to justify himself as a victim of society but shows no such sympathy for the victims of Boyle. He is portayed as the wrong guy gone good and constantly claims that he was wrongly convicted on many occasions. He married Miss Trevelyan in prison – he was allowed out to the Edinburgh Festival and she was allowed in for a conjugal festival. Thus he obtained a heroism for his misdeeds which brave and good men rarely obtain for valour. Such is the inverted guilt and squinted value of today's intelligentisa. Immediately following this incident, Boyle departed for London where he was bravely arrested by

Detective-Superintendent Elphistone Dalglish and Detective-Superintendent Stewart Fraser sixty-seven days later. Wilson was rightly acquitted of any complicity in this frightful deed, and Lord Cameron sentenced Boyle, at last, to life imprisonment, recommending that he should serve not less than fifteen years in prison. Suffice it to say that eight witnesses had to receive police protection after the trial for their honesty and pluck in giving the evidence that convicted him. He was sent to what is affectionately termed the 'Nutcracker Suite' at Barlinnie where hopefuls imagine they can cure frightfuls. I view their claims with extreme reserve.

In Scotland there is a sacred, wise and salutary protection which is the equivalent of, but preferable to, the habeas corpus rule in England, whereby no person may be detained in custody after his full committal for more than 110 days, by which time his trial must be concluded. Her Majesty's advocate indicted Greenshields with the attempted murder of a policeman. Greenshields was granted bail, but took some forty days to find it. He failed to appear at his pleading diet and was rearrested. Eventually his trial came up at the Glasgow circuit before Lord Milligan, but it was apparent to his advisers, Mr Beltrami and myself, that he had been detained in custody in excess of 100 days. We breathed not a word except, unwisely, to the client who was so delighted that he told the turnkey who told the other police who told the Crown. So our surprise was not as great as we had hoped, but our plea was unanswerable, Greenshields was released by Lord Milligan – renowned for running as fast as a boy, drinking Guinness as fast as a man and cracking jokes at both ages – 'from all further pain or penalties of law', which is mandatorily prescribed by the law of Scotland if a man is detained for more than 110 days for whatever purpose after his full committal. The case went unreported, as did several other momentous cases that week, on account of the fact that the Press were on strike.

That week there was also a very interesting case which was to be sent to five judges for judgment. A man had been found in possession of a forged five-pound note of a Scottish bank, and the question arose as to whether any offence had been committed. Lord Fraser, with his brilliant, nimble lawyer's mind and retiring nature, remitted the matter to a higher court. They found that for the purpose of criminal offences, at any rate, Scottish notes were legal tender. 'That sounds like nonsense, my dear,' wrote Scott in *Guy Mannering*. 'May be so, my dear, but it may be very good law for all that.' I argued in the Appeal Court that it was clear the Act did not have in mind Scottish banknotes since subsequently the offence of forging Scottish banknotes was created by the Burgh Police (Scotland) Act 1892, an offence punishable by a fine of £5.00. The argument was rejected. But it is worth recording how the Burgh Police (Scotland) Act came to be compiled. A request was sent to every burgh clerk in Scotland to make a list of the misdemeanours which were causing nuisance in their town and to qualify their invitation by allotting to them a fine of £10, £5, £2, £1, 10s, 5s, or 2s 6d. In Oban, forged notes were a nuisance, hence the crime.

I exhibited a painting in the Royal Scottish Academy for the first time. It is not easy for so-called amateurs like myself to persuade so-called professionals, like them, to exhibit our feeble work. Indeed, I have come to the conclusion that the difference between an amateur and a professional painter is this: a professional is a painter who has been trained to paint but who cannot sell his pictures, and frequently cannot paint either, so he teaches instead; and an amateur is one who has not been trained, but who can sell his pictures, although he frequently can't paint either.

One of the quirks of the public attitude to law and order is that we tend to admire a really good professional thief. Such was Hugh Kelly Mannion, a gentleman safe-breaker, who stood trial in Edinburgh High Court in November 1967, along with John Fee and John Anthony Lyon, for whom I was instructed to appear. They were charged with breaking into Clydesdale Bank in Princes Street, and stealing a large sum of money and valuables therefrom. It was a perfect setting for the crime and was not lost on Mannion's cunning eye. The New Club, a building of much distinction by William Burn, had been demolished to the eternal shame of the members who organized its destruction; and the hole where it had been was full of McAlpine's scaffolding and cranes, ready to erect the brash, farraginous monstrosity which now stands in its place. Pneumatic drills played their merry tune all day and all night. Next to this noisy hole was the bank on the ground floor and basement, which was the prey of the thieves. Above it were empty premises advertising prospective vacancy by a notice that they were sold. You do not have to be a professional thief to see the chance that that opportunity presented, but if you are one, you take it. The team entered the empty premises at the rear after closing time on Friday, and they obtained access to the premises of the bank through the floor, or ceiling, as one looks at it. They had all weekend, or so they thought, and took their time. Alas! for some of them. There were two safes, and they successfully drilled and blew the first, despite a vast notice on the door which gave a warning, 'This safe is fitted with a time lock and anti-explosive device'. They removed its contents, which amounted to some hundred thousand pounds' worth of junk, such as rose-bowls and hideous clocks which were regarded by their owners as valuables and worthy of incarceration in the vault. They then set about the second safe which contained money. This they drilled with equal skill. Indeed, the evidence of the safe mechanic at the trial was that the drilling was done so precisely that the only point which would not have set off the alarm, and which rendered the anti-explosive device neutral, was struck with meticulous precision. Someone clearly knew his job.

At this point the professionals' luck turned on a poignant event of saturnine banality; the manager of the bank had been asked by a friend at his golf club if he could possibly provide him with an income tax form. Whoever asked a strange bank manager for an income tax form at a golf club on a Sunday? It could only happen in Edinburgh, and happen it did. This meticulous curmudgeon duly and dutifully set off to the bank on Sunday morning after church to do his second good deed of the holy day. Opening the front door with his key, he found the light on in the bank. To his surprise, he saw what he divined was a transistor radio sitting on the top step of the stair to the vault. It was in fact the thieves' hastily abandoned walkie-talkie to the look-out on the roof. Concentrating the full powers of his intuitive and detective mind, he came to the reassuring conclusion that the cleaner must be in the vaults (what bank has a cleaner in the vaults on Sunday?) He called to her and got no reply and, once again applying his singular powers of reasoning, he decided that she probably could not hear him on account of her radio (which, as we already know, he thought was silent at the top of the stair), so he went into his office and got his form, and decided to spend some time, as good deed three, tidying up odds and ends to ensure that his desk had that traditional workless look so beloved of bank managers on Monday morning. While he performed these menial tasks with immaculate and sinless application, eight exasperated thieves, fleet of foot and laden with a few golden sovereigns and little else, were seen by two men working on the New Club site to skelter from the rear of the premises like rice crispies and hurtle along Rose Street. Emerging from his room the manager called to the cleaner once more to indulge his Samaritan concern for her welfare, and thinking that she might be ill (she would have had to be ill to be cleaning a bank in Edinburgh on Sunday morning), he descended to the vault, where to his glump amazement he found the discommodious scene in his very own beloved bank on Sunday. With electronic wit, he decided that it would be right to telephone the police, though not before he had checked the rear of the premises. Who knows how much better a place the world would be if the expertise of the thieves had been drafted into banking and the craft of robbers was restricted to the naïvieties of the bank manager?

Two of the men who emerged from the rear of the bank were identified in court by the men working on the New Club cavity as Mannion and Lyon. But Lyon had a special defence of alibi. He said that on Sunday at twelve o'clock he was on Glasgow Green with his children, one of whom had pointed a gun at a dog which belonged to a man who spoke with a foreign voice. As a result of this canine hold-up, he and his father had got into conversation with the owner, and asked, in view of his voice, if he was a visitor, but he said he had in fact lived in Glasgow for twenty-five years near Monteith Row, once the dwelling-place of the great and now more often the haunt of all manner of clunches and trulls and cockchafers and organ-grinders in general. Lyon, after being apprehended and charged, had been released on bail and had spent his time looking for this man. He found him. He was Monsieur Eugene Desire Maran, aged 62. He remembered the incident clearly. He identified the boys in court and their father. He remembered it was a Sunday morning, but the crucial question was *which* Sunday morning. Anyone can describe an incident and transfer it to a date to suit an alibi. That is the Crown's constant line of assault on alibi and it usually succeeds. His English being poor despite twenty-five years in Glasgow, or perhaps because of it, an interpreter was called from the University. Monsieur Maran pin-pointed the date as being the Sunday between the name-day of his daughter and Easter Day. The interpreter misinterpreted his answer. 'That is not what he said,' I objected. 'Well,' said the interpreter, 'it's not my fault. His French is even worse than his English.'

However bad either may have appeared to the interpreter, his tongue was silver to the jury and to Lyon, for his alibi was upheld. It is the only occasion I have ever known an alibi to succeed. Manion and Fee were convicted. *Nisi Dominus frustra* – the proud motto of Edinburgh – took on new meaning: unless the manager guards the bank on Sunday, they labour in vain that make thief-resistant safes.

For a long time I had been increasingly distressed and alarmed by the terrible consequences of unintended pregnancies – in and out of marriage. In the divorce courts most cases I dealt with started with a pregnant bride, which could not wholly be explained by the old Scottish practice of being allowed to ensure that a bride was fecund before you marry her. 'He ploughed her and she cropped.' In the criminal courts most of my clients were from large families, where the mother's emotional reserves and the father's material resources were insufficient to provide for all the children whom she had inconsequentially conceived. I was also impressed by the fact that if everybody had only the number of children they wanted, or intended to conceive, there would be no world population crisis at all. We could all have as many as we wanted, if we all wanted as many as we have. My work on the Board of World Population Crisis had brought me in contact with Mrs June Bedford and Mrs Jackson, wife of Professor Jackson, among others, and they were interested in setting up a birth control clinic in Edinburgh. I was asked to give them some legal advice and found myself, as a result, elected chairman of the committee to set up such a clinic. We quickly found a house in Lower Gilmore Place in Edinburgh, which was quiet, discreet and central, and we converted the premises to the needs of the clinic. The clinic opened, unannounced, in the middle of what was called 'The Pot and Pill Row' and it was not long before the storm, which started in the University, enveloped us. Anna Coote, editor of *The Student*, Edinburgh University's undergraduate magazine, had written an article attacking Malcolm Muggeridge's pronouncement on the pill. He resigned from the post of Lord Rector of the University in petulant protest. I could hear him think aloud about the beautiful Anna Coote, John Dryden's words:

> The holy priests gaze on her when she smiles
> And with heaved hands, forgetting gravity
> They bless her wanton eyes; even I, who hate her,
> With a malignant joy, behold such beauty
> And while I curse, admire it.

So the Press brought our clinic to light and Malcolm Muggeridge was not long in condemning it. 'I deplore this whole thing. To me it is extremely distasteful and extremely ominous.' Ominous indeed, and for many, a good omen. Typical of the story which justified its foundations in this one printed in the *Daily Record* on 31 January 1968 in an article by Margaret Hignet:

I always knew I should have been on the pill before I married. I never had the guts to go to my family doctor and confess that I was sleeping with my boyfriend. Then I got pregnant. We had to marry, and eighteen months later he walked out. Now I have to work to keep myself and the baby. I can't count the number of times I wish I had been brave enough to go to my doctor before I got pregnant and had to marry.

Wise solicitors do not keep the company of their criminal clients except in cells and docks. James Latta, my instructing solicitor in the recent case of Wilson and Boyle, never learned that imperant lesson. Latta was charged, along with Wilson's brother, 'Tarzan', and a man, John 'Bandit' Rooney, with attempting to pervert the course of justice by concocting a false defence of alibi for Boyle, who was not even his client. I was called to give evidence as a witness to my instructions, for I had had no instructions on Wilson's behalf for a defence of alibi.

The false defence was to be that two other men had run down the stair in slouch hats and raincoats – reminiscent of Al Capone – and that Wilson and Boyle had come upon the scene of the crime committed by these villains. These events were observed and detected by Detective-Inspector Beattie, whose legendary capacity for pluripresence and skill at disguising himself as anything from a mouse to a maiden earned him the title of 'the Flea'. It was sad to see a professional man in the dock who only a few weeks before had been sitting beside me as an instructing solicitor. The rail of the dock is a thin line but a big jump. All three were convicted and received long and appropriate sentences from Lord Grant. The purity of the legal profession is essential.

For some two years, old folk and women in general had been frightened to go out of their homes in Glasgow on account of a spate of horrific murders and terrible rapes in the areas of Cardonald, Craigton and Govan. Eventually, Samuel Gilbert McCloy was arrested and charged with attempting to ravish a woman at knife-point on 20 August 1966 in Craigton Road, Glasgow; secondly with attempting to ravish a woman in Levernside Road, on 18 September 1967; thirdly, with ravishing and murdering Mrs McAllister on 20 October 1967 in Craigton Road, Glasgow; fourthly, with murdering James Wright Brown, aged eighty-one, at 10 Montrave Park, Glasgow; fifthly, with raping and murdering his seventy-five-year-old wife. On his apprehension, McCloy confessed in elaborate detail to all of these satanic crimes, some of which he had not, at that time, even been charged with. McCloy was a shy, painfully awkward, unforthcoming, bed-wetting youth with a freckled face and spectacles. One of the officers who arrested this venomed worm could not believe that out of so timid a stripling could come the rage and hate which had been manifested by his murderous carnivoracities. He thought they were looking for a mad wild beast. The worst beasts are men, as he should have known with his vast experience of the abominable sadisms which the clustifists of Glasgow inflict on their hapless victims. But perhaps he believed, like Lord Monboddo, the glaikit Scots Judge, that orang-utans are a class of the human species. I was instructed to enter the rare plea that he was insane at the time of committing these atrocities. The homicidal assaults with which he was charged showed a brutality and viciousness of unthinkable fedity which the court photographs displayed. The Crown were determined to have him convicted of murder as a matter of public policy, for they felt perhaps rightly that to accept a plea of guilty, but insane at the time, would be tantamount to a public pardon, and the public would be too angry to accept, or concur, in the view that he couldn't help it. So the battle was over McCloy's sanity.

The principal evidence for the Crown was given by Dr Hunter Gillies. Dr Hunter Gillies is a distinguished psychiatrist – his hard eyes gaze out from behind his rimless, clinical glasses and from beneath the enormous, bald, marmorate dome of his hairless head like iron bullets waiting to be fired. He has regularly given evidence for the Crown in the High Court over many years, and he always describes in detail and with precision the bowel movements of the patients in his report on their mental health. He was in no doubt of McCloy's sanity and of the rightness of his judgement. Psychiatrists rarely are. I had once asked him in a previous case if he was aware that one of his colleagues had changed their opinion, and invited him to reconsider his own. 'I do not change my opinion,' came the groutly reply. 'Does that mean,' I naively enquired, 'that you never make a mistake or that you never correct one?' A glance of frigid indifference was the only reply. In the circumstances, I elected to forgo the delight of repeating Dr Johnson's taunt to a vacillating Highlander: 'Answer me yea or nay, sir, if your barbarous language permit of so subtle a distinction.' 'In my opinion,' he said, 'McCloy is sane and fit to plead. I find no evidence to suggest that his responsibility for his actions is in any way diminished, and I am not aware of any evidence,' he went on, 'to suggest that he was other than *completely* sane at the time of the offences.' He added that investigations of his past disclosed 'no sign of mental disturbance' and that he had never complained about such a condition, nor had he consulted a doctor or a psychiatrist. He opined further that McCloy had abnormally strong sexual urges, but in cross-examination he said that McCloy was perfectly aware that it was something that he should control, and he controlled it when it was expedient and safer for him to do so.

'Apparently,' he said, 'he gets some twisted form of pleasure from inflicting violence on helpless people.' I showed him the photographs of the brutalities that McCloy had inflicted and asked him this question: 'If I came to you with these photographs and said "This is what I have done", would you say, "You are abnormal but I cannot do anything for you because you are not insane"? If I said I had a compulsion to waylay old women and bludgeon them to death, and masturbate over their bloody corpses, would you say I was not completely sane?' Dr Gillies replied, 'I would say you were seriously abnormal, but not of unsound mind.' 'So you would let me go out on the streets again, having taken no action?' 'I might advise you to go into a mental hospital,' he said, 'but I could not do anything because you would not be of unsound mind.' This testimony was supported somewhat timidly by Dr David Anderson, then Chief Medical Officer in Barlinnie Prison. For the defence, these two opinions were contradicted flatly and vehemently by Dr George Swinney, the shy genial superintendent of Woodilee Mental Hospital, a man of great charm and much culture, running an Arts Festival of his own. His evidence ran thus: McCloy had been insane at the time of the murders of Mr and Mrs Brand and Mrs McAllister. McCloy's abnormal sexual urges towards old women could build up to such an extent that McCloy would simply explode and at these times he would commit such offences. McCloy had also admitted to spying on female ablutions and fetishism and all these, in the opinion of Dr Swinney, were part of a grave mental disorder. He was supported by Dr Wolffgang Kiernan, then a Consultant Psychiatrist at Gartnavel Mental Hospital, a man of prodigious experience and a fascinating mind. Amongst the abnormalities of McCloy which he listed were kleptomania, bed-wetting, exhibitionism, fetishism, transvestism, fantasism and sadism. McCloy was only capable of indulging in sexual experience of a perverted kind with old women and in association with the infliction of pain upon his victim. He said that in his wide experience of abnormal patients he had never known anyone to have all the abnormalities and anomalies present in McCloy. He had no doubt that these were the product of mental illness rather than voluntary lack of control. Dr Kiernan replied to a question from the judge as to what remedial treatment might be given, 'The possibility of an improvement in the accused's condition is so slim as to be non-existent.' This was the man whom Dr Gillies described as completely sane. There was no dispute about the facts that McCloy did all these vile things. The only question was whether he was sane at the time of committing his feculent crimes. Lord Cameron, who presided with great interest and awe over this frightful tale, was less than enthusiastic about the defence plea, having been the last person, as senior counsel, to put it forward equally unsuccessfully himself. The jury took seventy-five minutes to decide what the Crown felt the members of the public would think: that the crimes were too monstrous to forgive or mitigate by the explanation of insanity. McCloy was found guilty of all the charges. Lord Cameron, with just gravity, sentenced this condign sadist to life imprisonment and recommend that he should not be released for fifteen years. Fifteen years! The irony is that if the Crown had accepted the defence plea, McCloy would have been sent to a state mental institution at Carstairs for ever.

The particular interest of the case is that this aggressive and sadistic conduct started only with the death of his mother, who died of cancer. During her terminal illness, he showed not the slightest interest in her, believing that his mother of all mothers was safe from death and that her athanasy was inevitable on account of his wish for it. When, however, she did die, he immediately began to manifest aggressive behaviour towards his sister with whom he lived, and to the victims of whom we know, but he was always polite to his girlfriend and made no sexual advances to her. The poor victims whom he killed were all old women, with the exception of poor Mr Brand who just happened to be in the way; the victims whom he let go after attacking them from behind were all younger women, and they were granted liberty and life when he discovered their tender age. The pattern was very clear: he was killing his mother for dying on him, and no doubt for a hundred other deprivations as well.

The very next case was of a totally different character, but it involved the question of sanity again. Murray Swann was charged that on 21 March 1968 he assaulted Ellen McGregor, with whom he lived, and that he pushed her through an open window, causing her to fall to the street below, whereby he killed her. Swann had lived for some time with this gravid trull at a flat in 4 Craigmore Street. Neither had a change of clothing, there was no source of heat and the only furnishing in the flat, which had five rooms, was an iron bedstead with a lumpy mattress and one blanket in the room where they slept, and a table and stove in the kitchen. Otherwise the flat was totally bare, as was the body of Ellen McGregor when it was found, face down, in Craigmore Street in fourteen degrees of frost. Swann was casually employed and they lived this simple life confricating in their unheated and unfurnished house on the lumpy mattress on the iron bedstead. Swann claimed that he woke up and saw Ellen standing on the window-sill, naked, and when he spoke to her and ran to try and pull her in, she jumped – or fell. The police did numerous experiments with a dummy and made the startling claim that it always landed face-side up, unless it was pushed out, when it always landed face-side down. Swann was convicted, not of murder but of culpable homicide on the strange ground that his responsibility was diminished. Dr Hunter Gillies gave evidence that in his opinion Swann's responsibility was diminished, in a report which presumably did not overlook his bowel movements. So McCloy, illiterate, shy, maniacal, was completely sane and fit to roam the streets, though almost abnormal. Swann, humble, active, rational and with no previous convictions was not; he was detained in a mental institution.

It was now time for James Boyle, having only served one year of his life sentence, to appear in the High Court for the second time since being imprisoned for life. This time it was in Aberdeen High Court. He was charged that he assaulted Alister Sim, a prison officer, and did punch and kick him. Secondly, that he assaulted Thomas McGorry, a prison officer, and kicked him and punched him with his fists, and thirdly that he assaulted John Watt Gordon, another prison officer, and jumped on his back and bit his neck. Following the incidents in charges one and two, James Boyle had had his boots removed and had been taken to a cell by a troop of officers, including those concerned, with batons drawn.

There seemed little doubt on the evidence that he was there 'given the treatment' as a reward for incidents one and two, since he ended up with several parallel linear lacerations of the skull, covered in blood. That at any rate is what he claimed had happened. The officers claimed that he jumped on Mr Gordon's back and so tight was his grip that they had to hit him with batons, aiming only for his arms, and that he fell off and split the top of his head on the wooden bed-board – some feat. Since all the blood was spattered on the wall in the corner where Boyle claimed he was given his 'treatment', and none was near the bed-board, it was obvious which version was the truth. The jury returned a fascinating verdict which illustrates the equity which juries bring to their decisions, and how essential it is that they are forever part of our system of justice. They found Boyle guilty of charge one under provocation – which was what started the whole trouble, a row between him and Mr Sim. Boyle had claimed that the officer hit him first and he hit him back; the jury believed him. They found him not guilty of charge two; in other words, they believed Boyle again, and they disbelieved the very same officers who were the participants in charge three and the witnesses in charges one and two. They found him guilty of charge three. Why did they believe Boyle and disbelieve the officers in charges one and two, but the reverse in charges three? I don't think, in fact, they did, but the jury knew that if they returned a verdict of not guilty on charge three, they would in effect be finding the officers guilty of criminal assault. Knowing the nature of Boyle, and his record and the terrible risks these brave men have to run each day, and understanding human nature and the urge for revenge which runs in the blood of most men, the jury gave the jailers a verdict of acquittal rather than Boyle a verdict of conviction. He got four more years which, presumably, he will serve post-mortally in eternity.

Next month took me to the relaxed and intimate dignity of the Sheriff Court in Fort William to appear for a man who was charged with contravention of section 7 of the Criminal Law Amendment Act, the libertines' highway code. No prosecution had been taken under Section 7, which makes it a criminal offence to remove a girl out of the care of her parents with the intention of having carnal knowledge of her until she is eighteen, though it is perfectly legitimate for a gallant to have had carnal knowledge of her for the two years before. The logic of this was lost on me but not on the honourable mind of Sheriff Douglas Campbell QC, the then proud Sheriff Principal of Inverness-shire, a part-time post since regrettably abolished by reason of administrative logic – the art of going wrong with confidence. He had a thin prim face, reddened by his penchant for port and forerun by a considerable nose which preferred to sense those activities which he believed fell within the four decent walls of the word 'gent'. He held himself, his narrow interests and his office in high regard and had the appearance of a genial rodent emerging purposefully from its nest. With the rodent's characteristics of confidence and fear he explained to the jury in unforgettable terms the origin of this section in a voice which had all the sweetness of sugar. 'Ladies and gentlemen of the jury, this section was passed as long ago as 1885 in the reign of our late lamented Sovereign Queen Victoria. It has never before been used and was enacted to put a stop to the White Slave trade.' Thus enlightened the jury acquitted and Sheriff Campbell worked on to be worthily awarded the CBE and died a rich man.

Francesca Katherine Nicola Fairbairn came into the world on 15 January 1969 to complete our trinity of little women. Each of our children was baptized, like Jesus Christ, with the water of the river of Jordan, brought back and distilled in 1890 by a chemist named Stitt and given to my father who forgot to use it for the baptism of any of his three offspring, so I used it at the christening of mine.

Defamation is something which the Scots are much less sensitive about than the English, believing that 'Sticks and stanes may brak yir banes, but words will never hard huirt ye.' Two elderly Glaswegian ladies, however, proved the exception to this sage tolerance. They lived in a house in Glasgow let out in single rooms: Mrs Stewart, eight-four years of age, lived on the ground floor, Miss Stevenson, sixty-six, my client and crippled, lived on the top floor. Each got their newspapers from different newsagents, Miss Stevenson buying the *Glasgow Herald* and the *Scottish Daily Express*, and Mrs Stewart only the *Glasgow Herald*. Mrs Stewart's paper was often late in delivery, or didn't come at all and on such occasions she nipped out and removed Miss Stevenson's *Glasgow Herald*, leaving behind her *Express*. This annoyed Miss Stevenson as she had to scale the stairs twice with her hirpling gait. She determined to put an end to it and accordingly asked the landlord to accompany her to Mrs Stewart's room so that he could witness what occurred. She asked Mrs Stewart (in front of him) to desist from removing her *Glasgow Herald* when hers didn't come. No such infandous infamy had previously been uttered to Mrs Stewart. Indeed Mrs Stewart claimed that the allegation so embarrassed and insulted her that she was unable to eat or sleep and had to lie in bed, nervous and ill for many weeks, such was the wound to her pride, and the righteousness of her indignation. Strangely, however, the professional adviser for whom she sent in this ailing state was not her doctor but her solicitor. There was nothing for it but to sue. This momentous litigation was conducted before Sheriff Irvine Smith, a gifted orator and reciter of the works of Robert Burns. Short, virile and gruff with black hair, black eyes, a dusky skin and Charlie Chaplin moustache, he has an acidulous tongue and a taste for shooting and good claret, which is as pronounced as his distaste for the criminals who appear before him whom he used to defend with such gusto at the Bar. One of Miss Stevenson's essential witnesses was one Miss Ella Marshall, aged sixty-seven, who wrote to explain that she could not attend the trial as she was engaged to be married to the gerontic Sir Harold Danckwerts, a Lord Justice of Appeal in England. She must have read her Bible: 'I have taken a husband who is a High Court judge and therefore I cannot come.'

Without demur and spurred on by his thoughts of the epicurean delights which London had to offer at the expense of these two senile litigants, the learned Sheriff therefore decided that we must all travel, at great expense, to the highways and byways of London to hear her evidence. The mountain was to be moved to Lady Mohammed. But before it did, her honeymoon over, the happy couple travelled to Scotland to see that justice was done: and how justice was done! The Sheriff, confounding the judgment of Solomon, divided the baby. He found in favour of Miss Stevenson that Mrs Stewart had been not defamed, but he made no award of expenses against this impecunious and disgruntled old blain. Who said, '*De minimus non curat lex*'? The expenses were the only big thing in the case. Pope summed it up:

> Once, says an author (where I need not say)
> Two travellers found an oyster in their way
> Both fierce, both hungry, the dispute grew strong,
> While, scale in hand, Dame Justice moved along.
> Before her, each with clamour pleads the laws,
> Explained the matter and would win the cause.
> Dame Justice, weighing long the doubtful right,
> Takes, opens, swallows it before their sight.
> The cause of strife removed so rarely well
> 'There, take,' says Justice, 'take each one a shell.
> We thrive at Westminster on fools like you.
> 'Twas a fat oyster. Live in peace. Adieu.'

In August 1969 I was invited to address the Forensic Science Society, and this I did. This was the first of a number of starching speeches which were prompted by my increasing dismay that impartiality had not been an invisible feature of judgment in various recent cases. The First Division Appeal Court was then universally recognized by all members of the legal profession who appeared before it to be blind in one eye and to look through a telescope to see the word 'guilty' and reverse it to see the word 'law'. In the course of my address to these learned medicals I said:

> If a football referee were to behave with the partiality that some judges sometimes do he would probably be lynched by the crowd or brought before a panel of arbiters and dismissed. There are judges both historical and living of whom one can make predictions of the sentence he will pass and of the attitude he will take. That may be the product of idiosyncrasy and a well reasoned attitude. It may be the exercise of a deliberate partiality, but it is mythical to pretend that the Appeal Court can protect us against the partiality of such judges. There are so many judges who exercise that beautiful impartiality which is the grace of the law that it is unnecessary for the law to accommodate those who don't, can't or won't.

For this 'general and exceptless rashness' I got many letters of gratitude from members of the profession. This one will do to illustrate: 'Before you are blown to smithereens by the wrath of the judges, may I congratualte you on your fighting speech last night. It has needed saying for a very long time, and you deserve much praise for having said it. They can stick your head on your castle tolbooth.' They very nearly did. In contemplation of my fate, I comforted myself with the balm of the words of Robert Louis Stevenson: 'For God's sake, give me your man who has brains enough to make a fool of himself.' But was I, like Joan of Arc, to achieve martyrdom by roasting? Not quite.

For some time the Traverse Theatre had been in difficulties over its old premises in the Lawnmarket. They were too small and were judged by delighted officials to be unsafe. The crucial question was: should we move, or should we try to repair the home in which we had been born. We had no money to do either, so faith eventually triumphed over caution as it always should in matters of culture. We rented an old warehouse in the Grassmarket which had the benefits of prospective enlargement. We laboured night and day to transform it and create a theatre and a club. Every known technical, bureaucratic obstacle was raised by the entrenched obstructors of change. What a dangerous world we live in! It's hardly safe to breathe under the fire regulations, although I must say that the fire-master's chief concern was that the male and female actors had to change in the same dressing-room. The opening, by Jennie Lee, first Minister and Grand Duchess of the Arts, was planned for Sunday 24 August 1969. A week before, we had a visit from Bingo Mavor, then head of the Arts Council, son of the great James Barrie and the master of many arts and talents which he has lavished with abundant grace on the Edinburgh Festival and culture in general. With controlled and aloof concern, he surveyed the shambolic mess which was the object of his patronage. 'There is no chance,' he said sardonically, 'that you will be ready in a week.' This was the challenge that we needed, so we worked without sleep, some of us, for 128 hours, and the impossible was achieved. The miracle of paying for it took rather longer. James Ferguson, Vice-Chairman of the Club, shy, retiring and diligent, wrote me a kind letter:

My dear Nicky,
It was very kind of you to write and acknowledge our bagatelle. Lest the author of creation be forgotten, I want to say thank you on behalf of all those members who appreciate that the same hands which are transforming Fordell made possible the miracle in the Grassmarket.

Earlier in the day, the anandrious Malcolm Muggeridge had preached from the pulpit of John Knox in the High Kirk of St Giles the inaugural sermon of the Edinburgh Festival. It was on his usual theme, which he had preached since his miraculous conversion on the onset of age, abhorring virgins' wombs, thus canonizing himself for his involuntary sinlessness and blaming everyone for the lusts he could no longer indulge. Mustering every son of Christian charity, he described every fellow citizen as being a member of 'the most crime-ridden, sex-ridden, and sensually unstable society'. He condemned all modern arts as

> being so drenched and impregnated with erotic obsessions, so insanely preoccupied with our animal nature and its appetites, so remote from any other consideration – intellectual, moral or spiritual – that posterity [he said, presuming they interested themselves in the matter at all] would be astonished to the point of incredulity that writers like Henry Miller and William Burroughs should ever have been taken seriously. In a way, the whole thing is hilariously funny. All this vast extensive edifice of public culture, the Arts Council, Miss Jennie Lee, the National Theatre, Lord Goodman, the BBC, Kenneth Tynan and Kenneth Clark, the ever-multiplying and ever-growing universities where the half-baked received contemptuously the ministrations and instructions of the half-hearted.

It must be painful for so good a man to have to live in such an all-embracing cacotopia.

I introduced Jennie Lee in our new theatre in the evening thus: 'Miss Lee, Lords, Ladies, Gentlemen, John Knox, Malcolm Muggeridge, and other aspirant divines. I think we may ignore the decadent mutterings of the decrepit Mr Muggeridge from the pulpit of John Knox. Pray, Miss Lee, it is more important you convey a message to the Lord Provost of Edinburgh. Tell him we have presented Edinburgh with the most modern and exciting theatre in Europe and ask whether as a *quid pro quo*, he would like to present us with an opera house.' Jennie Lee graciously congratulated the theatre on a record of eighty-four world and international *premières* in the six and a half years we had lived in the Lawnmarket, and she launched this great adventure that has grown and thrived ever since.

On Sunday 3 November we had lunch at Newton Don the home of Mrs Auriole Balfour, a noble woman who always had the best roast beef and the most virile butlers throughout the years of rationing and call-up in the war. Moira and Ludovic Kennedy were also guests. It happened to be Ludo Kennedy's birthday – his forty-ninth birthday – so I composed a song in his honour which we sang to the tune of 'Darling Clementine' in the drawing-room after lunch. Here it is:

In the old manse at Mackerstoun
Always shooting a new line
Dwelt a diner, forty-niner
And his mistress most divine.

Oh my handsome, oh my brilliant
Oh my Ludo, so sublime,
Are they gone and lost forever,
Are your powers all past their prime?

Light he went, unlike a fairy
And his *métier* was a crime
He made lotses out of corpses
Scandals were his favourite line.

Oh my handsome, oh my brilliant
Oh my Ludo so divine
Have you really gone forever?
Promise fails at forty-nine.

Once a Liberal, now a National
Scottish National to the bone
Full of loyalty to the Royalty –
Cannot wait to mount the throne.

You're a genius, you're a wonder
Casanova in your time
What a shame then that already
You have gone into decline.

Little did I know I was about to embark on a case which would underline the irony of the second and third verses.

I was next instructed in the case of Her Majesty's advocate against Patrick Connolly Meehan: a case of infamous and historic reputation. A full account of this terrible miscarriage of justice has already been written by Ludovic Kennedy in his book *A Presumption of Innocence*, which was written before Meehan was pardoned, but which did so much to bring about that pardon. Nevertheless, perhaps as one of the prime actors, I may give my own account. Before the summer recess, I was instructed, as so often, by Joseph Beltrami. The main charge against Meehan was 'that on the 6th July 1969, he broke into the house occupied by Abraham Ross at 2 Blackburn Place, Ayr, and there he assaulted Abraham Ross and Esther Friedman or Ross, his wife, punched him and tied him up all to his severe injury, punched her and tied her up on the floor all to her severe injury and did further abandon them in said house where they lay without assistance for a period of thirty hours, in consequence whereof Esther Rachel Friedman or Ross died in Ayr County Hospital on the 18th July 1969, and you did murder her.'

Meehan had been the subject of a routine interview on Saturday 12 July, and he had frankly told the police that he and James Griffiths had passed Ayr on their way from Stranraer to Glasgow during the night of the commission of the crime. He told his whole story, omitting not unnaturally the criminal intentions and activities which had taken them to Stranraer in the first place. The Ayrshire police, desperate to produce results in this terrible case which had caused great public unrest in the sleepy seaside resort, thought that this coincidence was too good to be true – or at any rate was good enough to be true. Two men with criminal records called Pat and Jim had admitted, or one of them had, being near the scene of the crime on the night of the crime. According to Mr. Ross, Pat and Jim were the names of the assailants. The police made the classic mistake, a mistake men make in all walks of life and a mistake always to be avoided: having come to, or been handed, the evidence which could possibly suggest that Meehan and Griffiths could have been involved, they closed their minds to every other possibility. They never again tested the frail, basic premise, which after all was no more than a hunch. For them enough was as good as a feast. Consciously or unconsciously they determined that these two would do, and as the days went by they forgot the basis upon which Meehan and Griffiths came to be their suspects in the first instance and convinced themselves with hindsight that these were the culprits. And they did so to such an extent that they excluded evidence of the clearest nature implicating the actual killers, Waddell and MacGuinness, and fabricated evidence to convict their first choices.

Meehan was arrested on a warrant on 14 July. He said to Detective-Inspector McAlister, who arrested him: 'You are making the biggest mistake of your life. I can prove that I was in Stranraer that night.' Both observations were true. By the time I was instructed, Meehan had appeared on an identification parade and had been identified by voice only by Mr Ross, having spoken eight words. To Mr Ross he said instinctively, 'You're mistaken, laddie. Sir, you've got the wrong man. Honest.' No one else on the parade had spoken at all. Meehan was charged and detained. When he reached Glasgow, in custody and in desperation, he told Detective Chief Superintendent Goodall, head of Glasgow CID, that he had been with Griffiths who had an English voice; to which the detective replied that he was lying since both raiders had Glasgow voices and he had better tell the truth. Griffiths, on reading the startling news of Meehan's arrest and charge, telephoned Mr Goodall in person immediately to tell him that Meehan was with him that night, and was innocent. Mr Goodall told Griffiths to give himself up and all would be well, but Griffiths, knowing what had happened to Meehan, not unnaturally refused – mice are wiser not to fall for the blandishments of cats – though had he done so the tale would have been no different! Meehan had also been formally charged with the crime (while acting along with James Griffiths) in the sheriff court at Ayr. On his exit from the court he was assaulted by a hostile crowd. Feelings ran high in Ayr. Not unnaturally he thereafter, in desperation, divulged Griffiths's address to the police in order to establish his innocence. The police went to arrest Griffiths and were greeted with a hail of bullets and gun-fire. They retired to summon sharpshooters and cannon and in the ensuing round of battle in Glasgow, after inflicting many casualties, Griffiths was fatally shot. What more did one need – the Ayrshire police thought – to confirm the rightness of their judgment and the guilt of Meehan and Griffiths than such conduct? If they had ever doubted Meehan's guilt they certainly never doubted it again before Meehan's conviction.

The Crown Office therefore issued a statement of singular prejudice and warped impropriety: 'With the death of Griffiths and the apprehension of Patrick Meehan, the police are no longer looking for any other person suspected of implication in the incident concerning Mr and Mrs Ross at Ayr.' Ironically, as the years went on after Meehan's conviction, the pat answer which the Crown Office and the police gave to the evidence which pointed to the fact that the crime was really committed by Waddell and McGuinness, was that Meehan and Griffiths were in it and there too (i.e. that four men committed the raid). Indeed that was the standard refuge of the establishment – if Meehan and Griffiths didn't do it, they were guilty somehow; and that was the finding of the laborious and exorbitantly expensive report of Lord Hunter to Parliament in defiance of his terms of reference by Parliament that in no circumstances must he question the innocence of Meehan and Griffiths. They must have forgotten that awful Crown Office statement.

Joe Beltrami was horrified and thunderstruck. He immediately telephoned me and wrote, with my agreement, at once to the Crown Office in these terms:

It will now be nearly impossible for my client to have a fair trial before any jury. The Crown Office statement with regard to the finality of the police enquiries perturbs me. It would appear to me that the police are satisfied that they can exclude any possibility of error or mistake. I am far from satisfied that this possibility can be excluded. My client is entitled to a presumption of innocence. Following the Crown Office statement, it might well appear to some that he is now required to prove his innocence, whereas Scots law requires the prosecution to prove his guilt.

That letter demonstrates a remarkable piece of prescience. Even then Joe Beltrami realized that they had the wrong man. How poignant that letter is now. In answer the Crown, to show whose hand was uppermost, leaked the criminal record of the late James Griffiths to the Press for all prospective jurors to read.

So when I had my first consultation with Patrick Connolly Meehan in Barlinnie Prison the clouds were black indeed: I met him just as I had met so many before him in the hospital wing, where he was confined as a C.C. – a capital case. Had capital punishment still applied he'd have been wrongfully hanged.

He had a fresh, freckled but rather mean and resentful face. He had no charm and some cunning, sandy hair and a habit of putting his angular chin on his hand. The insistence of his innocence was urgent and desperate. He was a caged lion, entitled to the freedom of the plain, obsessively anxious to prove his right to acquittal but morbidly conscious of his inability to do so. At Mr Beltrami's suggestion, Meehan willingly agreed to be professionally examined under the influence of the 'truth drug'. We consulted Dr Wolffgang Kiernan who had given evidence for the defence recently in the case of McCloy. He explained that while it might be possible to invent experiences which one had not had under the truth drug, it was almost impossible to deny experiences which one had had. In my absence in Italy, staying with Islay and Rohais Campbell and our families at Villa Girosi which we had rented for a month, the petition was presented to the High Court by R.I. Sutherland QC, a suave, curt, incisive Silk with a taste for gin and a mind as sharp as his manner is glib. His cigarettes are many and his words are few. Lord

Clyde presided. The petition was refused most abruptly. 'The court has a duty,' Lord Cameron acidly, pointedly and personally observed in his judgment, 'to protect an accused person from the folly of his legal advisers.' From that moment on, for the next seven years, the court extremely effectively protected Meehan from the folly of all the legal advisers who pressed his right claim of innocence. Our folly eventually resulted in his belated pardon.

The stage was set for the trial in October. I was apprehensive. I did not, for one minute, doubt Meehan's innocence, or Waddell's guilt. I did not doubt as on so many occasions before, that I could persuade the jury of the truth, and knock a hole in every link in the Crown case, because it was so manifestly false and wrong. But I was worried by the furiant determination of the Crown and the police to secure a conviction at any price, and by any trick, and I was worried by the fervency of the Solicitor-General's belief that they had the right man.

I forefelt a great apprehension that once again it was Lord Grant on the Bench and Ewan Stewart QC for the prosecution. There had been too many replays. I, both separately and then together, asked Joe Beltrami and Patrick Meehan if they did not feel in all the circumstances that another counsel would be a wiser choice, recalling Homer's warning: 'Victory often changes sides'. Neither would countenance it. It would be a concession that the tactics of the Crown had paid off. Both insisted that I conduct the case. Whether they made the right choice or whether it would have made any difference we will never know, but the thought has haunted me since. Perhaps the terrible miscarriage of justice might never have happened if my catalytic presence had been absent from the trial. Certainly its conduct became very personal and most abusive. It is a heavy thought for me to think.

My co-adjuvant was a dear friend John Smith, a portly, homely genial advocate, now Labour Member of Parliament for North Lanarkshire, obstetrician to the stillborn devolution bills and the first advocate ever to be appointed a non-legal Minister of the Crown, Member of the Cabinet and Privy Councillor, which his considerable talents and quick wit certainly deserved. We were in no doubts as to the herculean scale of our task. The defence was supremely well-prepared by Mr Beltrami and his staff. Nothing had been left undone. We assembled that Monday morning in court no. 3 where Oscar Slater had been wrongly convicted as Meehan was about to be, and where, to the chargrin of the Solicitor-General and the dismay of Lord Grant, only a few months before Walter Scott Ellis had been acquitted of writing threatening letters to a sheriff. Announced by the thunderous call of the macer the Lord Justice Clerk now entered, tall, gruff and rough, his pock-marked face surmounted by squint spectacles, commanding authority and concealing a very good brain with a very low flash-point occasioned by his recent serious illness and his generous and appropriate patronage of the national tope. We got off to a bad start. Before pleading, I moved to separate the charges since the two subsidiary charges of stealing a car with Griffiths and falsely obtaining a passport with him were, in my submission, grossly prejudicial and in any event, Griffiths was not there to answer them.

Lord Grant glumply dismissed my plea with these words: 'This court has to keep in mind not only the interests of the accused [which it didn't] but the interests of the public [which it didn't either]. That has been laid down more than once recently, and it is possibly putting an end to a trend by certain judges in the past who tended to give greater weight to the accused's interests than was justified, to the detriment of the public itself, and to the administration of justice.' No judge ever gave clearer notice that the interests of the accused were not paramount. The die was indeed cast against us.

Abraham Ross was first to give evidence. He was small, dapper and plump and bore the wounds of his terrible experience. He blinked constantly behind spectacles which he never stopped pushing up his nose. He was clearly nervous. One can now see why. Having relayed the frightful experience of the night his home was invaded and his wife was murdered, he agreed to his identification of the voice at the identification parade, but with distinct hesitation. Listening to him I did not doubt that he was co-operating with the Crown authorities with either compulsion or Solomon's reluctance or both. This is what he said, hoping to grant half a baby to each mother – and perhaps keep a bit for himself: 'Well at that time I was kind of sure but I think it must be difficult to recognize a voice. I was very upset. It sounded so like the voice.' He knew he was merely identifying whom he was told to. To me he conceded and confirmed that both men had Scottish voices. He was *sure* of that, and that both men had *Glasgow* voices, and certainly the man called Jim spoke in a Glasgow accent.

Now in addition to pleading not guilty, Meehan had instructed me to submit two special defences: a special defence of alibi that he was in Stranraer, or Kilmarnock at the time the crime was believed to have been committed; and also a special defence of incrimination of Ian Waddell and another man. I now brought Ian Waddell into court. I made him read out the words 'Shut up! Shut up! We'll send an ambulance,' – the words which Meehan had had to read out at the identification parade. 'Was that like the voice of either of the men?' I

170

asked. 'It was like the voice, yes,' said Mr Ross. 'The one who said "Shut up! Shut up! We'll send an ambulance." Could you say it was the voice?' 'I couldn't say for sure.' 'Is it as like the one you heard at the police station at the identification parade?' 'It is very difficult to remember how the other fellow spoke, but that also sounds something like it.' For the first time, and by no means the last, Lord Grant, realizing that the defence of impeachment might well torpedo the Crown case, intervened: 'Is your recollection as clear now, three months later, as it was when you went to the identification parade?' 'No,' said Mr Ross, 'it is not as clear as it was then.' The Crown had two batsmen. Though in fact what Lord Grant had done in trying to equal the score, was to demonstrate the absurdity of the claim that you can identify a voice you have never heard before, having heard it speak eight words a fortnight earlier.

Meehan's instructions to me were simple and firm. And from them he never wavered. He had gone with James Griffiths to case and break into the motor taxation office in Stranraer in order to steal log-books with which to market the cars which Griffiths regularly stole. They had left Stranraer without breaking into the taxation office, and had broken into various cars in the car park of the Glenryan Hotel. They had left there after hearing the band play the National Anthem, having seen the proprietor's dog put out for its last micturition, and the barmaid walk home to her cottage, and that was between 1.30 and 2.00 A.M. They had then driven north, skirting Ayr. Near Prestwick Airport, in a lay-by, they had been flagged down by a girl called Irene Burns. They stopped. She told them that she and her pal, Isobel Smith, had gone to the terminal at Prestwick Airport which is Don Juan's strip, and had picked up two boys. They had set off back home with the boys in their car to Kilmarnock and they had stopped in a lay-by so that they could indulge in a little innocent canoodling. The Don Juans had begun necking, but her beau went further or faster than her moral code would permit. She had therefore got out of the car in real or protested indignation whereupon her frustrated Adonis had driven off with Isobel and her *amore* in the back.

When Meehan stopped his car to assist her, Griffiths told her to jump in and they raced ahead and overtook the car containing Isobel and the two frustrated gallants south of Kilmarnock. Meehan and Griffiths rescued Isobel from her fate, not that it is recorded that such was her wish, and then took each of the girls to their respective homes in Kilmarnock. At the time they overtook this romantic chariot, according to the Knights-errant, Mackie and Bell, it was still dark: by the time they got the girls to their homes it was, according to the girls, beginning to get light.

Mr Ross had said in evidence that five or ten minutes after the raiders left, he shook off the blanket which covered his face and it was then full daylight. So the raiders could not have been Meehan and Griffiths because they were north of Ayr and Kilmarnock and on their way to Glasgow when it was only beginning to get light, whereas it was full daylight only five or ten minutes after the actual raiders left. In the course of his charge, Lord Grant laboriously ensured that that point was astutely smothered.

But if the Crown case was right, here we had two men fleeing from the scene of a brutal murder which for all they knew had already been discovered, and only some ten miles from the scene of it, with the loot in the boot, unnecessarily identifying themselves to two young women and two young men, and equally unnecessarily delaying their flight by taking these damsels to their homes, when every road between them and Glasgow might well even then, so far as they knew, have had police blocks set up on it. This one might think seemed a little unlikely, but the Crown suggested that it was all an elaborate double-take to confound their guilt by identifying themselves to innocent citizens as people going about their lawful business.

Mr Ross made only one other point, again unhelpful to the Crown, but immensely significant. He said he did not think that there was any paper in the drawer of his safe, or in the cupboard where it was kept.

Next of importance came the two errant amorettos who gave evidence that Meehan and Griffiths appeared to be two normal, relaxed, perfectly ordinary people driving along with nothing on their consciences and time on their hands. They passed several strolling policemen in Kilmarnock without reaction from either men. They were not agitated or anxious or shifty in any way. They said that Meehan and Griffiths picked them up about 3.30, a time later confirmed by the two boys. Meehan's alibi confirmed that he was still at the Glenryan Hotel until 2.00 A.M. So if the Crown had the right man they had travelled fifty-two miles from Lochryanhead to the lay-by in one and a half hours, popping into the Ross's house on the way to execute the robbery and Mrs Ross. Whatever else might be in doubt about this crime one thing was certain beyond the need of proof: it had been elaborately and carefully reconnaissanced and planned, down to the timing of the robbery and entry to the house and the cutting of the telephone wire, so it seemed a little unlikely that Meehan and Griffiths would squeeze it in between their other established nocturnal escapades and misdemeanours.

In addition Ross gave evidence that the raiders were in the house for several hours, but Lord Grant in his charge succeeded in arguing away all the little difficulties of time.

Next came Detective-Sergeant Inglis, the officer in charge of the indentification parade. He entered the witness box and swore to tell the whole truth and nothing but the truth, and, if he did not, to answer for it at the Great Day of Judgment. He then swore that Ross was the first man to view the indentification parade, and he produced the parade form, written in his own hand contemporaneously in order to adminiculate his sworn word. Meehan instantly and instinctively tugged my gown. 'Ross wasn't first,' he urgently insisted, 'he was last.' At the time, the order in which the witness had identified him did not seem to me to matter. It was only after the appeal had been dismissed that the light dawned bright and clear, when Meehan's son traced and questioned the witnesses and stand-ins on the parade and Mr Beltrami completed the process by talking to the solicitor, Mr Peter McCann, as well. All these statements claimed that Mr Ross was last in fact to view the parade, but the first to be taken out of the witness room with his 'nurse' as if to view the parade. It was also established by the filial piety and diligence of Meehan's son that Mr Ross was in the receiving-room with his 'nurse' when the second witness to leave the witness room entered, *having viewed the parade*, and that Ross remained there until all other witnesses had viewed the parade. When the last witness entered having viewed the parade, Mr Ross apparently became ill and on this excuse he and his 'nurse' were hurried out of the receiving-room. In fact he was not ill but then viewed the parade for the first time. The reader should remember that when Meehan spontaneously tugged my gown in court, he did not have access to the statements of all these witnesses, though he would have known that if he were deceiving me they would contradict him. So Mr Ross was deliberately put in a position to talk to the witnesses who had identified, and were in a position to identify Meehan before he viewed the parade. It should be remembered that he had already told the police that he had not seen the faces of the raiders, and so Mr Ross could not claim to identify them by face. Thus was the charade of the voice identification fabricated. It has now been established by his real nurse's testimony that his 'nurse' was in fact a policewoman in plain clothes and that his real nurse was separated from her patient on arrival at the police station and only reunited with him at the end of the parade. Had he been first to view the parade he would have left earlier. Had he been ill she would have been summoned. The whole parade was an elaborate plot.

Significantly also the normal assembly room for the witnesses was allegedly being redecorated, so the witnesses gathered in the detective-constables' retiring-room instead. From the normal assembly the witnesses *must* go through the parade room in order to reach the receiving-room, but from the detective-constables' retiring-room they could, and Mr Ross did, go to the receiving-room without viewing the parade. When Ludovic Kennedy asked to see the lay-out of these rooms five years after Meehan's appeal had been dismissed, the then Chief Constables of Glasgow, Mr David McNee, refused to grant his permission on the grounds that the case was *sub judice* – 'under what judge?' one may ask – and, secondly, that the murder took place not in Glasgow, but in Ayr. What flapdoodle! What had he to hide? How could the viewing of that boring room, which I have seen so often, and which the defence solicitor in Glasgow knows better than his bedroom, by even so bland and adonic a communicator as Ludovic Kennedy, disturb the public peace? It certainly disturbed Mr McNee's peace and the reader can allot in the hindsight of history whatever reason he may deem appropriate. The reader should also remember that without Mr Ross's identification, the police could not have arrested Meehan or charged him, and Griffiths would still have been alive.

But it was the next chapter of evidence which was in fact fatal to Meehan, and it was palpably false. Detective-Superintendent Currie, who was in charge of the case, had gone on leave in August. He reported back on 18 August. The case, in his absence, had advanced not one whit by the time of his return. At that moment all the evidence the police had was Mr Ross's vocal identification, Meehan's account which put him near Ayr on the particular night and near the relevant time and the coincidence – very telling – of the names Pat and Jim. Nothing else. Detective-Inspector Cook, the police forensic expert, a tall, sallow bloodhound of few words and great charm and equal skill, had examined the safe, the cupboard, the clothes and the productions on 7 and 8 July, and he and his colleagues found *nothing* in the safe or in the cupboard. And when a forensic expert says nothing, he means *nothing* and not nothing of value, or nothing but paper. Because everything, however menial, is prospectively of value to the forensic scientist. Miraculously for the police, on Detective-Superintendent Currie's return in August, with the case no further forward, some fragments of paper turned up in the pockets of the car coat which the deranged Griffiths was wearing when he was shot, in their ambuscade, by the police. Mr Ross had said in evidence that neither of the raiders were wearing coats during the raid, and he had described their attire, of which car coats formed no part. When Mr Currie 'heard about' these scraps of paper, he 'recollected' having seen something similar in the drawers of the safe in the house at Blackburn Place. This was the safe examined by Mr Currie on 11 July and by Detective-Inspector Cook on 7/8 July and found to contain 'nothing'. These scraps of paper and the paper said to come from the safe were now shown on Mr Currie's orders to Mr Cook. *Mirabile dictu* – they matched. And they matched totally; they matched microscopically, they matched in colour on chromatographical comparison, and they fitted where they had been torn. Inspector Cook and his assistant, Detective-Constable Beaton, were of the opinion that they were of a common origin. They had no doubt in their minds, and there was no doubt in mine either. They were honest and right, because if a piece of paper is torn in two and one piece is planted in one place and one in another the pieces are bound to match under scientific scrutiny. The inference, of course, was absurd. What it involved was this: Griffiths had taken, inadvertently, these scraps of paper at the time of the raid and had somehow transferred them into a coat which he was not wearing at the time, but in which he was to be shot a fortnight later by the police. In my experience the corners of pieces of paper and banknotes have a tendency to 'break off' only in the hands of thieves on a criminal charge. We know now that Meehan and Griffiths were never in the Ross's house in Blackburn Place. We know they didn't commit the crime, so how did this paper of common origin from Mr Ross's safe get into the pocket of the coat in which Griffiths was shot? It was planted by the police who had no other evidence to convict two men whom they genuinely but grievously wrongly believed to be the culprits. By whom or on whose suggestion may never be known, but the fact that it was planted should be remembered for ever. The police having manufactured a false vocal identification which enabled them to arrest Meehan, and having shot Griffiths, albeit justifiably and courageously, had no evidence upon which to proceed against his admitted companion so they had to plant something, albeit in genuine belief of his involvement. It was fatal for Meehan, and it should now be fatal for them. Who planted it is a matter for the Crown to discover, but that the paper evidence was planted is beyond a sliver of doubt. Thereafter the rest of the case didn't matter. With such certain evidence all the discrepancies and the other evidence in the Crown case could be explained away, and explained away they were, both during the evidence and the speech of the presiding judge. The defence established through the mouth of Mrs Murray that Griffiths spoke with a pronounced Lancashire voice, and could not ever have been mistaken for a Scot, far less a Glaswegian. The Crown then called Donald Carmichael, a seasoned varlet, in order to give Ian Waddell a false alibi. He gave a confused and contradictory story. The police had shown a particular interest in Carmichael in order to check Waddell's alibi, and so alarmed was Carmichael by their prescient nosiness that he had telephoned a solicitor at midnight to ask this lawyer to protect his rights or wrongs. I asked him some questions:

Q: Isn't the reason you telephoned a solicitor because you knew your story was false and you were frightened of getting involved?
A: No.
Q: What was your reason for 'phoning a solicitor?
A: Well, sir, any time I'd ever been in trouble with the police I've always 'phoned my solicitor.
Q: But you weren't in trouble with the police, you were, according to you, giving a perfectly genuine alibi for Ian Waddell.
A: Yes.
Q: Well, how on earth, if you were telling the truth about Ian Waddell not being able to do the Ayr murder, could you be in trouble with the police for telling them the truth about that?
A: I couldn't have been in trouble with them.
Q: Well you told us that the reason you 'phoned your solicitor was that every time you were in trouble with the police you phoned your solicitor . . .
A: That's right.
Q: Did you regard yourself on this occasion as being in trouble with the police?
A: No.
Q: Well will you give the jury the reason why you telephoned your solicitor?
A: Well as I've already said before, any time I've been in trouble with the police I've always asked for legal advice if I could possibly manage it.

At this point Lord Grant, anxious to confirm and retrieve Waddell's credibility and to scuttle and confound our defence of impeachment came to Carmichael's much-needed rescue. 'I imagine you realize,' he said, 'that whether you are guilty of an offence or not, a person who is summoned to the police office is always wise to consult his solicitor, and that solicitors always advise their clients to that effect – if he is a reputable and able solicitor,' he added gazing despisingly at the one sitting on my right. 'The courts have said frequently that it is always desirable that a solicitor should be present if anyone is summoned to the police office in order to make a statement. Do you realize that,' he enquired to confirm this tract of misinformation. 'Yes,' said Carmichael: it was news to every lawyer in court. I made one last attempt: 'Why did you consult a solicitor?' 'Well, I says, I'm getting pulled in on this –' Carmichael was at last telling the truth. The police lost interest in Carmichael when they arrested Meehan. It took them another seven and a half years to regain their interest. I had expected the Crown to call Ian Waddell as a Crown Witness. It was, after all, their belief that Meehan was guilty, and therefore that Wadell was innocent, but for some reason – probably that it would give me the chance to cross-examine him if he was called for the Crown, whereas I could only examine him in chief if he was called for the defence – they decided not to call him, and the Solicitor-General informed me of their decision at this point. Waddell had refused to give a statement to the defence. Had he been called as a Crown witness he would have been immune from prosecution for the murder, to which he frequently admitted and for which he was subsequently and consequently tried seven years later. Whether the Crown, in their certainty of Meehan's guilt, had a lingering fear that Waddell might admit to the murder in the box if they called him, I do not know: but one thing is certain, he could not have been prosecuted for murder if they had chanced to call him on that occasion, and his many public confessions might have had less weight and Meehan might never have been pardoned. The Crown, not knowing what it had done, closed its case. Justice is strange. It was now Meehan's turn.

He took the oath and the stand. He told his whole story as he had told it to me, over and over again: He and James Griffiths had driven to Stranraer about five o'clock to look over the motor tax office and if possible to break into it and steal log-books. He gave, in full detail as he had in his routine questionnaire on 12 July, the details of his activities in Stranraer; his visit to a café, his enquiries about buying a car and having a meal at Spencer's Hotel, all of which were substantially confirmed by various Stranraer citizens who were defence witnesses. He went on to describe how they left Stranraer and stopped at Lochryanhead and broke into various cars at the Glenryan Hotel car park. Then they heard 'God Save the Queen' being played and saw the proprietor exercise his dog, and turn off his sitting-room light – all of this confirmed by the evidence of Mr Stanyer and doubly confirmed by the barmaid, Miss Priestly, who had walked to her house 100 yards away between 1.30 and 2.00 A.M.. Only in two respects did his account differ from the account he gave to the police in the routine questionnaire on 12 July: whereas in that account he had said they went to Stranraer to buy a car, they did in fact only look over one in Reid and Adams, and secondly he omitted the whole of the Grenryan Hotel episode, terminating his account of their adventures with leaving Stranraer at midnight. This untruthfulness was not lost on the Crown or the court. Knowing that both would ask him about these matters I preferred to anticipate their enquiry:

Q: Does that statement say that you left Glasgow to go to Stranraer to see a motor car which was for sale at a garage near Stranraer police office?
A: Yes.
Q: Now what in fact was the purpose of your visit?
A: To look over the motor taxation office.
Q: Does the account you gave say that at any stage you looked at the motor taxation office?
A: Well obviously not.
Q: Why not?
A: Well you don't tell the police these things when they come to ask you.
Q: Did you leave Stranraer at midnight?
A No.
Q: You say when you left, you think it would be near midnight?
A: Yes, but obviously I couldn't tell the police that I was standing in a Ministry of Defence yard watching a hotel.

Lord Grant now saw another chance to catch him out: 'But you had invented a reason for going to Stranraer. Why didn't you invent a reason for staying on in Stranraer until two o'clock? Or was that beyond your powers of invention?' he added sarcastically. It was now Ewan Stewart's turn to cross-examine. Having often appeared both with and against him I knew his superlative mastery of all the arts of advocacy and guile in cross-examination and I admired him for them but he did not need a judge to help him in the style of mutilating and vapid sarcasm which he adopted towards Meehan and his case. The next unfairness which Meehan had to suffer was when James Griffiths's record from the *Police Gazette* was read out. This, of course, had already been leaked and broadcast to the Press by the Crown office but the memory of the jury would, we hoped, have dimmed and, even more hopefully, none of them might have read it, or if they had, recalled the connection.

Had Griffiths been alive and sitting in the dock and able to admit, or deny, or explain the evidence against him, which by inference was also against Meehan, no mention of any of Griffiths's previous convictions could have been made. How much more unfair then to raise his record in his mortal absence? I objected, predictably in vain. One more stroke of mischief was to spurt from the judge's tongue as Mr Stewart concluded his merciless mauling of Meehan.

Q: Your idea in your evidence is to mix up something false with something true, isn't it?
A: That is not my idea at all.
Q: Isn't this the whole technique you have adopted since that weekend?
A: Sir, you are constantly calling me a liar.
Q: You are a self-confessed liar, aren't you?
A: Yes, I have asked some months ago to be given the truth drug and be interrogated under the truth drug.

The judge could not hold himself silent: 'Can't you tell the truth without having a truth drug?' he gleefully enquired.

Brutus triumphant plunged his forked tongue into the writhing corpse of the dying Caesar. Meehan endured seven years of living death before his resurrection. The Solicitor-General's cross-examination was more than enough to corroborate the planted paper. Only a man dexterous in giving forensic evidence could have so convincingly branded Meehan and Griffiths as two nasty and dangerous crooks as he unswervingly believed them to be throughout the case. The following witnesses, Mr Downey, the car salesman in Stranraer; the staff of Spencer's Hotel; the proprietor and the staff of Laurencehall Hotel all confirmed Meehan's story to the point that the Crown accepted that Meehan and Griffiths were still at the Glenryan Hotel between 1.30 and 2.00 A.M.. Mrs Meehan, a slight, pathetic, eternally tolerant and loyal wife was the next witness for the defence. She confirmed that it was she and her daughter who had persuaded Meehan to telephone the police about the two boys and the two girls he had picked up.

Next came William McIntyre, a convicted felon who had been approached by Andrew Dick with a suggestion that he should take part in a robbery with Ian Waddell. On the occasion of the trial Andrew Dick could not be traced by the whole force of the Glasgow police who had been asked to find him for the defence, though they found him quickly enough when they wanted to prosecute him. The Solicitor-General objected to my examination of McIntyre as to what Dick and Waddell had said to him on the grounds that such evidence was hearsay. Lord Grant shared that view and I explained that Dick was not available, but in any event it was perfectly competent for a witness to say what someone had said to him in order to prove the fact that it was said to him, but not of course to prove the truth of what was said. After further objections Lord Grant allowed the questions under reservation. So McIntyre told us of the details of Dick's proposition, and that he had initially agreed to it. He then related his meeting with Waddell in Dick's house. The Solicitor-General objected again. 'This,' he said, 'is a most blatant and deliberate attempt to elicit a quite improper and inadmissible hearsay, and I have no hesitation to say that my friend is clearly doing this quite deliberately.' This acetous attack and inappropriate cockfighting was one of the most disturbing features of the trial. I repeated the argument that it was perfectly competent in my submission to prove that somebody had said something without attempting to prove what he had said was a truthful statement. I was bound, I felt, as Disraeli said, 'to furnish my opponents with arguments if not with comprehension'.

'I understand,' said Lord Grant, 'that you have a defence of incrimination under which you say Waddell committed the crime. You are therefore attempting to prove that Waddell committed it and you are giving evidence from this witness that would tend to show out of Waddell's own mouth that he was at any rate party to the crime and that seems to me thoroughly improper.'

'If I may make the distinction,' I repeated, 'I am not trying to prove that what Waddell said was true, I am trying to prove that it is true that Waddell said it.'

'In order to establish what?' he enquired.

'In order to establish what Waddell said.'

'You are bringing evidence of what Waddell said in order to show that he said it. But in order to establish what?'

'That he said it.'

Unable to move me from my ground, the judge ignited into a paraphrenetic rage:

'Fairbairn,' snarled Lord Grant, 'would you please not be more stupid than you really are, or than even you can help?' I did not know how long I could stay tame.

I cite this logomachy to show the reader the extreme hostility to which Meehan's defence was subjected by the court. I had had many hot and searing exchanges, perfectly justified, over the years but in no other case and before no other court had I been the object of such a course of deliberate obstruction as that to which I was subjected in the defence of Meehan. But I was allowed to proceed and McIntyre described

Waddell's proposition. Next I called Ian Waddell himself, since charged with and acquitted on a technicality of the crime he was about to deny on oath. First I asked him to read the words 'Shut up! Shut up! We'll get an ambulance' which were the words which Mr Ross had identified.

'Have you ever said those words before, apart from in this court?'

'I refuse to answer that,' he said.

'You refuse to say whether you have ever used those words before, do you?'

'Yes,' said Waddell.

'Well,' said Lord Grant, intervening quickly to Waddell's relief and on his behalf, 'we must leave it there Mr Fairbairn. No persuasion is allowed.'

Would he have given Meehan this nervous protection, or would he have given it to Waddell if Waddell had been in the dock and not on the stand? The question does not require its inevitable answer. Waddell then told a tale about his relations with Carmichael and Dich which contradicted entirely the story which Carmichael had told. So we came to the most important part of his evidence. When Waddell was wanted by the police for interview, he was taken by Mr Skivington, manager of the Club bar, to see a solicitor, Mr Carlin, and there he gave Mr Carlin £200 in notes and asked him to act on his behalf if he was perchance arrested and charged with the Ayr murder.

Q: Is it not the case that you gave Mr Carlin, the solicitor, £200?
A: No.
Q: That is a lie, is it not?

Lord Grant intervened once more to say that dealings between a client and his solicitor were privileged and that only the client could waive the rules.

Q: Are you willing [I asked Waddell] that Mr Carlin should tell us whether or not you gave him any money on that occasion?
A: Yes [he said unexpectedly and very unwisely].
Q: Is your evidence that no money passed from you to Mr Carlin on the occasion when you went to him and asked him to accompany you to the police office where you were to be asked about your whereabouts on the 5th and 6th of July?
A: Yes.
Q: I suggest to you that on that occasion you gave to Mr Carlin a substantial sum of money in £5 notes.

181

Lord Grant again intervened to explain to Waddell that his dealings with his solicitor were private, and he could refuse to answer that question if he wished but Waddell surprisingly replied:

'I will answer it – I never gave him any money at all.'

This evidence was contradicted entirely by the last major witness, the solicitor in question, Mr William Carlin, who deponed thus:

'He was brought to my office by another client of mine who introduced him and told me that he had received information that the Glasgow Criminal Investigation Department wished to question him.'

Mr Carlin said that Waddell claimed he did not know the reason for the police interest in him. 'I pressed him further,' he said, 'and asked him if he had any idea at all what it might be, and he said it had been told to him that it could well be in connection with a robbery which had taken place recently in the town of Ayr.' Mr Carlin went on to describe how at Waddell's request he had telephoned Mr McAlister and told him that he had in his office a man whom he might wish to see regarding a serious crime.

Q: Did Waddell give you any money?
A: He did. He produced the money from a pocket after Skivington had said 'If Mr Carlin is going to act for you then you had better give him a fee.' He gave me £200 in new £20 notes.
Q: Did this surprise you?
A: Yes, to a certain extent it did. I didn't ask for a fee. No question had been raised at that time, but he said to me that he wanted me to act in his defence if he was charged with this particularly serious crime.

In a subsequent conversation Mr Carlin asked Waddell why he had lied about giving him the money when he knew the evidence would be contradicted. Waddell replied that he preferred to face a charge of perjury than a charge of murder. In the end he ended up by facing both and very nearly being convicted of both. As a result of his palpably false testimony he was charged with perjury, admitted it and was jailed for three years. Sentencing him Lord Cameron said most rightly, 'If the jury had known that Ian Waddell was lying they might have taken a very different view of Meehan's guilt.' Never was a truer word spoken. What now of the court's duty to protect clients against the folly of their legal advisers?

Thereafter various witnesses from Ayr spoke of seeing a suspicious-looking man casing the joint of whom they could say no more than that

Waddell was not unlike him. The case for the defence of innocence, incrimination and alibi was made out as far as it could be. Skivington had sent a predictably convenient medical certificate and was not present. Dick had apparently disappeared. I closed my uncompleted case.

The court then rose and I went through to Glasgow to take part in a rectorial debate at the request of the Very Reverend George McLeod, now Lord McLeod of Fuinary – that big, tall, brave divine, with his white hair and wise eyes whose restoration of the Abbey and ecclesiastical buildings of Iona is chief among his many contributions to the life and spirit of twentieth-century Scotland. The subject of debate was 'That permissiveness has gone far enough'. For the motion, apart from Lord McLeod himself, were two young students, Ian Valentine and Brian Gibb, the late Very Reverend John Gray, then the virile and upright minister of Dunblane Cathedral whose ecclesiastical excellence earned him the role of Moderator in jubilee year, and Lady Lothian the beautiful protector of the unborn child. Against, beside myself were Malcolm McKenzie of the Education Department, Donald Dewar, then the articulate Member of Parliament for South Aberdeen, Colin MacKay, the blonde teddy bear of Scottish Television, and Ludovic Kennedy. At dinner before the debate, I sat next to Lady Lothian and told her all the details of the Meehan case and of my faith in his innocence. When the verdict came out she sent me this generous and sensitive letter (despite the fact that we won the debate!):

My dear Nicky,
I believed you so much when you said he is innocent that I have thought of it ever since and feel so sad for you tonight.

Love, Tony.

The debate concluded, and permissiveness having received a vote of indulgent confidence by the indulgent students, I travelled back to Edinburgh with Ludovic Kennedy, and convinced him on the journey of Meehan's innocence. He insisted that I stay in Edinburgh for the night rather than travel back to my home in Fife, so after beer and sandwiches in the North British Hotel I went to bed there, to resolve my thoughts for the speech in the morning, for as a habit I have never written my speeches to a jury. They do not make notes and they will only remember as much, at most, as you do yourself. It is the balance of impressions they retain and judge upon.

The Solicitor-General started his brackish address to the jury first thing on Friday 24 October. He stressed the important points for the Crown; the coincidence of Pat and Jim; the voice identification of Mr Ross; the bits of paper found in the safe and in Griffiths's car coat; Griffiths's action in shooting his way out when attempts were made to arrest him and Griffiths's record for robbery; and he mocked and belittled the defence attack upon these points and divellicated the positive characteristics of the defence case. Of the salient pillars of the Crown case, the coincidence of Pat and Jim was in fact a coincidence, the voice identification was deliberately falsified to justify Meehan's arrest, the bits of paper were deliberately planted in order to obtain his conviction and Griffiths's conduct was yet to have its explanation revealed. By such evidence his conviction was most wrongously obtained. It was my turn; I knew it all might turn on my speech.

I went through the contradiction of the voices and accents of the raiders and of Griffiths; of the timing of their journey to the exclusion of the Ross raid; the contradiction of the light; of the unlikelihood that they would identify themselves to the girls after committing so difficult and so dangerous a crime; of the unlikelihood that they would drop in to do such a crime hurriedly and casually when it was obviously so carefully prepared. I stressed the considerable evidence pointing to Waddell's guilt and his very unsatisfactory performance in the witness box. Everything, when argued cogently, fitted Meehan's claim that he was innocent and that Waddell was guilty. It is an unwritten rule that except in the most exceptional circumstances, judges do not interrupt counsel during their speech to the jury. Lord Grant twice interrupted mine and by doing so mussed the thread and impact of my argument, once with the remark, 'Mr Fairbairn will you stop trying to mislead the jury?' and on another occasion, 'The jury will know how to deal with those sort of submissions.' As on several occasions when under rixatious attack in the course of that trial, I was close to losing self-control and bursting into tears. It took more than a few minutes to get back into the stride of my speech on each occasion, but the effect on the jury must have been very strong indeed.

I finished at lunch-time. Everyone to whom I spoke thought that Meehan must be acquitted but they had only heard, however, one speech for the Crown; the second, the charge of the Lord Justice Clerk, started at two o'clock. He started by making all the usual directions in law, and then he came to special defences. If a judge is going to give any special direction to the jury, such as that there is insufficient evidence in law on any matter, it is usual for him to do so before either counsel addresses the jury, so as neither to confuse the jury nor waste counsel's and the court's time. Lord Grant now proceeded in the middle of his charge, and without warning to say, 'I propose to direct you that the defence of incrimination has not yet been established; indeed, there is not even remotely sufficient evidence to establish it, and that you would not be entitled to hold it established.' At that time the law was that a special defence only had to be established on the balance of probability, though it was sufficient that if having considered the evidence of the special defence of incrimineation the jury were left with a reasonable doubt, then they must acquit. What was the evidence which was not even remotely sufficient?

Firstly, McIntyre, if believed, had retailed Waddell's description of the plan of the raid in detail; secondly, Waddell's voice could have been the voice of one of the attackers; thirdly, he had refused to answer simple questions when no other explanation other than guilt was available; fourthly, he had denied giving Mr Carlin £200 in sequenced notes such as had been stolen from Mr Ross's safe which an unemployed labourer might have difficulty in explaining having in his possession two days after the crime; fifthly, he apparently thought it neccessary to have a solicitor with him, as an innocent man going to give an explanation to the police of something in which he was not involved; sixthly, he evidently expected to be arrested for this crime; and lastly, he was, according to witnesses, similar to the man who had been seen loping about casing the joint. That was what was held not to be remotely sufficient to establish his involvement on the balance of probability. It had been clear from Lord Grant's over-zealous protection of Waddell's defectuous evidence and his overbearing manner when McIntyre was giving evidence of what Waddell proposed to him that he was worried that Waddell's evidence might well cause the jury to have doubts about Meehan's guilt. Perhaps he thought Waddell was correctly named as the perpetrator – if so, he got that right. It is difficult to see otherwise why he was so anxious to exclude, or restrict, Waddell's evidence from the jury's consideration. Both the Solicitor-General and I had addressed the jury on the special defence of incrimination, the former saying that it was not a defence but a device to divert the jury's attention, while I had emphasized the crucial importance of the jury's impression of Waddell, an importance which was to be re-emphasized by Lord Cameron at the time of his sentence of Waddell for perjury. By withdrawing the special defence in these terms at this time, the Lord Justice Clerk was effectively excluding Waddell from the case, and from the jury's consideration. Irony could not have invented a worse wrong. It was to take seven years of Meehan's life and a thousand hours of effort and pain

185

by his advisers to reverse Lord Grant's absolution of Waddell and see him rightly indicted at last.

Bit by bit throughout the charge the judge attacked the defence case; first the timing, then the light, then the voices. The charge concluded at 3.50 P.M. In view of the magnitude of the case I had asked Elizabeth if she would like to attend and listen to its summing-up. Rarely had I ever done that before. I had told her that though he was often partial during the conduct of the case, Lord Grant was always fair during his charge. After listening to it, she observed: 'You had better revise your opinion.' The jury returned a verdict of guilty by a majority of nine to six. I had failed to convince sufficient of them by two. With a fair trial, even despite the false evidence which had been planted, there can be little doubt that the jury would have acquitted. Lord Grant sentenced Meehan to imprisonment for life. After sentence prisoners sometimes break down, but they very rarely speak. Gaunt, sallow and enraged, Patrick Connolly Meehan addressed the court in a trembling but deliberate voice: 'I want to say this, sir,' he said, 'I am innocent of the crime and so is James Griffiths. You have made a terrible mistake.' More terrible unfairnesses were still to compound it. With a last beshrewing look at the Lord Justice Clerk, he turned and descended indignantly to serve his sentence.

I instructed an appeal to be marked forthwith, knowing that it would almost inevitably come before the first division of the Appeal Court with Lord Clyde in the chair, since the Lord Justice Clerk, chairman of the second division, had taken the trial. I knew therefore that the appeal was destined, almost inevitably, to be dismissed. I didn't know how strong were to be the grounds to support it. After the trial it came to light that the BBC had a recording of Griffiths's voice taken in prison for a religious programme. It was an unmistakably English voice, with a strong Northern accent. Not only that, but in the course of the interview Griffiths said that he could not bear to return to prison, and that if the police ever came for him again once he got out, he would shoot his way out rather than risk being arrested. So two of the Crown's main planks – the voice and their argument that Griffiths shot his way out because he knew he was guilty – were demolished. The police had also now, miraculously, found Andrew Dick. I asked the Appeal Court that Mr Ross should be allowed to hear a recording of Griffiths's voice, because if Griffiths wasn't there, Meehan wasn't there either. That request was curtly refused. When the tape was played to Mr Ross afterwards, he said it was not the voice of either intruder. I then asked that Dick's evidence be heard. It will be remembered that the basis for Lord Grant's so angrily stopping McIntyre's evidence was that Dick was not present. My request was refused with one of Lord Clyde's fribbling observations during the appeal: 'Where is this to end ?' he asked. 'Are you asking us to have a kind of retrial to rake about in the hope that something will emerge from a witness, whose evidence you don't know?' The third ground was that Lord Grant had wrongly removed the special defence of incrimination of Waddell. 'There was no corroboration,' said Lord Guthrie gridely from his painful, hunched, rheumatoid frame. I would not have given Waddell the chance of a bird in a cat-house if he had been tried and convicted of the crime on the evidence and had appealed that there was insufficient evidence to convict.

The fourth ground was that the presiding judge had not put the defence case fairly to the jury. 'The court is quite satisfied,' said Lord Clyde with splenetic hyprocrisy, 'that there is no ground whatever for these criticisms.' The court must have been alone in that view. With that, he jumped up and scooted from the Bench as if he was about to take part in a gavotte. The appeal was thus refused, and had there been capital punishment Meehan would have had ten days to live. The prerogative of mercy would never have been entertained for a villain like him. And the resistance of the authorities to admit their mistake (and their motive for denying it) had he hanged would have been even stronger, if it could have been, than it was to prove to be when he lived.

In the early days thereafter Mr Beltrami and I did our best to interest people of influence in Meehan's wrong conviction. I remembered the urgent words quoted by the Sovereign in one of her Christmas broadcasts.

> Tho' you have conquered Earth and charted sea,
> And planned the courses of all stars that be,
> Adventure on, more wonders are in thee.
> Adventure on, for from the littlest clue,
> Has come whatever worth man ever knew.
> The next to enlighten men may be you.

It wasn't I who eventually enlightened the stone-hearted men of power. Above all, it was the desperate wronged urge of Meehan himself, the boundless faith of Joe Beltrami and the telling pen of Ludovic Kennedy which won the final triumph for justice. But I did my little bit to help. We involved his MP Frank McElhone, the congenial and bluff jester from the Gorbals, and together we visited Meehan in Peterhead, that grim, smelly fortress, overlooking the grey North Sea on the Aberdeenshire coast. Meehan was already in self-imposed solitary confinement and I saw a grave change in his mental and physical health. It was not long before he was making paranoid suggestions that I had been bribed by the police not to defend him properly. I fully understood and forgave these tormented wanderings.

In April 1970, Waddell had pled guilty to committing perjury at Meehan's trial. In the July following the return of a Conservative Government we presented a dossier of precognitions to the new Lord Advocate Norman Wylie for consideration by the new Secretary of State, Gordon Campbell. These included precognitions of all the witnesses and stand-ins at the identification parade which established that the identification parade was falsified. They had been collected in the main by Meehan's son. Matters drifted on always with the same answer 'no reason to interfere'. On three separate occasions the Queen's pardon was curtly refused. What further could be done? Meehan, desperate and deluded by solitary confinement changed solicitors several times. He convinced all of them of his innocence, and they, though not acting as his professional advisers, all became members of the Patrick Meehan Committee. It cost us all years of what was called obstinacy: 'Quae enim pertinacia quibusdam eadem allis constantia videri potest' ('For what to some appears obstinacy can be seen by others to be constancy').

In 1971 Meehan eventually persuaded Ludovic Kennedy to take an interest in his case which had smouldered since our conversation in the train the night before his conviction. Though at times it had almost flickered out, quenched by doubt, now it burst into flame. What rekindled it was a chance event which occurred on 28 July 1972.

Waddell was released from jail after serving his sentence for perjury in June 1972. On 4 June he was rearrested on a charge of being in possession of a loaded revolver. Waddell instructed William Dunn, Mr Beltrami's rotund and genial partner. The pleading diet was to be held on 28 July, by which time Mr Dunn was on holiday and Mr Beltrami therefore asked Waddell if he wished him to act in place of his partner. Waddell agreed and Mr Beltrami pled guilty on his behalf. Waddell was sentenced to twelve months' imprisonment. After sentence he asked to see his solicitor, and told him he would like to help Meehan. He said that he would be willing to give evidence – which he said was true – under the truth drug, that he and another man had in fact committed the offence for which Meehan was wrongly imprisoned. He had remembered that the High Court had opined as part of 'their duty to protect clients from the folly of their legal advisers', that evidence under the truth drug was not evidence, so Waddell thought he might be able to help Meehan without harming himself. He wanted the experiment to take place in the BBC studios and for the press to be present. Just before 7 A.M., the traditional time for release, on the morning of 2 February 1973, Waddell was released from Barlinnie, when a BBC reporter, David Scott, and a producer, Ken Vass, lately seconded from the press, were there to greet him. They asked him to give them details of the crime, and in answer to various questions he gave a fairly full account. That afternoon, David Scott went to see Waddell's new solicitor, Mr Robert Gibson, and was informed by them that Waddell with venal cheek would like £30,000 if the experiment was successful, but nothing if it wasn't: he generously agreed. Later, Ludovic Kennedy was involved and David Scott and Ken Vass made further enquiries saying that Mr Kennedy was not yet sufficiently convinced of the detail of his confession to justify payment of such a large sum, so Waddell gave further details, all of which were followed up and were confirmed to be true. None of them had been published in the newspapers at the time of the Meehan trial or could have been known to any except those who had an intimate knowledge of the Ross house. Unknown to Waddell, David Scott had had a small microphone secreted under his tie and had recorded all the interviews. The BBC proposed to broadcast these interviews in a BBC television programme, whereupon Waddell instructed his solicitor to interdict the BBC from so doing – not on the grounds that what he said was untrue, but on the grounds that he hadn't said it. Waddell failed on appeal to the Court of Session. The broadcast went out in July, and all the new evidence and details of the confession were sent again to the Secretary of State. In October 1973 he once again refused a Royal pardon. But the broadcast had had the effect of convincing many people that Waddell must, in fact, be the culprit since he revealed so much detail which nobody else knew.

When the Conservative Government fell in February 1974, a fresh approach was made to Mr William Ross, who was once again Secretary of State for Scotland and, incidentally, the Member for Kilmarnock, which may have had its bearing on his judgments. In August yet again he said that he had come to the conclusion that there were no grounds that would justify recommending the exercise of the Royal prerogative of mercy or of taking any action in the case. Later that year, Waddell, now emboldened by the fact that the Crown had taken no action against him despite his detailed confession, became braver and justifiably so; he gave interviews to the *Scottish Daily Record* in which he disclosed even more details which were unknown to anybody even, in some cases, to Mr Ross himself. Principal among the many details which he disclosed in these interviews was that he had ripped a gold bracelet watch from the wrist of Mrs Ross. No mention had ever been made at the trial of Mrs Ross's watch and nobody had ever been charged with stealing it. Indeed, Mr Ross's explanation as to why he had not mentioned it to the police was that he assumed that it had been destroyed with her bloodstained effects at the mortuary.

In September 1974, Meehan finally made his first application for a Bill of Criminal Letters against the three detectives who had been involved in the identification parade. A Bill of Criminal Letters is a sort of private prosecution in Scotland. It was stoutly opposed by the Lord Advocate and was refused by Lord Wheatley sitting with Lord Fraser and Lord Kissen on the grounds that it would open the flood-gates to private prosecution which our system of principal prosecution had been devised and developed to prevent. Since this format of prosecution has not been allowed since 1908, it was difficult to see where the flood was going to come from. It had been dry for three-quarters of a century. In the spring of 1975 Meehan made further application for a Bill of Criminal Letters, and once again was turned down. But Meehan persisted – '*Quand on a raison, le succes n'est qu'une question de temps!*' In June 1975, the Secretary of State asked to see a manuscript copy of Ludovic Kennedy's book, and it was sent to him with the approval of the Committee and disappeared from sight or mention. Four months later, during which I raised the matter in Parliament several times, and obtained all-party signatures to a motion asking the Secretary of State to set up an independent enquiry, Mr William Ross once more announced on 10 October that he had come to the conclusion that there were no grounds that would justify the exercise of the Royal Prerogative of Mercy, or taking any other action in the case. We had hoped, after the press conference which launched Ludovic Kennedy's book in London, and the vast amount of responsible interest which the press showed thereafter, that at least we would have a better reception than that, but ears which are pestiferously deaf don't hear. Then in March of 1976, within the space of a few days, two most extraordinary coincidences occurred. At last Meehan, who had been the subject of such cruel coincidences, became the beneficiary of them.

Mr Beltrami was having dinner in the Carousel Restaurant in Motherwell with his lovely wife Delia, at whose hand I have received many kindnesses over the years, when the doorman asked him if he were still interested in the Meehan case, and if he would be interested in having Mrs Ross's watch, the existence of which Waddell had revealed. Sceptical of such breaks, for we had seen so many false dawns, he said he would. On Tuesday the 23rd, a man brought a watch to his desk and Mr Beltrami immediately went to Detective Chief Superintendent Elphinstone Dalglish with the watch and gave him a statement. A few days later, 'Tank' McGuinness, called McTurk in Ludovic Kennedy's book, was murdered in Glasgow, and in the evening his wife and son telephoned Mr Beltrami in his office and told him full details implicating McGuinness in the crime as Waddell's accomplice. The next day they called at the office and gave the whole tale in detail, a tale much of which Mr Beltrami had already heard from McGuinness's own lips as a client, but which hitherto he had been prevented by professional confidentiality from revealing. He at once obtained minutes of waiver from all McGuinness's next of kin and informed the police. He obtained my opinion that he was entitled to reveal what he knew. The Law Society waived his confidentiality. The Chief Constable appointed Chief Superintendent John McDougall and Assistant Chief Constable Arthur Bell, both of whom have been good friends to me, to investigate the matter. They sent a report to the Lord Advocate. I raised the matter again in Parliament on the 12 May, and the Lord Advocate gave the results of the enquiries which he had put in motion, and we would have to wait.

On 19 May 1976 the New Secretary of State for Scotland, Mr Bruce Millan, made a statement to the House. 'In the past few days I have received new information following the death of William McGuinness, a man with a record of crimes and dishonesty and violence. It was revealed after his death that he made statements to the effect that he participated in the Ross robbery to the exclusion of Mr Meehan. The value of these statements must remain a matter of judgment, but there is independent evidence establishing that McGuinness was in Ayr on the night of the murder.' He went on:

in the circumstances I have reached the conclusion that falls to me as Secretary of State to reach a decision on whether or not to recommend the exercise of the Royal prerogative. The new information which has become available since the death of McGuinness, taken along with the earlier considerations relevant to the case, have convinced me that it would be wrong for Patrick Meehan to remain in prison convicted of murder. I have therefore decided to recommend the exercise of the Royal prerogative to grant a free pardon. Mr Meehan is being released today.

It was a brave and most righteous decision and great credit is due to

Bruce Millan for the fortitude and sagacity of his judgment. He had only been Secretary of State for a few weeks. Had he not been, Meehan might still have been kept wrongly in prison; for his predecessor William Ross immediately rose in the chamber and said, 'While not necessarily disagreeing with the final decision which my Right Honourable friend reached, may I ask whether he appreciates that in this case there has been a confusion and duplication of confessions, not all from unimpeachable sources. Bearing in mind the important implicit consequences of his decision for many people in Scotland, is he satisfied that this is the only action which was open to him?' He might have found another way if the decision had still been his. I asked this question: 'Does the House appreciate that we must have an explanation of how the Lord Advocate and those preceding him took the right of their office to oppose Bills of Criminal Letters, which would have established the very facts that are now admitted in the name of the Secretary of State?' The House was not too pleased. So, most belatedly, justice was done. 'Judge not the play before the play is done. Her plot hath many changes. Every day speaks a new scene. The last act crowns the play.'

Injustice would never have been done had the evidence not been falsified, but even standing that, if the trial had been fairly and impartially conducted, it is inconceivable that the jury would have convicted Meehan as they did. It required, after all, only two of them who voted for guilty to vote the other way. Following Meehan's conviction on 24 October 1969, but before his appeal was heard on 25 November 1969, I had addressed the Law Society of Edinburgh University on his very matter, in the course of a lecture entitled 'The Presumption of Guilt':

> One of the most essential principles of the criminal law of Scotland is the presumption of innocence. A presumption which every member of the jury is supposed to make, and every judge is required scrupulously to apply, in favour of an accused. That it is a fiction of our law rather than a reality is always a risk, but it is a risk which is increased as society is stampeded into assuming that law and order are breaking down, and as the courts react by reducing the safeguards of the presumption of innocence.

I reminded them of the Lord Justice Clerk's words at the beginning of Meehan's trial, and added 'We have been warned.'

That is [I said] the ideal and the principle of our system, but in practice, it does not necessarily work in that way. There are notorious cases, past and present, trivial and serious, in the sheriff and High Courts where justice is not only not done, but it is manifestly seen not to be done because the judge himself, presuming the guilt of the accused has ensured the conviction of the accused by his conduct of the trial and his charge to the jury. The acquittal of a guilty man is not in the interests of the public, but the conviction of an innocent one is even less so, and while we have a system of trial by jury and impartial judgment, justice is not done if a judge perceptibly departs from the presumption of innocence.

My anxiety had been increasing over several recent cases, but it was the conduct of the court in the case of Meehan which forced me to break my silence.

If I were asked [I said] by a solicitor to write an opinion on the following memorial 'My client was convicted of murder and robbery on the following evidence' – I then related the evidence against Waddell on the special defence of incrimination in the case – 'what are his chances of successful appeal before a First Division Court?', there is only one opinion I could give. His application would be refused. He would have more chance of kindling fire with snow. The court would hold that there was ample evidence to convict beyond reasonable doubt. But that was the very evidence that the Lord Justice Clerk said was not remotely sufficient to establish Meehan's special defence of incrimination of Waddell on a mere balance of probabilities, and I predict that the appeal courts will unanimously uphold the Lord Justice Clerk's views.

It makes strange and chilling reading now and it received an immediate reaction from the establishment. On 7 November 1969, following that incautious speech, I had a letter from Lord Cameron:

Dear Fairbairn,
I have read a report of your recent address to the University Law Society in the current issue of *The Student*. I am afraid this goes too far and coming in public from a member of the Bar addressing a legal audience. I have referred the matter to the Dean.

The Dean of Faculty, George Emslie, asked for a copy of my address which I sent him. It was not long before the matter became a major public issue. John Mackintosh, Member of Parliament for Berwick and East Lothian, asked questions in Parliament. He asked the Secretary of State if he could introduce legislation to permit reasonable and responsible public discussions of a judge's handling of a case, and he asked how many judges of the Court of Session had had judicial experience prior to their appointment. Various others wrote articles on this important subject in the press. For many months I was the unlit faggot on this blazing pyre and I tried to keep the mighty anguish in and force out a smile. Keith Bovey, a concerned Glasgow solicitor, wrote a letter to the *Scotsman* from which I quote part:

> What Mackintosh said, and what is of great importance is that judges are as often as not chosen because of political allegiance and not for merit. The Lord Advocate makes these choices. The appointments of lords ordinary and sheriffs in this way is undesirable but not critical. What is critical is the appointment of the Lord President and the Lord Justice Clerk in this way. The holder of these offices, especially the President, have a profound and far-reaching effect on the conduct and administration of the law. Moreover Presidents sometimes preside for long periods. Is it not therefore a matter for acute public concern to see that the judge or advocate most suited for the post should be appointed to it, rather than that those who happen to hold political office at the time can grab these posts for themselves or their appointees? The position is made worse by the fact that political advocates only go into politics in order to obtain a seat on the Bench.

This was the hub and source of the trouble – appointment at the top. Following on this letter, the BBC did a programme about the subject in which the Dean asked me to appear. Norman Wylie, the Lord Advocate, also appeared and he said, there and then, that he would never appoint himself to either of the two chairs, but would appoint the most suitable and eminent person from the Bench. He was as good as his word, and when the time came he appointed George Emslie (who by then had been on the Bench for more than a year) pre-eminently appropriately, to the office of Lord President and Lord Justice General, and Lord Wheatley to the office of Lord Justice Clerk. Eventually my misdemeanour was forgiven and I was not disbarred for saying what I believed to be true, as for so long had seemed possible. It was a time of terrible strain, and many a time I rued my words and mused with Dryden's Cleopatra: 'Why was I framed with this plain honest heart which knows not to disguise its grief and weakness but bears its workings outward to the world?' But penalty was worth the reward of a purified legal system. The Dean's Council invoked the liberty of 1789: 'No man should be molested for his opinions provided his conduct does not injure the community.' I hoped I had protected the community, however incautious I had been of my own salvation. 'A cat that sits on a hot stove lid,' observed Mark Twain, 'will never sit on another hot stove lid. For that matter it won't sit on a cold stove lid either.' I have often yearned for a cat's caution, but I trust I would suffer for the right once more.

CHAPTER 10

In July 1969 the first of a number of bank robberies had occurred in Glasgow which puzzled the CID. They could find no matching fingerprints, they could get no whisper from any of the underworld sources, and the technique of the raiders differed from that of any criminal team known to them or their records. The team were nicknamed 'The Gentlemen Raiders'. On 30 December 1969, Inspector Andrew Hislop, driving up to the Southern police office in the company of PC Sellars in Allison Street noticed two men carrying a heavy black box and two suitcases into a close. He decided to investigate. He sent PC Sellars to the close and went for assistance in the persons of Acting Detective-Constable Mackenzie, PC Barnet and Detective-Constable Campbell. The time was 4.25 P.M. When he returned, PC Sellars was at the close speaking to Howard Wilson whom Hislop recognized as an ex-policeman who had been with the City of Glasgow police for nine years. Wilson invited them into the house and offered them a drink. It was the last supper. In the house were John Sim, Ian Donaldson and the suitcases. The police enquired what was in the suitcases and where was the black box. Wilson indulged in some bluff badinage which failed to deter the officers' curiosity so he offered to go and get the black box. What in fact he went to get, and what he got, was a loaded pistol. He returned to the hall, took aim at Inspector Hislop's head and fired. There was a click. He rearmed the weapon, fired again and hit the Inspector smack in the face. Wilson then shot Mackenzie and Barnet in the head as they rushed to Hislop's aid in the hall. Barnet was fatally wounded and died in hospital five days later leaving a widow and young family. Wilson then put the gun to the prostrate face of Mackenzie, murdering him at point-blank range. He now turned his attention to PC Sellars who was radioing for help from the tenuous sanctuary of the bathroom. PC Campbell, with magnificent courage, for he could have crossed the road to the Southern police station for help, flew at and overpowered Wilson and managed to get the gun from him. The three bankraiders were thus arrested in this abattoir.

The news of these crimes, committed on the second last day of the year, left Glasgow stunned and incredulous. Wilson was born in 1938 and received an excellent education at Glasgow Academy. He was bright, smart and popular. He was an accomplished sportsman and a good police officer, being twice commended. But lack of promotion forced him to leave the Force after nine years. He used his police annuity to set up a fruiterer's shop and, unwisely, opened a second and discovered that far from being better off than he was as a police officer, he was worse off. He took the risks which self-improvement requires, but he was inexperienced and too impatient of success. Debt is a cruel and relentless master, and in debt Wilson turned to crime. Debt creates in its victim the fantasy that once it is paid off all will be well; just commit the perfect crime once and retire, which is the dream of most robbers and the imagination of many who never rob at all. And if you have no record, no criminal associates and no fingerprint record, you are off to a great advantage. But as the Train Robbers discovered before Wilson, however much pelf you get, it is never enough. All prospective thieves would do well to remember that. Wilson started by robbing the British Linen Bank in Giffnock of £21,000 in July and finished by robbing the Clydesdale Bank in Lynwood of £14,000 in December. Tax free, it sounds plenty, but it is never enough. It was aurivorous greed in the end that caught him. Not content with the chievance of his last raid he and his associates stole the silver and copper as well as the notes; that was what was in the suitcases that attracted Inspector Hislop's alert attention. Four men took part in the first raid, three in the last. No trace of the fourth man, dead or alive, has ever been found. Some say he is in the foundations of the Erskine Bridge, that superfluous white elephant built over the Clyde at such expense by the profligate nuttersacks of the bureaucracy. If he is no one has ever been able to establish how he got there, and I doubt if anyone will ever find him. There was little, if anything, to be said in mitigation; except to point the awful lesson for us all. 'And so, step by step,' I said to the ugglesome Lord Grant,

this tragedy moves inexorably to its fatal climax. One more lesson that crime does not pay, and ill-gotten gains will not resolve financial plight. Even the best man – even policemen – have a low guard against temptation at times, and can give way to it, not seeing what lies beyond; even the most exalted can succumb. It is quite clear that when these men embarked on the first robbery, they had no idea of the length the path their need and greed would compel them to walk along. It is a chastening thought that Wilson was no different from the rest of us, or indeed the best of us.

Lord Grant imposed sentence, observing that those of us who play for high stakes must expect equally high penalties. Wilson was sentenced to life imprisonment, and ordered to be detained for not less than twenty-five years. Being perhaps the most shocking crime in Scottish legal history on account of its combination of public treachery and personal tragedy, it was appropriate that it attracted the longest sentence ever imposed, for with remission that was the equivalent of thirty-seven years' imprisonment. But for the widows and families the sentence was for ever. Time and pride alone can be their comforters.

In April 1970 a great character retired from the Glasgow legal scene: Dr James Imrie, Chief Medical Officer in the City of Glasgow police for over thirty years. Like all Glaswegians he was a rough diamond with a core of burnished gold. He had given evidence in many, if not most, of the cases I had appeared in in Glasgow. Inevitably one develops a familiarity and fondness for those with whom one is in association, even if one is on the other side. Jimmy Imrie was usually on the other side from me, and always very much on his own side. He was small, rugged, bandy-legged, brisk and jovial. His face was purple, sometimes blotched black, and ever creased into a grin beneath his bosky eyebrows, for he always had a joke on his tongue and a whisky down his throat. A great character and a good friend, he was castrated, as so many are, by the trauma of his retirement and limped a lonely life to his death soon after. To die is easy, to come to terms with life which has lost its purpose is often insurmountable. Retirement for some can be the acolyte of death.

I had been on the Board of Ledlanet Nights since its birth. Several times a year there was a short festival season at Ledlanet, then the home of John Calder, the diminutive, intellectual and impudent publisher and a most energetic entrepreneur. These excellent seasons brought some supremely good artists, and found some very promising talent including the beautiful Jill Gomez, then entirely unknown, and not yet known as well as her talent deserves. They were a part of the renaissance of culture which had swept Scotland inspired by the Edinburgh Festival and its many legitimate and unintended offspring. Ledlanet Nights depended on the devotion and effort of a few loyal and unswerving committee members under the chairmanship of Jim Fraser, the gargantuan, bibulophile director of a Dundee building firm of great success, whose devotion to the arts, and especially the operatic arts, and to Ledlanet were exceeded only by his size, his kindness and his generosity.

199

In the summer of 1970, Ledlanet Nights put on a season for Beethoven's bicentenary. Alas, despite the loyalty and love it received, the festival died of lack of funds and of its author's stubborn unorthodoxy in 1972.

August 1970 saw my first one-man exhibition for eight years, during which time all my creative energies had been devoted to the restoration of the house and garden of Fordell. The exhibition was opened with genial kindness by Emilio Coia, the electric and dapper caricaturist who has made painting, and especially Scottish painting, so popular and widely known on television. The exhibition was held in the Great King Street Gallery owned by the unflappable and sardonic George Neilson, then an antique dealer. Coia wrote in the catalogue:

> Temperamentally attuned to the professional as I am . . . in the case of an amateur as talented as the irrepressible Nicholas Fairbairn, it would be ungracious and unjust if I did not welcome his reappearance in the role of painter . . .
>
> Those who think they know Nicholas Fairbairn will discern many facets of his diverse personality in his painting. There are here, it seems to me, warm expressions of his ebullient nature; indications of his disarming honesty and apparent comprehension of current attitudes; brittle reflections of his sharp intelligence; examples revealing his innate sensibility and, most pertinent to the purpose, a certain painterly and picture-making skill possessed by comparatively few among that perpetually proliferating population of part-time performers. To be less prolix, I wish Nicky well.

Of the many occasions on which I had appeared instructed by Lawrence Dowdall – the first, or one of the first, being the case of the Festival nude Anna Kesselar – none illustrated his intuition and genius more than a case which was tried in Dumbartonshire Court in August 1970.

Two Italians from the local Roman Catholic College were charged that they recklessly discharged a loaded firearm at a gamekeeper and his brother. The gamekeeper and his brother claimed that they had caught the two incoming renegades poaching, and that on being challenged one had pointed and fired the shotgun at them, encouraged to do so by the other. It was Craig and Bentley all over again. Both accused were dark and swarthy, and were obviously foreign to look at. But since neither spoke English an interpreter was necessary for the trial, and since he had to interpret for both the accused, the clerk of court enquired of us where we thought he should sit. 'I suggest he sits in the dock between the two of them,' Lawrence Dowdall immediately replied with a nonchalance which did not betray his guile. So the fair-haired Scot from Glasgow University who had been sent to interpret sat between the two swarthy, alleged malefactors. They denied discharging the gun at all. The gamekeeper, under examination-in-chief by the Procurator-fiscal, confidently nodded to the dock to identify his assailants unspecifically. I rose to cross-examine. 'Which of the three in the dock do you say you were identifying?' Discomfited he eventually picked the two on the right, the interpreter and Mr De Luca. 'And which of these had the gun?' 'The one on the right,' he said. His brother then followed him into the witness-box. He told the same horrific tale of how close to death they had come, with equal emotion and detail, and alarming similarity. He, too, nodded to the dock in identification. In cross-examination he picked the two on the left, but unlike his brother he placed the gun in the hands of the interpreter. Needless to say, the two Italians were acquitted.

This case says much about identification. No evidence is more convincing, none easier to get genuinely wrong, even if it is untainted by coaching. Had there been only two men in the dock and no interpreter, both men would have been positively identified and wrongly convicted. Human beings tend – given three – to pick the middle one and, given four, to pick the third. Thus this exaggerated and false testimony was exposed, but only by the chance of Lawrence Dowdall's quick-witted suggestion. It is on such threads that justice, and injustice, hang. And it is on such genius that Lawrence Dowdall established his enormous reputation. There was however a nice ending to this unfortunate story. When Mr De Luca went into the witness box I said 'You are a married man with no family?' 'I have a family,' he replied. My information was that he had no children. 'But you have no children,' I said. 'Yes, I have, a son born at six o'clock this morning.' If his acquittal was ever in doubt, it wasn't now. De Luca's baby boy was christened Nicholas Lawrence De Luca. I hope he lives to be as lucky as his father was that day.

May 1971 took me to Aberdeen for a very rare case. Five men, including William Bremner Mitchell Massie, my client, were charged with the crime of piracy. It was the first case of piracy to be tried in Scotland for 150 years. They were charged 'that they unlawfully deprived the skipper of command of the trawler *Mary Craig*, robbed him of his keys, took possession of the stores, put him and his crew ashore and did thus take masterful possession of the trawler and appropriated it to their own use'. They were also charged with wilfully navigating the trawler intending to cause a collision with the trawler *Coastal Empress*.

The preliminary plea that their acts did not amount to piracy failed, so the trial commenced.

The story was simple: it is apparently a habit of some fishermen to get drunk before they set off on a voyage and in such cases the employers have to collect the crew and roll them on board. On this occasion the cook was rolled aboard. No sooner is a trawler out of harbour than the booze lockers, with their restricted supply of beer are opened in the hope that, with luck, all the booze will be drunk, and the crew will have ceased to be by the time the vessel reaches the fishing grounds. On 8 October, when the *Mary Craig* set out, 168 tins of beer were aboard. Two hours and 161 tins of beer later the *Mary Craig* put back to port at the demand of one of the crew who reported that the cook was comatose and they would therefore get no decent food. So the skipper put back to port, whereupon the crew were dumbfounded to discover that in accordance with civilized ethics but contrary to their concept of loyalty it was the cook who was relieved of his job and not the member of the crew who had complained about his state of intoxication. That would never do. That was against the spirit of union ethics. Delinquency must go unpunished. Moreover 'clyping' is a major sin in their code.

So the next day when the ship sailed with a new cook, the mutineers had a plan to teach the employers a lesson. They decided to take over the ship and run it ashore. They were very drunk, having again consumed the new supply of liquor. They were confused as to their intentions which appear to have included going to South America. It was all rather like the *Pirates of Penzance*. However, before either sobriety or shipwreck could be achieved, another of the company's ships, the *Coastal Empress* hove into sight. That was too good to be true: two men-of-war for the price of one. And so they agreed on a single objective and decided to ram the *Coastal Empress* with the *Mary Craig*. Fortunately for them, their condition saved both the ships and their lives, because try as they did, they failed to ram it. Eventually, as they came closer to sobriety, they put the skipper and his crew ashore, and on recovering in the cold light of day, their resolve vanished and they brought the *Mary Craig* back themselves to be arrested and charged with piracy. On the last occasion that piracy had been committed and that anyone had been convicted of it in Scotland, 20,000 turned out to see the execution of the culprits on the shore at Leith. Massie and his mates were more lucky. Lord Cameron imprisoned them for only two and a half years.

Travelling south I stopped at Perth to defend Charles Connolly who with another man was accused of 'assaulting Siegfried Pepper, an Antwerp Belgian and John Burt of Kelty in Scotland, striking them on the head with clubs, binding their hands and feet and robbing them of some diamonds and then locking them in a cupboard and barricading the door'. It was a most remarkable tale. Mr Burt claimed to be a diamond dealer in his spare time; he lived in the little mining village of Kelty and was a toy salesman. It seemed a strange way to conduct so sophisticated a profession. He obtained a client in Tayport of all places who was interested in some rather larger diamonds than he was normally accustomed to keep under his bed and so Mr Pepper was brought over from Belgium and travelled north with a selection of large diamonds from Shepherd's Market. On arriving at the house in Tayport they were quickly hustled into a cupboard, barricaded in and relieved of their diamonds. It all seemed too easy. Indeed, they managed to escape from their prison at the very moment the men had said they would be allowed to try to do so. They identified, though rather vaguely, Connolly and his accomplice as the robbers, but Connolly had a special defence of alibi. He said that he was in fact in England, in Hertfordshire, on the day of the robbery, and a large battalion of very respectable and well-to-do men and women with no criminal records came to attest that fact. The staff of a birth-control clinic brought their records showing that he had been there on that day. The staff of a shop brought their records which showed that he had purchased clothes for his daughter from them on that very day, and all of these witnesses were able to recall that he walked with a limp, spoke with an English accent and had a strange defect in one eye, which indeed he had, since the iris was missing from his left eye. Despite this most convincing and unrefuted body of evidence Connolly was convicted by the jury and sentenced to ten years' imprisonment. Many months later, I was instructed by his accomplice (who was also convicted) and I took the opportunity to ask him if Connolly was indeed there: he said he was. I asked him how he could explain the alibi. 'Money talks,' was his simple reply. It was the only alibi I ever believed. I must be gullible too.

I also had occasion to be stopped in the street in Perth years later by a man who had been a member of the jury and I asked him how they had got over this enormous body of apparently genuine witnesses who spoke to the alibi. 'I can't remember that,' the juror replied, 'but what I do remember is that we spent a great deal of time discussing the boots which you wore under your pin-stripe trousers.' Thus is justice done.

The twenty-second of August 1971 saw the inaugural service of the twenty-fifth Edinburgh International Festival, to whose council I had been elected shortly before. The Festival was conceived by the genius of Sir John Falconer, then the Lord Provost of Edinburgh, and Rudolph

Bing its first director, and it had for twenty-five years gone from strength to strength as undoubtedly the greatest and most varied international festival in the world. It had many traumas and anxieties mostly caused by the fact that part of its funds came from the local authority and many of the paynim councillors felt it unjustified that money should be spent on anything so flippant as culture when it was needed for such necessary things as wash-houses and public lavatories, as if they were alternatives. Little did they realize that for an investment of £90,000, that is a penny per citizen a day, while it was on, a mere three weeks, they generated wealth in the region of £20m. Not a bad investment. The Silver Jubilee got off to a magnificent start in St Giles Cathedral with the BBC Symphony Orchestra playing its joyous din in the echo of the great kirk. The Festival began with a brilliant experiment – a free concert in the Usher Hall, which was attended by many who probably had never been to a concert before, and they loved it. I wish the Festival would open with a free open-air concert every year in the forecourt of Holyrood Palace so that the citizens of Edinburgh could listen to the music blaring out over loudspeakers from the slopes of Arthur's Seat. I made that suggestion but so far it has never been followed. Towards the end of that Festival my 1971 exhibition began, once more in the Great King Street Gallery, and Sir William McTaggart, the then past President of the Royal Scottish Academy was kind enough to write the introduction in the programme:

I first met Nicholas Fairbairn in the 1930s. He may not remember the occasion as he was being pushed in his pram at the time. Over the years I have watched his development with admiration and interest. He is a man of many talents and painting is not the least of them and this exhibition proves it. I can remember him having a studio in his father's lovely garden, and my first visit was always there to see what he was painting. He already had a fine gift for colour and fearless use of it. He has developed this talent as the years have gone by and today he is a vital and assured painter.

Willie McTaggart was one of the people I remember earliest in my life. His short, stocky stature, and mighty rugged head with its shock of white hair and his wide sensitive face combined into a most gentle presence which one could not ignore. His grandfather, also William McTaggart, the great landscape painter, thought he had invented painting, because living on an island in the west of Scotland he had never seen anyone paint. Willie McTaggart produced in his lifetime some great, seething, rugged, luminous landscapes, and his contribution to Scottish painting and to the Academy have the mark of that quality and excellence which his character and presence bestowed. He was one of the most forgiving and undemanding men in Scottish public life, one of those rare painters who was a painter and nothing else and did not earn a living as a teacher and paint when he could find some time. He really could lay claim to being a true professional – and a truly good man.

It is rare as counsel to be able to prove that evidence has been planted. However much one may suspect it it is very rare to be able to establish it. But I now appeared in a case in which I actually had a photograph of planted evidence. The accused were charged with, amongst other things, breaking into the Toll House Café in Crieff Road, Perth, and in order to obtain access and certainly in order to leave, they had opened a trap-door in the roof which had a nail which stuck out. This trap-door was photographed *in situ* in the café, and was then unscrewed and taken to the police office in Perth where it was photographed again, and in particular the offending nail was photographed in the police office and it had, adhering to it and wound round it, a healthy morsel of human hair some two or three inches long. This hair was wound round the nail in a way that would be difficult to achieve other than manually and the remarkable thing about it was that in the photograph *in situ* there was no hair wound around the nail. The detective sergeant in charge of the case conceded that there was no explanation except that the evidence had been planted. The Advocate-depute generously dropped the charge to prevent his other colleagues from the fate he suffered himself. He is no longer a policeman.

In March 1972, Lord Clyde who had dominated the legal profession so personally and so jealously resigned. He was succeeded by Lord Emslie.

My practice next took me to Ayr to appear for a police constable who, along with another constable and a sergeant, was charged with perverting the course of justice by assaulting two youths of sixteen and eighteen years and intimidating them to the extent that they admitted and pled guilty to stealing a van which they had not stolen. This was a very serious matter for the three policemen involved, but it had a very interesting lesson for me. In an ordinary case, the Crown has all the assistance. They have at their disposal the whole powers and offices of the Procurator-fiscal and his staff, who need but tap their fingers and all witnesses will come to the office to give their statements. They have the whole police force to go and get what they want or find what they need. They have all their specialist advice, whereas the defence had then but ten days after the service of the indictment to burrow about attempting to discover the whereabouts of the witnesses on the Crown list and persuade them to give a statement if they catch them in a state in which they are capable of doing so.

In this case the normal procedure and powers and balance of advantage were reversed. I had at my disposal all the forces of the Ayrshire police and every assistance that willing detectives and uniformed officers could provide. The Crown on the other hand had a reluctant team in their prosecution. The jury, which tends to be on the side of law and order naturally sympathized with the accused, and so I experienced confirmation of the enormous imbalance of the forces which are normally on the side of the Crown as against those on the side of the defence. Only the presumption of innocence is on the defence side and that is difficult to presume when the innocent man is caged and flanked by policemen with batons drawn. In the course of the trial we practically established – if we did not establish – that the youths had in fact committed the crime to which they had apparently wrongly pled. At any rate, if we did not do that, we established to the satisfaction of the jury that at no time had any of the officers assaulted either of the youths or used any pressure to bring them to plead to something they hadn't done. It was not so much that the defence knife was sharp but the prosecution cheese was soft. The policemen were, to their intense relief and mine, unanimously found not guilty and returned to their duty to the public. Police run many hazards.

My next clients of interest were aspirant revolutionaries: William MacPherson (whom I was to see again in an attempt to break out of Inverness Prison), Ian Doran, Matthew Lygate and Colin Lawson who were charged with a variety of bank robberies and other offences, facing twenty-three charges in all. The police had tracked these evil deeds to a variety of flats and a shop from which the Workers' Party of Scotland, a Marxist-Leninist organization, was run, and there they found, apart from a great deal of military pamphlets and other anarchistic junk, the proceeds of these many robberies. I appeared for Lygate and in the course of the day's trial it transpired that I had constructed a strawless brick, for there was little to go on. But he was as determined on his own destruction, as he was on the lives of the likes of me, so the brick was smashed. In evidence Lygate described bank robbery as a means of liberating money to furnish materials for us to move forward in the people's struggle – the people being his lot and the struggle being for the bondage of communist dictatorship. At the conclusion of the evidence before I addressed the jury Lygate dismissed me from any further conduct of his case because he was anxious to make a political statement to the jury. What impressed me and frightened me in the course of this terrible case and my meetings with my client was the strength of the aggressive determination and staring hatred which motivated these outwardly decent and jovial men. Political slogans like 'liberation' and 'working class' were used to dress up their hatreds and justify their evil in their own minds. Truth and honesty found no place in their code. The end – the brutal end – justified the bestial means.

I now returned to Ayr for another case which involved three very different young men. They were charged with murdering another youth by sticking an umbrella into his eye. This single blow occurred in an incident outside a fish-shop and although a crowd was present, menacing the three youths, none saw the fatal blow struck. Indeed, when the police arrived, they did not appreciate he had received any injury of consequence at all. The judge was Lord Johnston, a former Labour politician, having been Member for Paisley and Solicitor-General until the rout of the socialists in 1951. His mannerisms and voice were more appropriate to a successless suburban squire than a socialist tub-thumper. After his fall he moped around Parliament House with suave dignity until he was elevated to the Bench where he constantly seems to be having to remind himself of the tenure of his office, which he discharged with condescending grace, and characteristic kindness. He was a very good man.

To the utter astonishment and horror of all the court, the jury found all three fresh young men unanimously guilty of murder and they were sentenced to life imprisonment or to be detained as was appropriate during Her Majesty's pleasure. Very few verdicts have taken me so greatly by surprise or upset and shocked the public observer so much. Three young lives for a single thrust with an umbrella. We appealed immediately. The appeal was to be the last case which I was to do before taking silk, and I was thankful indeed when the Lord Justice Clerk, Lord Grant, and the judges sitting with him ruled that the misdirections of the trial judges were such that the verdicts could not, and should not stand. All three were hastily reunited with their families and excused from the blame of a death from circumstances which were unique. None of the youths had been in trouble before and so far as I know none has been in trouble since. And so with this last rewarding appeal and having completed my last four murder trials as a junior counsel, on the 7 July 1972 Elizabeth II 'by the grace of God Queen', generously referring to me as 'trusty and well beloved' constituted, ordained and appointed me to be one of her counsel learned in the law of Scotland. This momentous elevation of an advocate to the rank and dignity of Queen's counsel, has, alas, no ceremony. It would be nice at least to travel to receive the noble commission from the hand of the Sovereign herself or for there to be some public ceremony, not just a newspaper snippet like a notice of birth, or in some cases death. I had always said that I would not apply to take silk until Lord President Clyde abdicated the office of the presidency, and I was the first person along with my best man Kenny John Cameron, now the Lord Advocate, whose application was considered and recommended by Lord Emslie, the august new Lord President.

CHAPTER 11

My first case as a silk was a strange tale. Frank Jackson who owned a garage was charged with attempting to murder a girl, Sandra McKenna, by putting her under a hydraulic ramp and lowering it on to her face. Jackson had had an affair with the girl when she was his petrol pump attendant. He had broken it off, whereupon a girl had started telephoning his wife to tell her all about it. On 9 June she was given her books by Jackson. In the afternoon of 10 June the garage was robbed at knife-point. 'Hell hath no fury like a woman scorned.' Jackson was in no doubt that out of spite she had organized the raid and made the tainted telephone calls. He put her under the ramp in order to extract the truth out of her. In this objective he failed, though he nearly extracted something else, but the jury discerned where the truth lay, even if he were unable to extract it, and found him unanimously not guilty of attempted murder and assault to the danger of her life. He was sentenced to twelve months for simple assault by Lord Wheatley who regarded the offence as the more serious since the accused was in drink at the time. How different from the judgment of the great Lord Hermand, unlike Lord Wheatley, a Tory and a toper. Having presided *inter alia* at the trial of a man who had stabbed a friend in drink and been found guilty of culpable homicide, the great Hermand thought the case brought discredit on the virtue of drinking. 'We are told there was no malice, and that the prisoner must have been in liquor. In liquor! He was drunk! And yet he murdered the very man who had been drinking with him. They had been carousing all night and yet he stabbed him after drinking a whole bottle of rum with him. Good God, my Laards, if he will do this when he's drunk, what will he do when he's sober?'

In September, two deaths occurred with legal connections. Johnny Ramenski died in Perth Prison at the age of sixty-seven. Few brigands persist as long as that. Thief, safe-breaker and jail-breaker, his genial nature and war record had endeared him to his adopted countrymen. He was a character in his own right. I had the privilege of defending him for the last time when he was charged with a crime, which he vehemently denied, of breaking into a dairy. The police evidence seemed overwhelming. Every form of real evidence was available; paint flakes, safe-packing, glove patterns – everything matched except the gelignite which was sent for specialist examination by experts at the University. I was instructed by Joseph Beltrami. His assistant, Tom Hatfield, who became a Procurator-fiscal until his tragic death and whom I affectionately called 'Hatpin', had been a police officer before he had taken his degree in law. He knew the officers in charge of the investigation and was convinced that the evidence was bogus and could be broken. I had my doubts, but he was right and I was wrong. As it turned out the officer was neither qualified nor was he capable of doing the experiments which were necessary to establish the similarities he claimed. The Crown mercifully dropped the charge rather than embarrass his side-kick with having to give this bogus evidence as well and Ramenski went rightly free to go back and die where he had mainly lived – in prison.

On the other side of the law, Lord Grant, the Lord Justice Clerk, with whom I had had such difficulty at Meehan's trial, was tragically killed in a motor accident at Kincraig in Inverness-shire and his place on the Bench was taken by the Dean of Faculty, Bobby Johnston, who chose the judicial title of Lord Kincraig. Lord Grant's full life was devoted to the people of Scotland and to good causes in Scotland, among which Scottish opera was the major beneficiary. He was a really tall man in the world of the Bar and his sudden disappearance was a hefty shock. Had he lived a century or more before, he would I am sure have approved of the habit of judges having wine and biscuits on the bench. Black bottles of strong port were set down at the call of a wink, decently ignored for a few moments when argument was made to look more demanding than thirst and law more diverting than port, but not for long; and the feast of quaffing and munching made the Bench more tolerant if not more susceptible to persuasion or understanding. On circuit, a different practice prevailed. The temptation of what in Glasgow is called 'a refreshment' frequently caused a total stoppage of business, during which all concerned – judges and counsel, clerk and macers and even the jury – to keep all on a level – repaired to the tavern – much fairer than the judicial privilege in Edinburgh. Today, alchohol has taken on a taint of guilt which it did not then attract and which the swashbuckling Lord Grant's broad heart did not in any shred share. He drank deeply from the pool of life utterly unspoiled by success or office, though made tetchy by the curse of a mortal disease. There is no drinking after death.

It was not long before Scotland was robbed of a third character. Within sight of his ninetieth birthday, Sir Compton Mackenzie suddenly left this earth. None could regret the end of so full and congenial a life, except that we were deprived of the fun and sparkle of his company and the celebration of his impending ninetieth birthday. Lily, his widow, staunchly discharged his wishes and respected his memory with cheerful fortitude. She generously distributed some of his most precious belongings to his friends. To me she gave his box of tie-pins, and to the children some of his books. They are treasures beyond price. In his long life, Sir Compton Mackenzie must have given more pleasure to more people than any other Scotsman of his age by his wit and his company. He was a friend to all who came within his ken, spiteless but fearless and by his capacity to remember and retell tales, he was a source of amusement, entertainment and information such as few men can equal. Heaven now contains another Scotch romantic.

In January, the second of the twin great clerks of justiciary retired: Robert Johnston, whom I had nicknamed 'Bible Johnston' – a play on the nickname of an undetected murderer 'Bible John' and Robert Johnston's devotion to the railway mission. His place has been taken by many hands. He was a person of harmless habits and correct principles, a diligent servant of the court, prodigiously devoted to its etiquette and loyal to all who appeared in it. I was the recipient of many kindnesses at his hand. He was renowed for drinking nothing, keeping his temper and doing jobs quietly.

In February death called again and robbed Scotland of yet another kenspeckle, but quite different, character, Councillor John Kidd, who had the appearance of some deep sea monster washed ashore. His young years he had spent in England and he came to Edinburgh and local politics when he was at the zenith of his absurdity. For years he had been the champion of a number of preposterous causes which included the purity of art. The idiocy of many of his bellowed outbursts which were never vicious and always sincere, ensured him consistent attention from the press and media. He was in the tradition of pennimental gossoons who historically enlist in the town council of Edinburgh and had he been alive in 1789 would no doubt have been foremost in the town council's refusal to drink claret at meetings in the belief that they would ruin France! I remember appearing with him on a debate on television when he said that it wasn't the students from Edinburgh University who were promiscuous, but that all the trouble stemmed from the young bull students from the Black Isle who migrated south and stampeded them.

We laid this good character to rest in the Dean Cemetery. He had done well.

The Traverse was now ten years old. No one present at either its conception or its birth and certainly not in its infancy would have believed it possible that this delinquent and prodigious theatre would live to grow up. So we had a grand celebration of its tenth birthday with a variety programme in the King's Theatre on a Sunday night. Russell Hunter, creator of Cocky, Bill Simpson, alias Dr Findlay, John Cairney, alias Robert Burns, Polly James, Fenella Fielding and Andrew Cruikshank all took the stage, as I did myself. It was a night of great fun and the theatre benefited to the relief of those who had to run it, by some £1,500, thanks to that generous loyalty which is so much in the make-up of the actor.

From time to time I have been instructed to defend those who believe that the love of God is best expressed by hatred. In May, Joe Beltrami instructed me to appear on behalf of Caroline Renahan, an Irish girl, who was charged together with two men named Sweeney, with the possession of explosives under the Explosives Act. She lodged a special defence impeaching the Sweeneys and a priest named Father Bartholomew Burns, then aged thirty-eight-years. As the police watched them from look-out points, all three and Father Bartholomew Burns moved 150 pounds of gelignite from the chapel in Possil Park to a waiting car. Carefully allowing the priest to be driven away by Father Martin, aged sixty-eight, *en route* as it surprisingly happened for Dublin, the police arrested the other three red-handed in St Teresa's Chapel in Possil Park. Under Father Bartholomew Burns's bed were found training documents for the IRA and pamphlets which demonstrated how to make explosive devices under Republican instructions. The pile of torn collection envelopes of the faithful bore witness to the destination of these sacred funds. Miss Renahan said that Father Burns had asked her to meet him and trace the Sweeneys because he thought that the boxes which they had left in his confidential custody 'might contain explosives'. The fact that the police were now on to them all, and the fact that the word 'Explosives' was written all over the boxes in red letters, could perhaps have been the source of this suspicion. The point was not lost in court on Lord Cameron. 'Why this crescendo of urgency?' he asked icily. 'That question,' Miss Renahan replied, 'is very unfair.' By which she meant it was very fair but impossible to answer. Father Bartholomew Burns had told her that he thought it unwise to tell the police in case they didn't believe his story. There indeed was a Christian act: better a few hundreds of innocents were maimed and killed by those explosives than that a priest should be disbelieved by a policeman. 'We both decided,' she said, 'the previous evening, to make an anonymous telephone call to the police.' Needless to say neither did. She was, after all, as she admitted, a paid-up and active member of the Sinn Fein and the Sweeneys were, as evidence related, not by any means the only faithful who thought that the chapel was a good place to hide explosives and that Father Burns was a good custodian of them. Caroline Renahan's defence was that as a loyal and devout Christian she was the innocent messenger of the bidding of Father Burns in contacting James Sweeney. But that was of no avail as a defence to a statutory charge of handling the explosives which she had undoubtedly done. James Sweeney was convicted and sentenced to seven years. The charge against his brother John, who was on a visit from Ireland, was found 'Not proven'. Lord Cameron remanded Caroline Renahan in custody for two weeks for reports. 'It would appear,' said Lord Cameron generously, 'that your first association with these explosives came through your friendship with Father Burns, whose actions demonstrate very eloquently what would appear to be his own sense of criminality.' It was not long before Father Bartholomew Burns's code of ethics put Caroline Renahan's liberty above the secrecy of his seclusion. He revealed his whereabouts and sent a signed and sworn affidavit to Mr. Beltrami. It contained the following passages:

It may sound incredible but I saw no writing on the boxes to say that these were explosives, although I have read in reports of the trial that it was clearly printed on them. On Thursday 22 March Miss Renahan turned up in the morning with two men. Her sole purpose was to make certain the men who left the stuff there came to take it away. The explosives were taken from my room. For my own part I did take a box down from my room and put it in the boot of the car, but I did not know it was explosives. I saw shortly afterwards that there were police in the grounds, and I noticed a man being arrested. The next thing I heard was that she had been arrested. I looked out of the window and saw police all round the place, and I took fright. I asked the parish priest for the day off. He drove me to Parkhead and let me out in the street. I am admitting that I am technically guilty of harbouring gelignite unknowingly and on discovering this did so unwillingly. I have read that documents supposed to be associated with the IRA were found in my room. I have absolutely no knowledge of them, and can only assume they were put there along with the explosives by the same man. *I have never had, nor have I any desire to be associated with the IRA, nor do I support it in way.*

When the Glasgow police attempted to extradite Father Burns and bring him to trial in this country, he pled in the High Court in Dublin that he had committed a political crime and therefore he could not be extradited. He is still a priest, no doubt preaching the message 'Thou shalt not kill' and 'Thou shalt not bear false witness.' Such are the ethical priorities of some priests in the Irish Church. 'The long array of guards in golden arms and priests besides, singing their bloody hymns, whose garbs betray the blackness of the faith it seems to hide.'

One of the nightmares which has always haunted me is the thought of having my home compulsorily purchased. It is a nightmare that for many becomes a reality, and I have always been greatly hurt when little people who have lived in their beloved homes all their lives are turned out of it by some authority. Such a man was James Mitchell. 'You take my house, when you do take the prop whereby it stands. You take my life when you do take the means whereby I love.' So determined was he not to be turned out of his home and his shop for which the local authority had made a derisory offer, that he armed himself with a home-made petrol bomb which he hurled at the unfortunate police who were compelled to go and get Naboth out of his Vineyard for the King Ahabs of local authority. He was charged with the attempted murder of a sheriff officer and a police constable. He was found guilty of assault only and sentenced to twelve months, but he was successful on appeal.

> The law doth punish man or woman that steals the goose
> From the common, but lets the greater felon loose
> That steals the common from the goose.

Local authorities should read the account of Ahab's compulsory purchase order on Naboth. It is at I. Kings 21. ii: '. . . And Ahab spake unto Naboth saying "Give me thy vineyard . . . I will give thee for it a better . . . or . . . I will give thee the worth of it in money." And Naboth said to Ahab "The Lord forbid it me that I should give the inheritance of my fathers unto thee." '

Mitchell was deprived of his inheritance and no such offers as Ahab made were forthcoming from the ghouls who snitched his house and livelihood. Theirs was the assault upon justice.

Once more James Boyle attracted the attention of the Lord Advocate. He was charged with assaulting prison officers at Inverness Prison and of attempting to escape from the maximum security wing with three other maniacal convicts of whom one was Howard Wilson, the police killer for whom I had appeared. The four had issued an ultimatum of chilling lethality:

> We have taken a hostage with us, one of your screws, as you will by now be aware. His safety depends on your action between now and noon tomorrow. Our conditions are as follows: if we are approached, obstructed or accosted in any way by the police or other forces of authority he dies. If news of our departure is broadcast on radio or television before 12 noon tomorrow he dies. We are all four dead men in the estimation of the society which is sentencing each of us to a living death and in three of our cases in perpetuity. [Not a word of remorse for those they had sentenced without reason to real death.] We have been subject to brutality and violence at the hands of the uniformed thugs which society has placed in charge of us. [OK for their victims but not OK for them.] You thrust us into concrete boxes or steel cages; you brutalize, dehumanize and degrade us; you try to make us into degenerate, mindless vegetables – you call it rehabilitation. [What did they start as?] Worst of all you give us no vestige of hope, on the contrary, the hysterical mouthings of certain political dinosaurs set out to destroy any last faint glimmer of hope of future freedom with genuine retraining and rehabilitation.

This ultimatum demonstrates the complete lack of a sense of wrong, and the exaggerated sense of being wronged which psychopaths and their champions, in my experience, inevitably show. They are always the ones who are being wronged. In this case there was certainly a mighty conflict between these four and the 'screws' – as they called them – in the recreation room. According to the evidence a few of the 'screws' had a baton but none used one, so how all four accused had baton injuries, and broken batons were left at the scene of the battle, remains a mystery. The Chief Officer, or 'Super Screw' as he was called, had a very convincing reason for not carrying one: he claimed it was so heavy that it made his trousers fall down if he carried it, and in any event he had indented for a specially light baton so he would never hurt anyone with it; not that he would carry it anyway. So struck by nothing, Boyle ended up unconscious with a fractured skull and Wilson had five stitches in his forehead. Certainly a large number of extremely unlikely escape materials were found in bare empty cells – which were allegedly searched several times daily – from transistor radios to seven knotted bed-sheets, ropes and other things which were clearly planted after the stramash. Whether it was an escape attempt or a protest, as the accused claimed, we will never know. They all had six years added to their sentences, three being life sentences, and I had two delightful weeks of beautiful weather staying at Kinkell Castle which has been restored from a shell with loving care by the genius of Gerald Laing, the great Scottish international sculptor, and his beautiful Russian wife Galina.

The *Sunday Times* decided to conduct an experiment to test the claims of astrology. It was arranged by Nicholas Tomalin who was tragically killed reporting the war in Israel not long after. The subjects all had to be Scots as it is only in Scotland that we are meticulous enough to record the time as well as the date of our birth on birth certificates, and the astrologer must have that precise information, for the relationship of Venus to Uranus is all important. From the relative position of the stars the astrologer described the character of the chosen seven from their birth date and time, and we each had to choose which one was ourself out of the seven. Only one was right. I thought I was Ronnie Corbett and he thought he was me – perhaps he is. Bill Anderson, the champion caber-tosser in Scotland also thought he was me – that is less likely. At the same time an experiment was conducted by Professor Eysenck, the distinguished psychologist, who sent us all a questionnaire to fill in. From our answers he described the characters of the seven people. All but two of us recognized ourselves correctly. Earth beat heaven hands down.

One of the greatest rewards in life is to see one's efforts come to fruit, however stony the ground in which the seed was sown. When I founded the Society for the Preservation of Duddingston Village in 1959, it was against a bitter wind of haughty disdain and official resistance. Preservation – for the vulgar word 'conservation' had yet to be invented – was regarded as old-fashioned, anti-contemporary and the quirk of post-mortal romantics who wanted to live in the past. No help or encouragement was forthcoming from the Planning Department, indeed very much the reverse. What was old was finished: the old must die, long live the new! But the age of a building has nothing to do with its merits, or its beauty, though antiquity certainly attracts veneration and often bestows maturity on buildings as on men. It was therefore a matter of particular satisfaction that fifteen years on from the foundation of the Society, Edinburgh Corporation Planning Department did a whole case study on the 'conservation' of Duddingston Village. Never, in the bitter, lonely, early days and the destruction of George Square, did I believe that such a change would ever come about, any more than I would have predicted that ten years after its birth the Traverse would be strong and well, or that when we set up the Brook Clinic in whore-frosty Edinburgh that birth control would become government policy in a few years' time. You can only do what you believe is right, whatever the pain and the cost and the opinions that assault you; thus you will form the general opinion by your example – that is what is called leadership. It is an art presently lost but much needed in the practice of politics.

In June, a strange case occurred against two men – this time Protestant – William Campbell and George Taylor Martin, the last case tried by Lord Milligan before that most jovial judge was forced by his own Act of Parliament to be the first judge to resign at seventy-five. Not long after, he fell into his jokey tomb. They were charged with unlawfully and maliciously causing an explosion of a nature likely to endanger life and to cause serious injury to property in the Apprentice Boys of Derry Club in Landredie Street, Glasgow. This took place during a meeting of a number of loyal Protestants, when a vast explosion wrecked the hall and out of the smoke-charred remains staggered Campbell and Martin amongst others. The explosion was caused by the mixture of sodium chlorate and ammonium nitrate, in other words, fertilizer and weed-killer. Martin, for whom I appeared, was convicted and sentenced to five years' imprisonment, but not for long. The Lord Justice General, Lord Emslie, upheld his appeal on the grounds that there was insufficient evidence. So Martin was blown out of the dock as suddenly as he was blown out of the Apprentice Boys' Club.

At the end of June I appeared in a case of tantalizing contradiction in the High Court before Lord Avonside – Rhadamanthus himself – a huge man with a rageful red face, several chins, and large rolling, dangerous eyes; powerful, aloof, half-ice, half-fire, bursting with vilipendant indignation, slick brains and immense good manners, and as kind and generous off the Bench as he is mighty and commanding on it. Like the solar system he has never had any anxiety about his reputation, nor need he have. He is a brilliant gardener, a discerning collector of books and paintings and with his tasteful and elegant wife Janet he has restored the Mill House in the little village of Samuelston to be a jewel of civilization for cats and men.

The accused, John Preece, had been charged with murder in England but by the time the magistrates' hearing came to court, the Crown had decided not to prosecute. He was immediately rearrested and charged with murder in Scotland because though the body of Mrs Helen Will was found in England, he was charged that he murdered her in Scotland and transported the body to England in his lorry, and then drove back

217

again to Scotland. It was not immediately apparent to the defence at what time of the day or night in question the Crown were going to try and allege that Preece had made his drive from Kirkcaldy to England and back and deposited the body. He was charged with strangling Mrs Will in the cabin of a motor-lorry on a road between Dunfermline and Denny, or elsewhere in Scotland to the prosecutor unknown, and murdering her and depositing her body at Longtown in Cumberland. Preece had left Stoke, or left his house, at 6.20 A.M. but his lorry wouldn't start and he was drag-started by a man called Pepper who recalled that Preece was wearing brown overalls. At 7 A.M. he set off. He reached Cannock at 9 A.M. and stayed until 9.30 A.M. He stayed for about an hour at Wishaw. He passed Riggend at about 3.40 P.M. Thereafter all his movements and deliveries were confirmed by various witnesses and he left Stirling at about 5 P.M. and reached Kirkcaldy at 6 P.M. He went to a café and to a toilet. He was at bingo from 8 to 10.30 P.M. when he left with a woman and her husband who had won a prize. According to him he went to sleep about midnight and awoke at 6.50 A.M. in the car park at Kirkcaldy. His battery was again flat, and he required assistance to start his vehicle. All this was confirmed in evidence. Thereafter he set off for two days to the north of Scotland.

It therefore emerged during the course of the evidence that it would have been impossible, as the Crown had originally suggested, for Preece to have murdered Mrs Will in the afternoon and then nipped down to Longtown before arriving in Kirkcaldy. Their only alternative therefore was that he left at midnight, or thereafter, and was back in the car park by the morning. That of course meant that Preece would have driven for over forty-eight hours without sleep, which seemed unlikely. In addition, it would be strange, if having driven all through the night, with a few minutes to spare, his lorry at seven o'clock in the morning on his return was cold and unable to start. In order to establish the first theory which they set off on and later abandoned, the Crown had proved that the body had lain on its front for six hours and thereafter had lain on its back, the theory being that during its journey on the lorry it had lain face down and it had been deposited at Longtown thereafter on its back. But once Preece's programme for the day of the twelfth was proved completely it excluded his going to England in the afternoon, with the inevitable conclusion that he would have had to have taken the trouble to leave his bingo six hours after the murder and turn the body over in the lorry for reasons best known to no one. A number of witnesses gave contradictory evidence that they had seen him with a sober woman they thought could be Mrs Will in a café near Kincardine, and other witnesses gave evidence that they had seen Mrs Will on a roundabout not far from the café in a state of advanced intoxication. Moreover, two police officers gave evidence that his lorry was not in the car park at Kirkcaldy at three o'clock in the morning, and to crown the Crown case, a Dr Clift gave evidence that he found fibres in Preece's lorry which could have and probably did come from a coat of Mrs Will. Despite the fact that the timing was almost impossible, that it was inconsistent with the fact that his lorry would not start in the morning, and would not have been able to start at midnight when he would have had to leave to take the body from Kirkcaldy to Longtown, despite the fact that the evidence of hypostasis as to which way up the body was lying contradicted the Crown's theory and that he would have had to have driven for forty-eight hours without sleep, and despite his constant denial, the jury by a majority found him guilty, accepting the evidence of Dr Clift. Lord Avonside sentenced him to life imprisonment on 'the verdict of his peers'. After a long appeal in which the court scrutinized the whole conflicting evidence, that verdict was irrevocably confirmed.

In the course of the appeal Dr Clift began his evidence after luncheon on the Friday of the first week. He was hesitant, shifty and uncertain. He opined that fibres found on Mrs Will's coat matched fibres from a rug in Preece's lorry cabin and vice versa. He conceded that they might have come from another source, but he thought it unlikely. Such was his manner that I firmly believed he was hiding something. So I spent the entire weekend examining the slides with my microscope and learning the mysteries of fibrology. It was immediately clear that Clift's evidence did not bear scrutiny. His description of fibres was inaccurate. Some he described were not on the slides at all. I decided to demolish his evidence on Monday. I never made a worse forensic mistake. Into court on Monday came not the shambling, forlorn, absent-minded professor of Friday evening, but a neat, clinical, alert executioner. Every time I faulted his findings or observations he underlined the immutable certainty that the fibres definitely had a common origin. He convicted Preece. It took eight years to right that wrong. Clift had been suspended by the Home Office for giving false evidence in an English case. Another scientist investigating his work discovered that he had suppressed vital evidence in the Preece case, having decided himself that Preece was guilty. The matter again came before the Appeal Court, who immediately ordered Preece's release. Justice had at last been done – or had it? Preece received compensation of £77,000 for eight years in prison. Clift got rather more as a discredited civil servant. Preece and

Meehan are the only two clients of whose wrongful conviction I was certain. They have both, thank God, been pardoned.

In October I was instructed by Jim McCann, a solicitor in Dumbarton of jovial and wise disposition, on behalf of a teenage youth, Roy Myatt, who was charged with the brutal murder of Miss Esther Bendall, a fifty-eight-year-old retired teacher, at the home of a surgeon in Helensburgh. My junior was Malcolm Rifkind, a very shrewd young advocate fond of words, particularly his own, whose glasses like Lord Clyde's dwarf his narrow face and who like me travelled through the constituency of Central Edinburgh on his road to a seat in Parliament, where he sits for Edinburgh Pentlands with distinction and devotion. He is Secretary of State for Scotland at the present time.

Miss Bendall had been the war-time friend of the surgeon's wife and, as her colleague, she had kept up the friendship. She had agreed to come and stay and look after the bungalow where the family lived at Garelochhead while the surgeon and his family made a tour of America. I had last been at Garelochhead in my last CCF Camp at school, and I had very mixed feelings about returning to Greengayres Camp where I had contracted food poisoning from which I had thought I would never recover. Roy Myatt was the boyfriend of the daughter of the surgeon, Mr Ewan Cameron, and was frequently at the house at their invitation. He was the son of a storeman at the dockyard, and he was asked by Mrs Cameron if he would look in on Miss Bendall from time to time and see that she was all right, and also cut the grass in their absence. Mrs Cameron described him as a mild, pleasant and good-mannered boy. No witness had ever seen him lose his temper, and he had no history of assault or aggression of any kind at all.

Myatt gave the following account. He had asked his friend James Boyle (not mine) if he would care to go with him to cut the grass, but Boyle had declined so he had gone off himself on his motor-bike and had had a cup of tea with Miss Bendall. He had then gone for a ride, promising to come back. On his return, he saw through the inner front door what appeared to be her arm lying in the hall, and thinking something was wrong, and finding that the door was locked, he went round to the French windows and entered the house. On going into the hall he came upon a scene of unspeakable frightfulness which the jury were able to see for themselves from the photographs. The body of Miss Bendall was lying against a chest of drawers, covered in blood, her head smashed to pulp and surrounded by the objects which had inflicted these terrible injuries – broken pots, jars, pans, coffee percolators, ash-trays and two heavy gun cartridge cases. Her blood and brain-matter were scattered nine feet up the walls of the hall and over the ceiling. Myatt immediately, according to his account, fled from the scene and jumping upon his motor-bike went straight to the police station where he told them of his frightful discoveries. The senior police officers who interviewed him accepted at that stage his account as the truth, and the doctor noted that his hands were dirty, but there was not a spot of blood on either his body or clothes.

After a few days of enquiry the police interviewed James Boyle and discovered on his clothing a few spots of blood of the same, fairly rare group, as the unfortunate Miss Bendall. He had originally attracted their attention by going to the police station the same evening of the crime in order to report a motor accident which he claimed to have had on his motor-bike, but which had never in fact occurred. He claimed to have gone to hospital to have injuries attended to, which he had never suffered. Their suspicion fell on him but after further investigations the police discovered first of all that it was not possible to see Miss Bendall's arm from the inner front door from which Myatt had claimed to see it; secondly, that the inner front door was in fact opened and unlocked; and, thirdly, that Roy Myatt's fingerprints were on some of the objects with which her gentle head had been smashed. Accordingly Myatt and not Boyle was charged with murder, and he instructed a special defence of incrimination of James Boyle who after the murder had shown a concerned and morbid interest in how Myatt was getting on.

Both the Crown and Myatt were in difficulties in the case. Professor Forbes, the chief Crown pathologist, that distinguished, kindly and sapient man, tanned like a horse-chestnut in autumn, gave evidence that there was no question but that the assailant must have been heavily contaminated and covered in blood and brain tissue. In this dilemma, the Crown then asked his colleague, Dr Walter Pollock Weir, to contradict that view. Dr Weir advanced the theory that the assailant could have been naked at the time and could have so struck the victim from two positions at right-angles to one another so that the blood splashed forwards or sideways and never contaminated him. The jury did not find that theory digestible any more than anyone else. How would Myatt have washed all the blood off his naked body without washing the dirt off his hands and why on earth should he have taken the trouble to take his clothes off in order to do to death this innocent spinster? That contradiction combined with the remarkable blood on Boyle's sleeve and the false explanation of James Boyle compelled the jury to find the charge 'Not proven' by a majority. It was a remarkable and tragic tale, and the truth will never be known. Lord Leishman, that most vapid and imbellic of men, transparently honest and honestly transparent raised the gentlest hand that had ever wielded the sword of justice, and dismissed Myatt from the dock.

Lord Milligan, now retired, had for a long time shared my dislike of bad and complicated legislation and he kindly filled his final days sending me some examples of it which he had collected, the best of which is the statutory definition of a staggered weekend:

> Where a weekend which previously did not occur now falls in the middle of the week it shall be deemed to occur on any two days either preceding or following the days on which it previously occurred provided they are not the same days upon which it previously did not occur.

In other words, it can happen whenever you want, on any day of the week provided it is none of them. 'Better to have no laws at all than to have them in such abundance.'

CHAPTER 12

I was forty on the 24 December 1973. I did not know what an exciting and important year it would be. It started with a most unfortunate murder case in which Mrs Margaret Bain was charged with strangling her husband. She was a woman of gentleness and diligence. She had been worn out by her work as a waitress and the tempestous and tormenting treatment to which her drunken husband subjected her throughout her twenty-eight-years of married life. Finally, having seared her with a red-hot poker, he invited her to put a pair of tights round his neck and strangle him because, as he said, that is what she had always wanted to do, and certainly no one could but forgive her if she had. Being timid she declined, so he put the tights round his own neck and invited her to pull with him, which she did. The tights were so knotted by him that when pulled they did not loosen, and it was impossible to know whether she made any contribution thereafter to his inevitable death. Lord Kissen's electric mind presided over the tragic case. He agreed that whether she had made no contribution to his death or had been an agent of it was impossible to tell, and withdrew the charge from consideration by the jury. So this good woman was released to carry on her gentle life, and we hope she has lived more happily as a widow than she ever did as a wife.

Alas, May saw the closure of the St Enoch Hotel in Glasgow where I had always stayed so happily when on circuit. Its particular distinction was that being built in Victorian times the rooms were very quiet and solid, and its special pleasure was that Tommy the barman was one of the best cocktail mixers I have ever known. He is happily settled in a new job I'm glad to say, but I miss his concoctions very much. No doubt this grand building will be replaced by a crossword puzzle containing more government offices and a hotel whose rooms are separated by silver paper. When will we learn that these great buildings are irreplaceable?

I now appeared, for the first time in my practice, for an American citizen. A number of sailors from the US nuclear supply ship *Canopus* had been irritated by the arrest of one of their number following a return match fight in a dance hall, and were determined to release him from custody in the manner that one sees in western films. Accordingly a near riot occurred in respectable Dunoon which, but for the grace of God, would undoubtedly have ended in murder. As it was, a large number of citizens and policemen were badly injured, and all the slubber-degullions were convicted, and rightly convicted of these crimes and sentenced to a variety of terms of imprisonment. Like the mutineers in Aberdeen, they had a squint sense of outrage.

Sir Alec Douglas-Home now announced that he would not stand again for Parliament. Unlikely as I thought it was that I would obtain the nomination, I decided to apply. I took advice from Hugh Fraser, the distinguished, grave, eminent, courageous Member for Stafford and Stone with whom I had dinner at his magnificent house at Eilean Agus in Inverness-shire, once the home of the Sobieski Stuarts, who imagined quite falsely that they were the rightful heirs to the Scottish throne. Early in April I unbelievably reached the short leet and the fateful contest and play-off was fixed for Sunday 19 May at 4.55 P.M. in the office in King Street Crieff. On the day before it, I attended the Conservative Conference in Ayr where I met, amongst others, Donny McNeill, chairman of the Association of Kinross and West Perthshire, who was to be one of my judges on Sunday. I gave two speeches at the Conference, both of which went down well. I took much advice. Sunday came with great haste, and in terrified anticipation I went to Crieff. I gave my speech, jumped the penultimate fence and got on to a short leet of two, the other being Robert Henderson, my friend and colleague at the Bar. 200 to 62 to 6 to 2. Would I fail yet again? It was too much to think of. I have sympathy every year for the runner-up at Wimbledon who falls at the last net and must begin all over again. The jury returned their verdict at 8.15 P.M. I'd made it. The world was alight. I immediately telephoned Alec Home and other friends. Was it really true? I slept in Heaven.

I had the kindest of letters from Alec Douglas-Home and Edward Heath, and a mighty load of good wishes and congratulations, but perhaps the most generous letter of all I got was from Mr Cameron, chairman of Bute and North Ayrshire where I had been so disappointed to fail in my attempt for the nomination, which I thought was my last chance to make a political career. I now felt completely fulfilled. Life, indeed, begins at forty and anything that is to be added to me now would be a bonus. At last I could do my best, and all the frustrations which had tormented me for so long were suddenly resolved. With their departure there arrived a clarity of thought, a fluency of speech, a facility of words, an energy and a peace which were remarkable. Fate has indeed been kind to me.

And so, after ten busy, hectic, but fulfilling days I reached the haven of the glorious first of June. I got up even earlier than usual at a quarter to five, and dictated many letters and thoughts and sorted out all my papers and my library, which like my life had hitherto been so confused, and now fell into order. At half-past seven Francesca came down and we walked around the garden and picked some flowers, she, to give to her aunt, and I to give pleasure to myself. Solomon's seal and yellow irises I picked, poppies and purple irises she picked. It was the children's half-term and, late as usual, we all set off for Elizabeth's sister's farm for the weekend, Upper Huntley Wood – Aunt Maggie, as she is to the children, and Magpie as she is known to me. The children were in a state of excitement as arises from anticipation. I was in a state of excitement which arises from fulfilment and the knowledge of impending rest.

Alas, it was not long before my nomination was under attack. Mr Donald Jack, an elder of the Free Church of Scotland attacked the nomination of 'a prominent QC who had shown himself inimicable to the Gospel and a supporter of the Traverse Theatre in Edinburgh which had made its own nefarious contribution to the permissive society. It is to be hoped that at the appropriate time,' he said, 'the constituents will reject such a candidate.' Generously the press sought me out from a theatre where I was watching a Festival performance so that I could reply to the attack before it was printed. I immediately sent a telegram to the Moderator of the Assembly, the Very Reverend Alistair Ross which read as follows:

I do not agree with the opinions of your Assembly, but I will defend to the death your right to express them. I further request the right to address the Assembly at any time tomorrow to express my opinion and my reply. I am sure as Christians you will be willing to listen as Christ did, to the voice of one whom you have judged as a sinner:

I received an unstamped letter declining my request, and so I here print some of the text of what I would have said, which the *Scotsman* generously published:

Fathers and Brethren, I am both proud, relieved and humbled to receive your invitation to address the gathered Assembly of the Free

Church of Scotland, because the keystone of a civilized democracy, as of a vital church, is free speech . . . . No man and no Church has a monopoly of either wisdom, sanctity or love. Let us listen to those with a guid tongue in their heid. We might learn something from one another. I feel like Daniel in the lion's den, but beware brethren, Daniel won three nil against the lions. Rather am I like Abednigo in the fiery furnace, I am impervious to heat but very, very sensitive to warmth. Now is it not strange that in this world of universal and instant communication the gap between the image and the reality has not got narrower but wider . . . and the gap is never wider than between the image and the reality of the Free Church of Scotland . . . I hope in correcting your image of me that you will correct my image of you. Three motives inspire my actions and stimulate my energies: love of freedom; love of my country; and love of my fellow man. That thread runs through all my activities.

. . . I founded a birth control clinic for the unmarried, the Edinburgh Brook Advisory Centre, in the city of John Knox. And I founded it not only because of my concern for the quality of life for those on earth but because I saw every day in my professional life, people forced into unhappy marriage by unintended pregnancies . . . in short, my professional life became a diet of divorce and delinquency. I am sure you have stopped much misery in this world by preaching the warning 'Be good'. I hope I have saved a little by preaching to those who either didn't hear you, or wouldn't listen 'Be careful', and in aiding them to be careful if they wouldn't be good.

And then I championed and chaired the Traverse Theatre and saw it through its tempestuous birth-throes and delivered it to an astonished Edinburgh and an astounded Free Kirk. Art is the greatest gift of God and the highest attainment of man. The power of creation is the only capacity which man shares with God. I have no doubt that the contemporary Assembly of the Free Kirk was horrified by the plays of Fletcher and Saltoun and the contemporary paintings of Raeburn and Ramsay, and the contemporary poems of Robert Burns.

Art is not well judged by representatives of the generation that produces it. I am sure that many of the plays performed in the Traverse are trivial. Without a fertile soil for the seed of contemporary inspiration we condemn ourselves to live forever in the past, and we forbid the vital idealistic energetic young generation now alive in Scotland in our second Renaissance to make any contributions to the artistic treasure chest of Scotland, or the heritage of man. There lurks, no doubt, in your mind the pathetic spectre of the Festival nude whom I defended some fifteen years ago, her crime was that she was dressed in nothing but one of the most beautiful creations of God, which has been the inspiration of the highest attainments of man, the human female form. I say in mitigation 'Pity is a higher virtue than scorn.'

It is well to remember in our moments of partiality and stricture that inside the breast of every man, woman and child, be he a minister or a mugger or a ragamuffin or royalty, there beats a human heart and there lives a human soul. Why are so many young people delinquent? An ugly environment eventually produces an ugly person; an ugly home and an ugly atmosphere produces despair and undirected anger. Bad soil produces stunted trees. If you treat people like animals and abandon them to playless jungles, the law of the jungle comes to replace the law of Scotland and that is why I have been concerned to eradicate ugliness from our environment, be it in human or in concrete terms, and that is why I have tried to stimulate beauty in modern buildings, why I have encouraged the planting of trees and why I have tried to preserve in some small way and restore the heritage of Scotland.

Laughter wins more hearts than a frown. You and I have different means but surely we share a common end – the service of our fellow man, and the service of our beloved country in the service of God. Gentlemen I have had my say and leave you as I came to you, a miserable but now a confessed sinner, eager in the services of man and humble in the sight of God. May I be forgiven.

That week I went to visit Mrs Hadden, the ninety-nine-year-old widow of my grandfather's coachman in Montrose, and former 'guardian' of my aunts Jane and Georgina in the house at White's Place, and she told me in her crackling Angus voice that she had prayed for me every night of her life and she was now truly proud and could sleep humbly and proudly in her bed because all she had prayed for had come true. So could I. And, she added, she had prayed for many things and had not got them, and in the end it had always turned out for the best that those prayers went unanswered. Little did I realize that in a year's time I would return to her one hundredth birthday party with the then new leader of the Conservative Party, Mrs Thatcher.

On 11 June in Picardy Place in Edinburgh, a small ceremony occurred. I had long been horrified by the building which is called the St James Centre. It is a building of Alcatrazian vulgarity which the City Fathers had decided to erect. It ruins almost every view in Edinburgh, and is a monument to bad taste, and so I gave, in celebration of my fortieth birthday forty trees to the city. I handed them over to the Jack Cane, the most quiet, humble and northy Labour Lord Provost with these words:

Lord Provost, I hand over these trees to your care and keeping with the wish that Edinburgh and they will grow and flourish together. Edinburgh has a wonderful heritage and beautiful architecture, but the St James Centre is a major and terrible disgrace, and may it always be a lesson. It is a disgrace to planning, an offence to the eye, a wound to the city, and a monument to profligacy. We all make mistakes and all mistakes must be forgiven, provided we learn to do better. Let it stand as a warning never to make such a big mistake on such a terrible scale. Edinburgh is too perfect and too important for that. My Lord Provost, I bestow to your care these trees, in the hope that it will persuade many other citizens that even the best architecture is improved by the magnificence of nature, and I bestow them to you to salute and hopefully to stimulate the resurrection and restoration of our beloved capital city of which you are so worthy a first citizen.

In July the whole executive of the constituency came to Fordell for a lunch-party. Sir Alec Douglas-Home came too. We had a tent in the garden and Elizabeth made a very good lunch. In my speech I told the story of Sir Alec's visit to Peking when during lunch he turned to Chairman Mao and said: 'Tell me Mr Chairman, what do you think would have happened if Mr Khrushchev had been assassinated and Mr Kennedy had not been.' After a pause the Chairman replied, 'I do not believe that Mr Onassis would have married Mrs Khrushchev.' Sir Alec claims that the story is apocryphal. None the worse for that.

And so the summer was spent getting to know all the good people of my vast and beautiful constituency. Before the election broke upon us, I defended a few more cases, had a rest in Italy and visited Strathconon in Ross-shire where there lives a man of remarkable talent, called Oni Armstrong. He has a slow, soft voice, the eyes of the acute observer, the taste of nature, which is only out-matched by his taste for whisky which he bestows on his guests and friends whatever the time of their visit. Licensing hours are obscene for him. His home and habits are otherwise thrawn. This sturdy highlander makes the best and most distinguished crummocks that can be found and he made a magnificent one for me, carving Fordell out of the horn at the top of a stick and emblazoning my arms upon it. It is one of my most treasured possessions.

Then in September the election broke upon us, and for three hectic enervating weeks I tore around the constituency, sustained and encouraged by Hugh Fraser the wise, good-humoured, sardonic son of Lord Lovat, not to be confused with the grocer of the same name. I was, unfortunately, owing to the election unable to accept instructions from Patrick Meehan to present his Bill of Criminal Letters setting out the falsehood of the identification parade, but it was now turned down. How ironic! As it turned out my election was to be a more important service to his cause.

Finally the day of the count came. I had never doubted that we would win though I always knew it would be a hard and difficult fight. The tide of Nationalist dementia tartanica swept over rural Scotland, but we were able to keep it at bay in Kinross and West Perthshire by fifty-three votes. One was enough. And so I went to Westminster. Immediately, a Labour Member from the North East came up to me and said: 'Don't worry son, about t'majority. I never go to t'constituency except to sign nomination papers. I never speak in the Chamber, and if I get any letters or postcards from the constituency I put them in the bucket unopened.' My intention was to do the reverse. At noon on Wednesday 23 October I arrived at the House of Commons where I had never before been. To my amazement I was welcomed by the policeman and servants at the Members' Entrance in Palace Yard. I was introduced to John Marling the doughty Sergeant-Major of the Tory Whips' Office. Every possible civil offer of help and kindness was proffered. At 2.30 P.M. I entered the Chamber for the first time. It was strange to see all the celluloid people in reality. There was an air of boyishness especially from the Government benches. But one memory above all others is outstanding. I met Margaret Thatcher in the Members' Lobby. There I thought is the true leader of our party. I wrote such in the *Strathearn Herald*. It was not long before she was, and I was first to vote for her in both ballots. I received a most appropriate telegram from Oscar Wood, of Christ Church, Oxford. 'Sitting is better than standing.' All good messages like fresh biscuits are crisp. Impatient to begin, I made my maiden speech on 4 November 1974.

To my sons, Samuel and Joseph, and all the children of South Africa

First published in Great Britain in 2002 by Frances Lincoln Limited,
4 Torriano Mews, Torriano Avenue, London NW5 2RZ

British Cataloguing in Publication Data available on request

ISBN 0-7112-1934-6

Designed by Sophie Pelham

Printed in Singapore

1 3 5 7 9 8 6 4 2

The Publishers would like to thank Amanda Cairns for checking the text.

AUTHOR ACKNOWLEDGEMENTS
I would like to thank Bongani Mofokeng, his aunt, uncle and cousins, Manana, David, Flory and Thabi Coplan,
for allowing me a glimpse of their lives. To David Coplan, special thanks for all your time, advice and input.
To Mrs Ailsa Steyn (Principal of Emmarentia Primary School), Miss Layla van der Merwe (Bongani's teacher),
Bongani's classmates – thank you for your co-operation.
To my husband, Mark Turpin, thank you for your ever-present love and support.

BONGANI'S DAY

From Dawn to Dusk in a South African City

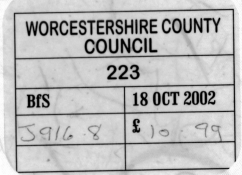

Gisèle Wulfsohn

FRANCES LINCOLN

AUTHOR'S NOTE

Bongani and his family live in Johannesburg, the largest city in South Africa. We sometimes call it 'Jo'burg' for short. Central Jo'burg is like city centres all over the world: full of noise, traffic and busy people rushing from one place to the next. Bongani is lucky because he lives in a suburb of the city where the streets are quieter and there are plenty of green spaces to enjoy. At weekends, he and his cousins love scrambling up the *koppies* (small rocky hills) near their house and collecting pine-cones. They sprinkle glitter on the pine-cones at Christmas time and hang them as decorations.

Bongani means 'we give thanks' in Zulu, one of the many languages spoken in South Africa. He belongs to the Basotho people who live in the Kingdom of Lesotho. Bongani lived in Lesotho until he was four years old, before moving to Johannesburg three years ago to stay with his aunt and uncle. It was a big change at first – especially because his home in Lesotho had no running water or electricity – but now Bongani cannot imagine living anywhere else.

AFRICA

Johannesburg

South Africa

Kingdom
of Lesotho

Bongani Mofokeng is seven years old.

He lives in a quiet suburb of Johannesburg called Westdene with his uncle David, his aunt Manana, and his two cousins, Thabi, aged ten, and Flory, aged seventeen. David is a professor at the University of the *Witwatersrand*. Manana runs a food caravan for minibus taxi drivers in the city centre.

THE WITWATERSRAND is a great rocky ridge surrounding Johannesburg. It contains some of the richest gold deposits in the world.

Bongani and Thabi are both fast asleep in their bunk beds when
Difedile, the family's domestic helper, comes to wake them up
at six o'clock. After a yawn and a stretch, they get dressed and go
to the bathroom to wash their faces and brush their teeth.

ready for breakfast. Bongani eats his cereal quickly so that he can watch Disney Cartoon Café on television before they have to leave for school.

Bongani prefers cereal, but many more South Africans start their day with mielie meal porridge. Mielie means 'corn' in Afrikaans (one of the languages spoken in South Africa), and is one of South Africa's biggest crops.

At 7 o'clock Bongani and Thabi jump into the *bakkie* (truck) and Uncle David drives them to Emmarentia Primary School about two miles away.

It's great fun sitting at the back in the open air. There is a mattress to sit on, so it's comfortable too.

4

When the school bell rings all the children organise themselves into lines in the courtyard. Each child has a special place in the line, which means there is no need for anyone to run or push. Once there is silence, they recite the school prayer. The prayer was specially written so that it has meaning for everyone, no matter what religion they are.

The first lesson of the day is English. Bongani's teacher, Miss *van der Merwe*, tells the class that they will be exploring the letter 'C'. To start them thinking, she gathers everyone together on the carpet and reads them a funny story about a character called Clever Cat.

VAN DER MERWE is a common surname amongst the Afrikaner people of South Africa. All the van der Merwes are descended from the same man, Willem van der Merwe, who came from Holland to settle in South Africa over three hundred years ago. These settlers from Holland and other countries in Europe developed a language called Afrikaans and became known as the Afrikaners.

words they can think of that begin with C. Bongani puts up his hand to ask whether he can do some drawings too.

After English, they put away their books and put on their art aprons. Miss van der Merwe shows them how to draw a clown face on a paper plate.

At breaktime, Bongani rushes outside to the climbing frame to play *Shaka Zulu* with his friends.

SHAKA ZULU King Shaka was a powerful chief who once ruled over the Zulu people – one of the main groups of people in South Africa. Bongani's game is based on a recent television series about the adventures of King Shaka and his Zulu warriors. When they reach the top of the tyre tunnel, they jump off and yell, "Bayete Nkosi", which means "Hail the chief!" in Zulu.

Back inside after break, it is time for Bongani's favourite subject – computer skills. This morning the class is trying out a new maths program.

The next lesson is PE (Physical Education). Bongani concentrates hard on every step as he walks across the balancing beam because he knows his friends will laugh at him if he falls off!

Water Adventures. Water is
their special project this term
so the children learn something
new about water every day.

At one o'clock the bell rings
for the end of school, and
everyone packs their bags.

After school, Uncle David takes Bongani to see Manana at her food caravan. Sometimes Bongani helps Manana sweep the pavement around the caravan, but today his friend James has asked him to help wash Manana's car. It is James' job to wash the minibus taxis while the drivers are having their lunch.

down together to enjoy their food while Manana's assistant watches over the big silver cooking pots on the stove.

AFRICAN PLATE *Manana's African Plate is made up of meat stew, mielie pap (a stiff white porridge made from corn), mashed potato, beetroot and chakalaka, a delicious dish made from tomatoes, onions and chillies.*

After lunch, Uncle David and Bongani pick up Thabi from school and head for home. They stop off at the supermarket on their way to buy some groceries. At the sweet section, they choose some chocolate for Manana as a present – and a bar each for themselves too!

Kirsty, the family's pet rabbit, is hungry

Then he crosses the street to his friend Lucky Boy's house. Lucky is very pleased to see Bongani because he has some smart new sunglasses and wants to show them off.

15

Later on, when the day starts to cool down, Bongani and Thabi take the new puppy Spencer for a walk up Banbury Street. As they walk past the high walls in front of the houses, Spencer wags his tail because he can hear the neighbourhood dogs (*dintja*) barking.

Security is important in Johannesburg because there is a lot of crime. Many people protect their houses with high walls, gates or electric fencing.

At about 6 o'clock Bongani settles down to his English homework. He wants to finish it before Manana comes home so that she can check it and sign it.

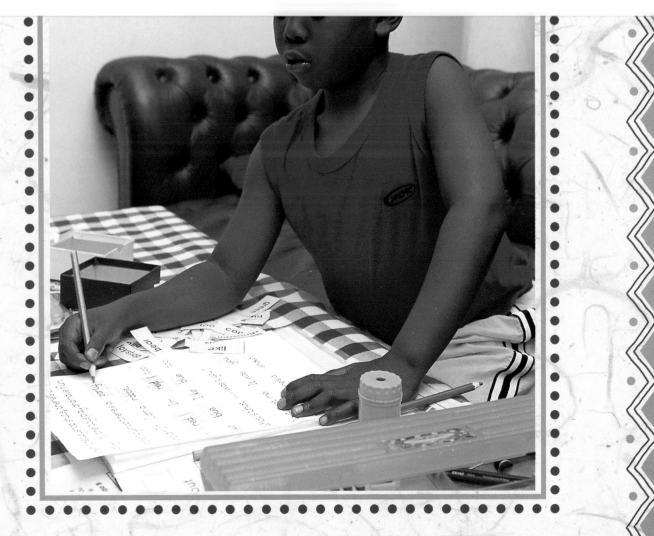

Every couple of weeks Flory shaves Bongani's head with an electric razor, rubs vaseline into the bare skin and then puts hair wax on his dreadlocks (thick, matted strands of hair) to keep them shiny.

Bongani's hairstyle is the same as Lucas Radebe's, the captain of *Bafana Bafana* – shaved round the sides with a mop of dreads on top.

BAFANA BAFANA means 'boys boys' in Zulu and is the nickname of the South African national football team.

David has made spaghetti bolognese for dinner and, for once, everyone sits down together. They are all so busy during the week that it is often easier for the children to eat earlier by themselves.

After dinner, Bongani, Flory, Thabi and baby cousin Nikita, who is visiting, dance the *kwasa kwasa* and watch some *kwaito* videos.

KWASA KWASA is a style of music and dance from central Africa. You shuffle backwards and forwards while swaying your shoulders and hips to the rhythms of the music.

KWAITO is a style of black South African dance music that is very popular with young people. The music is created in a studio using synthesizers and computers. The words are usually sung in Tsotsitaal, a South African street slang.

Bongani could dance all night, but Manana reminds him that he needs to take a bath.

Afterwards he treats Manana to a foot massage. He teases her by saying that he expects payment but really he enjoys spoiling his *rakhadi* (aunt) after her exhausting day.

21

There is just time for a quick family music session before bed.
Bongani plays the *balafon*, Uncle David has chosen the *apentemma*,
Thabi strums a guitar and Manana tries out a *dondon*.

BALAFON A wooden percussion instrument that is similar to a xylophone.
APENTEMMA A traditional drum from Ghana in West Africa.
DONDON A Nigerian 'talking' drum, which makes a sound like someone talking.

At nine o'clock, Bongani and Thabi kiss everyone good night and go to bed. Thabi reads to Bongani from Harry Potter until he cannot stay awake to listen any more.

Robala hantle aubuti. (Good night, little brother.)

MORE ABOUT SOUTH AFRICA

SOUTH AFRICA, THE LAND

The country of South Africa lies at the southern tip of the continent of Africa. It has many different kinds of landscape: a long and sunny coastline, vast mountain ranges, regions of lush farmland as well as large flat areas of scrub, national parklands – where herds of wild animals like elephant and buffalo roam – and a huge desert (the Karoo). It is also rich with natural resources, including gold, diamonds and almost every useful type of mineral.

SOUTH AFRICA, THE PAST

In the very beginning, the land of South Africa was inhabited by black tribespeople. The first white people to settle in the country came from Holland, France, Belgium and Germany in 1652. These settlers, who became known as the Afrikaners (or Boers), set to work farming the land, and fought brutal wars with the black tribespeople who already lived and worked on it. When the British settled in South Africa about two hundred years later, they also wanted the land for themselves so many more wars followed, including the 'Zulu Wars' between the British and the Zulus (the biggest group of black people in South Africa) and the 'Boer Wars' between the British and the Dutch settlers.

For a long time in South Africa's history, the white people ruling the country believed that they had more right than the black people to all the good things South Africa had to offer. The white government passed laws which meant that black South Africans had to live in different areas from white South Africans and go to separate schools. When the people protested that these laws were unfair, the government punished them severely. This system was called 'apartheid'.

The rest of the world condemned South Africa for its apartheid laws, but the South African government ignored them. They sent many black leaders, like Nelson Mandela, to prison, and they took many black South Africans from their homes and moved them to 'homelands' (areas miles from the cities where the land was poor). Eventually, however, the South African people and the rest of the world protested so much that the South African government had to give in. In 1990 the black leader Nelson Mandela was set free after 27 years in prison, and became the first black president of South Africa. The day he became president, 27 April 1994, is known as 'Freedom Day', and is celebrated every year.

PEOPLE IN SOUTH AFRICA

South Africa is often called the 'rainbow nation' because the people that live there come from so many different races and cultures. Unfortunately, because of its troubled history, South Africa is also a land of great inequality. While some South Africans are wealthy, many are still very poor. Diseases like HIV/AIDS and tuberculosis are widespread, and many people have to manage without decent housing, clean water or electricity.

RELIGION IN SOUTH AFRICA

Most South Africans are Christians. The churches and their leaders, such as Archbishop Desmond Tutu, gave important support to the South African people as they struggled under the apartheid system. There are also large numbers of Hindus, Muslims, Jews and African traditionalists. Traditionalists worship their ancestors – although they are no longer alive, they remain important members of the family.

LANGUAGE IN SOUTH AFRICA

South Africa has 11 official languages. The most widely spoken are English, Afrikaans, IsiZulu, IsiXhosa and Sesotho. (Although IsiZulu and IsiXhosa are the correct terms, people usually refer to these languages as Zulu and Xhosa.) Bongani speaks fluent Sesotho as well as English.

ENGLISH is spoken by almost half the white people living in South Africa (the others speak Afrikaans). Many more South Africans know how to speak English, but it is not the language they speak at home.

AFRIKAANS is spoken mainly by the Afrikaner people. It developed as a mixture of the languages spoken by the first European settlers – Dutch, French, German and English.

IsiZULU is spoken by the Zulu people. The Zulus live mainly in the KwaZulu Natal province in the east of the country, where the Zulu royal family has its palace.

IsiXHOSA is spoken by the Xhosa people who live in the southern area of South Africa. IsiXhosa is difficult to speak for non-Xhosa people because it has so many 'click' sounds.

SESOTHO is the language of the Basotho people who live in the Kingdom of Lesotho (the small country within South Africa where Bongani was born). It is also spoken widely in South Africa.

SOME SESOTHO WORDS AND PHRASES
Dumela. Lebitso la ka ke Bongani.
   – Hello. My name is Bongani.
O phela jwang? – How are you?
Ke phela hantle. – I am fine.
Ke leboha haholo.
   – Thank you very much.

GLOSSARY

African Plate – Manana's speciality dish, made up of popular African foods like meat stew and mielie pap

Afrikaans – a language spoken in South Africa

Afrikaners – the white African people whose ancestors came to South Africa from Holland, Belgium, France and Germany

apartheid – an Afrikaans word meaning 'being apart'. It is used to describe the way the previous white South African government kept black and white South Africans apart

apentemma – a traditional drum from Ghana in West Africa

Archbishop Desmond Tutu – the Christian leader who helped fight apartheid

Bafana Bafana – the nickname of the South African national football team

bakkie – a truck

balafon – an African musical instrument which is similar to a xylophone

Basotho – the people who live in Lesotho

Bayete Nkosi – 'Hail the Chief!' in Zulu

Boers – the Dutch farmers who settled in South Africa

chakalaka – a spicy mixture of vegetables

dintja – 'dogs' in Sesotho

dondon – a 'talking' drum from Nigeria

dreadlocks – thick, matted strands of hair

koppie – a small rocky hill

kwaito – a popular style of South African dance music

kwasa kwasa – a style of music and dance from central Africa

Lesotho – a small country within South Africa

mielie meal – ground mielies (corn)

mielie pap – a stiff white porridge made from mielie meal (ground corn)

Nelson Mandela – South Africa's first black president

rakhadi – 'aunt' in Sesotho

Robala hantle aubuti – 'Good night, little brother' in Sesotho

Sesotho – one of the languages spoken in South Africa, and by the Basotho people of Lesotho

Shaka Zulu – a famous Zulu chief

Tsotsitaal – a South African slang language

The Witwatersrand – a rocky ridge surrounding Johannesburg that is mined for gold and minerals

Zulu – the largest group of black people in South Africa. Zulu is also the name of the language they speak

27

INDEX

Afrikaner people 6, 24, 26
art lesson 7

bedtime 23
breakfast 3

cartoons 3
computer lesson 9
corn 3, 13

dancing 20
dinner 19
disease 25

English lesson 6–7

food caravan 1, 12–13
football 18
foot massage 21

geography 24
gold 1, 24

haircut 18
history of South Africa 6, 8, 24–25

homework 17

language 6, 26, 27
lunch 13

mealtimes 3, 13, 19
music 20, 22

PE lesson 10
pet rabbit 15
playtime 8, 15
prayers 5

religion 5, 25

school 5–11
security 16
storytime 6, 11, 23
supermarket 14

walking the dog 16
washing 2

Zulu people 8, 24, 26